Killing Finucane

Murder in Defence of the Realm

Killing Finucane

Murder in Defence of the Realm

Justin O'Brien

Gill & Macmillan

Gill & Macmillan Ltd
Hume Avenue, Park West, Dublin 12
with associated companies throughout the world
www.gillmacmillan.ie

© Justin O'Brien 2005
0 7171 3543 8

Index compiled by Helen Litton
Design by Make Communication
Print origination by Carole Lynch
Printed by ColourBooks Ltd, Dublin

This book is typeset in Linotype Minion and Neue Helvetica.

The paper used in this book comes from the wood pulp of
managed forests. For every tree felled, at least one tree is
planted, thereby renewing natural resources.

A CIP catalogue record for this book is available
from the British Library.

5 4 3 2 1

To my son Justin
that he may grow up in a society that recognises the
value of truth

I have thought it proper to represent things as they are in a real truth, rather than as they are imagined...A prince who wants to maintain his rule is often forced not to be good, because whenever that class of men on which you believe your continued rule depends is corrupt, whether it be the populace, or soldiers or nobles, you have to satisfy it by adopting the same disposition; and then good deeds are your enemies.

— NICCOLO MACHIAVELLI
THE PRINCE

Contents

ACKNOWLEDGEMENTS   XI

1. Terrorising the State   1
2. The Security Nexus   20
3. Crossing the Rubicon   54
4. Killing Finucane   78
5. Tactical Successes and Strategic Failures 106
6. Inquiring for Truth   127

APPENDIX 1   The Walker Report   150
APPENDIX 2   The Cory Report
              Conclusions   160
APPENDIX 3   Stevens 3 Conclusions   164
APPENDIX 4   Statement from the
              Secretary of State
              on Finucane Inquiry   166
APPENDIX 5   The Inquiries Bill
              Proposed Provisions   168

INDEX   201

Acknowledgements

Investigating collusion is a process fraught with professional and personal risk. In a world governed by duplicity, there is always the danger of manipulation. By its very nature, the subject matter necessitates extreme caution in its handling. Agent sources invariably inflate their contribution, minimise their complicity and often pursue secret agendas that, if unchecked, could cause immense damage to the fragile political process and considerable professional embarrassment. Differentiating between hearsay and actual knowledge is often impossible to adjudicate, necessitating judgement and integrity. Politicians hide behind the Official Secrets Act. The Ministry of Defence shows an alarming propensity to invoke national security in order to prevent the disclosure of material that it is in the public interest to reveal. Overarching all of this is the dismal reality that in a divided society, truth itself is bitterly contested.

In 1995 I returned to Northern Ireland to take up a position as a senior producer at the *Spotlight* programme with the BBC. For the next nine years I tracked the parallel development of the peace process and the unravelling of the security nexus that forms the focus of this book. Throughout my time as a journalist at the BBC and later with RTE in Dublin and UTV in Belfast, I had the privilege of working with some of the most astute observers of Northern politics in both journalism and academia. In particular, I would like to thank Chris Moore at UTV for his professional insights and friendship. As Editor, Current Affairs, at UTV I made the investigation of collusion a departmental priority. I am grateful for the determination of all current affairs staff, including Trevor Bernie, Jim Fitzpatrick, Mary Currie and Kate Reid, and for their work in translating this mission into important, well-crafted television outputs with the help of excellent camera, editing and post-production teams. I benefited too from the wise counsel offered by Ken Reid, the station's venerable political correspondent and Mike Nesbit, its premier news and current affairs anchor. As a corporation, UTV provided unstinting support. I am grateful to the station's

Managing Director, John McCann, Director of Programmes, Alan Bremner, and Head of News and Current Affairs, Rob Morrison, for their determination to ensure that this most important issue was given the prominence it deserved. I would also like to thank our legal advisors, in particular Brett Lockhart.

At Queen's, I was exceptionally fortunate to have the benefit of Paul Bew and Richard English as doctoral supervisors and later colleagues. Mel Dubnick, Kevin and Joan Gilmartin, Bronagh Hinds and Ciaron O'Kelly were always at hand to listen and provide encouragement as the book took final shape. I am grateful to Patrick Dobel of the University of Washington for what to me was an exceptionally important conversation about the nature of truth and truth-telling, which informs the final structure of the book.

It is important to thank Johnston Brown for his courage and integrity in coming forward, providing important new evidence about the reality of policing at the height of the prosecution of the Dirty War. I also wish to place on record my deep respect for John Ware of the *Panorama* series, who has been instrumental in ensuring that collusion was never off the political radar. His documentaries on Brian Nelson and the Force Research Unit, and the complicity of Special Branch in protecting a confessed killer, were vital contributions to the degree of public knowledge about the corrosive compact between the security forces and loyalist paramilitaries.

I would like to thank my family for once again providing a safe and secure environment in which to write this book. My wife Darina took the strain of additional work with little complaint, a feat more remarkable given the fact that she was carrying our third child at the time. Élise and Jack put up with the disappearance of their father with only the occasional subversive attempt to demand attention by switching off the computer. Peter and Mary Blake, as always, were on hand to help. We have all lived through this project for too long and with too many sacrifices. These pale in significance, however, when compared to the suffering felt by the Finucane family and others bereaved as a consequence of a state policy that was devoid of morality. I hope that the book serves as a reminder of the true cost of the politics of terror.

Chapter 1
Terrorising the State

All murders are, by definition, controversial. The private pain felt by those left behind is magnified if the perpetrator is not brought to justice, an all too common occurrence in the aftermath of the Northern Ireland conflict. While no one case can claim pre-eminence in terms of personal grief, the murder of Pat Finucane on 12 February 1989 by loyalist gunmen raises the most difficult public policy implications. The politically inspired killing of an officer of the court represents a profound assault on democracy. If the state itself, by commission or omission, allows the subversion of democratic values through complicity in murder because of wider security considerations, can it really retain the moral high ground in a war against terrorism? If loyalist paramilitaries, publicly condemned by the state as terrorists, were privately recruited as a proxy for the British army and other elements in the wider security nexus and allowed to murder with impunity, what are the consequences for democratic government itself?

The execution of Pat Finucane by loyalist gunmen as he ate dinner with his family encapsulates the ethical, political and moral dilemmas occasioned by a policy of rendering policing and criminal justice systems subservient to an overarching security policy. Such was the ferocity of the attack that the solicitor died clutching a fork, leading to one of those responsible boasting to police that he was responsible for introducing a new method of killing. In the macabre lexicography of loyalist paramilitaries, Finucane was not merely assassinated: he had been 'forked'.

The family of the Belfast solicitor has remained dogged in its insistence that the truth behind the killing can only be resolved by a full independent, international, judicial public inquiry. 'I have never thought a great deal about the person who actually killed my husband,' maintains Geraldine Finucane. 'At the time he was killed and probably even yet, gunmen in Belfast were two a penny. I've always focused attention on the people behind the gunmen who orchestrated it and decided it was going to happen.'[1]

The belated murder conviction in September 2004 of Ken Barrett, a loyalist paramilitary and Special Branch agent involved in the attack, paved the way for the British government to make a major policy reversal. On 23 September 2004, the Secretary of State for Northern Ireland, Paul Murphy, announced that there would be an inquiry, but his announcement included the caveat that the exceptional nature of the Finucane case necessitated the passage of new legislation (see Appendix 4). Since the Finucane killing, calls for an inquiry had always been trumped by a competing imperative: the stated need to safeguard the integrity of the criminal justice system.

The signing of the Good Friday Agreement in 1998 had weakened significantly the moral force of the argument. As a qualifying prisoner under the terms of the early release programme, legitimised by the public endorsement of the Agreement in referenda, Barrett's life sentence is merely a symbolic punishment.[2] His decision not to contest the charges, despite defence counsel intimating that there was no forensic evidence to link him directly to the killing, ensured that crucial information about what the security forces knew in advance of the killing, or the attempts to obstruct the criminal investigation in order to protect a serving agent, were not tested in court. Barrett claimed that to provide testimony would heighten the very real threat to his life from unidentified sources, a threat that could encompass loyalist paramilitaries or the wider security nexus. It is the pursuit of this wider context that forms the basis of the investigation conducted here but not necessarily the inquiry ceded by the government.

When making the announcement, London indicated that this inquiry could not be convened under the 1921 Tribunal of Inquiry Act, which underpins the governance of all other inquiries in the United Kingdom. The stated reason given was the protection of national security interests, a formulation that also covered the government's insistence that much of the inquiry would have to be held in private. Despite the fact that the 1921 Act was sufficient for the operation of the Saville Inquiry into the events of Bloody Sunday and will also underpin the other investigations into collusion, the exceptional nature of the Finucane case required exceptional measures to ensure the inquiry's smooth operation. In interviews conducted after the announcement, the Secretary of State for Northern Ireland repeatedly focused on cost and time issues, downplaying or evading the more important question of what national security interests were threatened by this case, who would adjudicate on whether these issues were genuinely threatened and how widely or narrowly set the terms of reference would be.[3]

Calibrating the exact nature and extent of collusion between loyalist paramilitaries and elements of the British intelligence agencies in the prosecution of a counter-insurgency strategy requires a carefully nuanced analysis. Divining the exact degree of political responsibility is fraught with legal and practical difficulty. The process is hampered by the fragmentary nature of the documents in the public domain, a reality that some fear is likely to remain the case given the framing of the Inquiries Bill.

Until the Barrett conviction in 2004, police investigations, even by outside forces, have proved inconclusive. In situations where the only opportunity to provide closure is to be found in inquests, the terms of reference governing their structure are too narrowly defined to generate light as to motives or strategies. This is compounded by a strategy to withhold documentation from defence teams on the grounds that publication breaches national security. The usual decision by army and police agents not to contest charges in court has ensured that only the broadest of outlines has been entered into the public record. The publication of the Cory Report into collusion in 2004 (see Appendix 2), complete with footnoted references to secret military communications, has allowed for a degree of granularity hitherto denied.[4]

The Cory Report has been criticised by some for its wide and potentially counter-productive definition of collusion, a less than compelling writing style and excessive concentration on the evidence provided by previous state-sponsored investigations, most notably the three inquiries into allegations of collusion conducted throughout the 1990s and the early part of the new millennium by Sir John

Stevens, the Metropolitan Police Commissioner.[5] The Cory Report does, however, provide limited access to source material that has explosive implications for our understanding of contemporary history.

Even before the publication of Cory, the factual issue of collusion was no longer in doubt. In the course of its three investigations, the Stevens Inquiry produced a staggering amount of information, released in piecemeal fashion through careful and selective leaking: '9,256 statements were taken, 10,391 documents recorded (totalling over 1 million pages) and 16,194 exhibits seized.'[6] In April 2003, Sir John Stevens travelled to Belfast to pass interim judgement in the form of a truncated summary of the voluminous evidence collated, without providing public disclosure of the material against which his claims could be substantiated. He stated: 'My enquiries have highlighted collusion, the wilful failure to keep records, the absence of accountability, the withholding of intelligence and evidence, and the extreme of agents being involved in murder. These serious acts and omissions have meant that people have been killed or seriously injured.'[7]

Stevens' conclusions in relation to the central case investigated in this book were stark: 'I have uncovered enough evidence to lead me to believe that the murder of Patrick Finucane could have been prevented. I also believe that the RUC investigation of Patrick Finucane's murder should have resulted in the early arrest and detection of his killers. I conclude that there was collusion.'[8] The Cory Report ran to 127 pages, and helps fill in a number of gaps. In a highly critical adjudication of state policy, Judge Cory concluded:

> If agents are not adequately controlled and prohibited from committing criminal acts they will increase, not decrease, the level of homicidal violence… [It] is the paramount duty of any government to establish and maintain the rule of law and to ensure that no one is above the law. This is a fundamental and requisite principle of democratic government. Accordingly, the need to gather intelligence cannot justify providing a mantle of protection to those who are parties to murder.[9]

Recognising the important role played by the security services in protecting that democracy, Judge Cory places equal weight on the need for public confidence that the methods employed do not circumvent the law. For this reason, in an implicit rebuke of how a provincial manifestation of a war on terror was prosecuted, he adopts an expansive definition of collusion:

> There cannot be public confidence in government agencies that are guilty of collusion or connivance in serious crimes. Because of the necessity for public confidence in the army and police, the definition of collusion must be reasonably broad when it is applied to actions of these agencies. This is to say that army and police forces must not act collusively by ignoring or turning a blind eye to the wrongful acts of their servants or agents or supplying information to assist them in their wrongful acts or encouraging them to commit wrongful acts. Any lesser definition would have the effect of condoning, or even encouraging, state involvement in crimes, thereby shattering all public confidence in these important agencies.[10]

In this context, it is significant that the British government, on national security grounds, redacted no less than ten crucial pages of the report relating to involvement and/or knowledge of the plan to execute Finucane. This lack of transparency is in sharp contrast to the substantial disclosure provided to the Hutton Inquiry in the United Kingdom, established in 2003 to inquire into the circumstances leading to the death of a weapons inspector who had leaked information to the BBC.[11] It is apparent that despite the partial closure of the Northern Ireland conflict, unearthing the intelligence secrets there remains too sensitive and potentially destabilising. There are domestic and external reasons for this reticence. Within the Northern Ireland peace process, establishing the truth behind operational policy without a parallel investigation of IRA activities risks legitimising the republican worldview and destabilises attempts to resuscitate a stalled political process. Perhaps more importantly, exposing the modus operandi of Special Branch delegitimises the export of intelligence-driven policing to Kosovo and other post-conflict countries. It undermines the British state precisely at the same time as it is playing a frontline position in the self-proclaimed international war on terror.

The aim of this book is to go beyond the narrow remit of the Cory Report, which was charged merely to ascertain whether or not the grounds exist for the establishment of a public inquiry into the

Finucane killing, a question already answered positively by the publication of the 2003 Stevens summary. To examine the Finucane murder in the context of the wider security nexus requires the penetration of the secretive world of intelligence gathering; the exploration of its form and function; and the triangulation of disparate and often contradictory, vague or inconclusive source material.

The book seeks to ascertain not just how the actions of the security forces transgressed the rule of law. It places these transgressions in an institutional context. Were the politicians aware of the consequences of allowing the security forces such leeway? If so, what were the terms of the calculation? If not, who bears ultimate responsibility for a policy that so denuded the state of its democratic legitimacy? Using a variety of investigative techniques, the circumstances that led to the killing of Pat Finucane, and the subsequent failure — until now — to bring those responsible to court, are excavated to reveal how security policy was created, refined and partially dismantled as a consequence of the ending of the IRA campaign. The specific impact of the Finucane murder on that policy is illustrated through interviews, court documents and official reports. The dynamic interchange between the various actors is explored and the consequences for the moral authority of the state are evaluated.

Piecing together the evidence exposes not only the tactical abuse of formal due process for strategic gain, but also the wider panoply of measures used to force the Provisional IRA to reposition its political and military strategy.[12] As such, my analysis moves beyond apportioning blame to rogue individuals, rogue commanders or rogue units for specific acts. Rather it argues that the policy of providing primacy within the police (already a quasi-military force) to Special Branch, while simultaneously downgrading legal safeguards, had a corrosive effect on the legitimacy of the state itself.

The factors that led to the supremacy of Special Branch were codified in a confidential document known as the Walker Report, the existence of which was first publicised by *Insight* (see Appendix 1) in 2001.[13] A set of internal guidelines designed to ensure the centralisation of all intelligence-gathering, the Walker Report provided the basis for a policing culture that gave a lower value to the detection of crime and its prosecution than to the accumulation of intelligence. Informers were run through two specialist units — E3 and E4A. Handling these informers was a dangerous occupation that undoubtedly saved many lives. The sense of danger was described by a constable who was handling an alleged high-ranking member of the Provisional IRA. He is quoted in the memoirs of Ian Phoenix, one of the most powerful members of Special Branch in the 1980s. Recounting plans to meet the informer in an isolated area, he says, 'I must be fuckin' mad sitting here, waiting for a fuckin' gunman.'[14] It is also unquestionably the case that there was a pressing need for intelligence to be collected, a fact acknowledged by most neutral observers, if not those with political axes to grind. The question is one of political control, or more accurately, the lack of it. The privileging of intelligence over criminal prosecution not only subverted both the legitimacy of the state and the credibility of its liberal rhetoric, it also led to the effective criminalisation of parts of the RUC itself.

The institutionalised re-ordering of priorities outlined in the Walker Report was a jealously guarded secret within the force itself and was aggressively defended from internal criticism from the Criminal Investigation Department and external scrutiny from the Policing Authority. The crucial thing to consider, however, is that security policy was not created in a vacuum. Charting how the democratic process was subverted to justify managing the threat posed by paramilitaries extends well beyond Special Branch. It requires challenging the received wisdom about the fundamental nature of the conflict, which mutated as a consequence of specific strategies that, in turn, had a direct impact on cause and effect. That process, we now know, included the refining of loyalist targeting through the placement of agents by Special Branch and other nodes of the security nexus within the terrorist organisations as well as classic counterinsurgency infiltration of republican groupings.

When Brian Nelson, one of the most notorious army agents recruited and run by the army's Force Research Unit, was facing trial on multiple counts of conspiracy to murder, he was provided with a character witness defence by his operational commander. Identified in court as Colonel J, former head of the Force Research Unit, Lieutenant Colonel Gordon Kerr, maintained his charge was 'motivated by team spirit and loyalty to the army, I have no doubt that it was not out of loyalty to the UDA'.[15] According to the logic employed by senior police and military commanders, the killing of innocent people was an unfortunate fact of life in the prosecution of a dirty war in which the boundaries of acceptable behaviour were blurred, judicial oversight weakened and a culture of impunity institutionalised.[16]

Sixteen years after Pat Finucane's death, his murder continues to cast a heavy pall over the nature of policing and criminal justice in Northern Ireland. The key questions can be usefully divided into four distinct but overlapping areas of inquiry. First, how was the intelligence arena structured? Second, how did the loyalist operation that led to the killing of Finucane fit into this structure? Third, did excessive discretion, coupled with myopia about who represented an 'acceptable target', distort the decision-making process? Fourth, what was the rationale, endorsed at the highest levels of the RUC and the British army, behind the predetermined obstruction of both the initial police investigation into Finucane's murder and the subsequent external inquiries held under the auspices of the Metropolitan Police?

It is important to state that to concentrate on the Finucane murder is not to privilege his death above all others. Rather, the case is used as a mechanism to unpick the reality of security policy in Northern Ireland. In so doing, it illuminates the inevitable consequence of a corrosive compact based on a vulgar interpretation of the Machiavellian dictum that the end justifies the means. A more appropriate epigram from the worldview promulgated by the same master political strategist — and one that underpins this book — is that 'those who study the ideal and neglect the real learn how to accomplish their destruction, not their salvation'.

It is also important to note at the outset that Pat Finucane was not a member of the IRA, a fact acknowledged at every stage by the RUC and its successor organisation, the Police Service of Northern Ireland, in official pronouncements (even if, privately, many officers continue to hint darkly at his connections and still despise the skill of his advocacy and the uses to which he put it). Finucane was an assertive and particularly adroit solicitor. He had successfully challenged the British government at the European Court of Human Rights over its incarceration policies in the mid-1970s. He had spearheaded the use of compensation claims in cases involving allegations of mistreatment and torture within interrogation centres.

He was also instrumental in galvanising opposition to the provisions of the Prevention of Terrorism Act, which was facing a barrage of international criticism from human rights organisations. In the Northern Ireland of the late 1980s these were dangerous measurements of success. The targeting of the lawyer was the result of a dangerous myopia that conflated a professional lawyer with his client base.[17] This was not an exceptional circumstance. A similar distortion of reality lies at the heart of the controversy over the killing of Rosemary Nelson in Lurgan a decade later and to the continued harassment of other prominent defence attorneys.[18]

The anger and frustration on the ground at the activities of defence attorneys being displayed in visceral fashion in the interview rooms of fortified barracks was matched by obvious antipathy at the highest levels of the RUC. In a House of Commons debate in January 1989, a junior Home Office minister, Douglas Hogg, provoked uproar when he proclaimed: 'I have to state as a fact, but with great regret, that there are in Northern Ireland a number of solicitors who are unduly sympathetic to the cause of the IRA.'[19] Hogg maintained that this assertion was based on informed intelligence. 'I state it on the basis of advice that I have received, guidance that I have been given by people who are dealing with these matters.' That guidance, provided at a briefing with the RUC Chief Constable, Jack Hermon, and later clarified in written form by Special Branch, was eventually published in part in Justice Cory's excoriating report into the Finucane killing.

Noting that two of Finucane's brothers had served prison sentences for IRA activity, the guidance provided to Hogg stated categorically: 'Finucane has continued to support the republican cause using his expertise in an advisory capacity and associating with PIRA/PSF personnel.'[20] From his review of the documentation, Judge Cory concluded: 'It could be inferred that RUC SB [Special Branch] tended to identify a solicitor with his clients.'[21]

Seamus Mallon, who was later to become Deputy First Minister in the Northern Ireland Assembly, gravely warned at the time of Hogg's incendiary remarks that the government was setting lawyers up to be killed. 'I have no doubt that there are lawyers who are walking the streets or driving on the roads of the North of Ireland who have become targets of assassins' bullets as a result of the statement that has been made tonight.'[22] It was a prophetic warning.

Three weeks later, Pat Finucane lay dead on the kitchen floor of his north Belfast home, the victim of an assassination team that had been heavily infiltrated by at least two arms of the security nexus — Special Branch and the Force Research Unit, an elite unit of British intelligence run by the elusive Colonel J. At least four members of the team had documented links with the security forces: the commander; one of the killers, Ken Barrett; the quartermaster, William Stobie; and the intelligence officer, Brian Nelson. The full details of state involvement in this murder and how the security network was structured will be unravelled in the course of this book, but it is useful to present at the outset a short summary of the facts of the case as they relate to both Special Branch and the FRU.[23]

There have been persistent allegations that Special Branch detectives had orchestrated the Finucane killing in advance. Ken Barrett, a self-confessed and now temporarily imprisoned member of the murder team, was recruited to Special Branch as an agent even after SB became aware of his complicity in the murder. He told the *Panorama* programme 'A Licence to Murder' in June 2002 that he had been given implicit sanction for the murder by a senior police officer. According to Barrett, at a meeting with Jim Spence, then a senior loyalist commander in Belfast, the officer made clear the force's antipathy towards the solicitor:

> Pat was an IRA man like and he was dealing in finances and stuff for them and IRA was a bad boy and if he was out, like, they'd have a lot of trouble replacing him, stuff like this. He says: 'He'll have to go. He'd have to go.' He said: 'He's a thorn in everybody's side. He'll have to go.' He was determined in pursuing that. That's the one he wanted. They didn't want any fucking about. They didn't want to wait months. They wanted it done.[24]

As preparations for the killing gathered pace, Barrett met with the UFF's intelligence officer, Brian Nelson, who gave him a photograph that included an image of the solicitor. Nelson, the recipient of the character statement from the FRU commander noted above, was, in reality, an army agent brought back to Northern Ireland to infiltrate the loyalists. Ostensibly, he was charged with gathering intelligence in order to save lives. In fact, he proved instrumental in the recalibration of loyalist capacity. An influential report forwarded to the British and Irish governments in 1999 by the British Irish Rights Watch, a respected human rights group, detailed the unassailable logic behind such a policy. According to this report, the Force Research Unit 'broke every rule in the book and committed some of the most serious crimes, including conspiracy to murder, collecting and providing information likely to be of use to terrorists and directing terrorists.'[25]

For Brian Nelson, the FRU's most successful agent within the ranks of the loyalist paramilitaries, the power of life and death was an addiction. 'I was bitten by a bug,' he wrote in his personal journal. 'Hooked is probably a more appropriate word. One becomes enmeshed in a web of intrigue, conspiracies, confidences, dangers and the power of being aware of things that others around you aren't. The power of this phenomenon acts like a drug.'[26]

Those administering the dosage to Nelson soothed any moral qualms he may have had about the consequences of his actions. Throughout his career as an army agent, Nelson was given impunity to commit criminal acts, including extortion, the intimidation of witnesses in criminal prosecutions and conspiracy to murder.[27] The journal has never been published in full but is given critical weight by Judge Cory in his assessment of the need to hold a public inquiry into the circumstances of the Finucane killing.[28] As Justice Cory concluded, in a formulation close to that put forward by the British Irish Rights Watch, 'FRU considered the normal rules — including the rule of law — to be suspended and the gathering of intelligence to be an end that was capable of justifying questionable means.'[29]

According to Barrett, in the undercover recording with the *Panorama* programme, there was no doubt that Finucane was the target; nor was there any doubt that Nelson knew it when he provided the picture showing the lawyer with an IRA suspect, Pat McGeown, following his acquittal on charges relating to the murder of two British corporals: 'He brought it out. It was in like a wee plastic bag. He [Finucane] was in a case at that time and he was outside the court or something with a top Provie and you seen him fucking jubilant. I just says: Right, that's dead on.'[30] For Cory, the lack of documentary evidence backing up this claim is not a barrier to coming to the conclusion that it has the ring of authenticity. Cory maintains that it is quite simply inconceivable that neither Nelson nor his handlers were aware that the solicitor faced a clear and present danger. The failure to alert him of this danger was, in itself, evidence of collusion.

The quartermaster of the murder team was William Stobie. Stobie had been recruited into Special Branch as an agent two years earlier. He had been arrested following the murder by the UFF of a Protestant teenager, Adam Lambert, in a case of mistaken identity. They thought he was Catholic, sufficient grounds for his killing. It was an early indication of the dangers inherent for the security forces in entering a

Faustian bargain with those it subsequently sought to control. Yet, rather than being charged, Stobie was recruited into the secret world of the security services, where rules were distorted for short-term gain. His job was to relay information to Special Branch about paramilitary activity in the loyalist heartlands of north and west Belfast. He proved useful and by 1989 he was responsible for sourcing weapons for one of the most active loyalist units in the city. A week before the Finucane killing, Stobie was tasked to procure the weapons required for a murder bid. He told his handlers in advance where the weapons would be stored and when they were to be moved. Inexplicably, no attempt was made to disable the weapons or install sophisticated tracking devices. The murder plan was simply allowed to unfold.

On the day of the murder, Stobie again alerted his handlers to an impending hit against what he termed 'a top Provie'.[31] Nothing was done with this intelligence. His handlers reasoned to their source that he should regard inaction as a matter of self-preservation: if the operation was compromised, Stobie would have been implicated. The informer accepted the reasoning. Ken Barrett went even further, telling *Panorama* that a senior police officer relayed information to the murder team that there would be no checkpoints to impede the assassins on their way to the Finucane house on the night of the killing. The Cory Report rejects any suggestion that the army checkpoints were deliberately removed to facilitate the operation, but pointedly remains neutral on whether the allegation that police officers may have provided scouting intelligence should be considered in a public inquiry.[32]

If serious concerns surround the manner in which the intelligence services handled the information gathered from agents in advance of the killing, their activities following the Finucane murder are even more questionable. These include the obstruction of the initial criminal investigation, perversion of the course of justice and the deployment of ever more desperate strategies, including arson, in order to prevent the truth from coming out, matters explored in detail in the later stages of this book.

It was indicative of the dismal zero-sum reality governing Northern Ireland politics that the Cory Report prompted tribal rather than rational responses. Rather than deal with the complexities of the issue, somewhat predictably, and not a little self-servingly, Sinn Féin, the political wing of the republican movement, saw justification for its war in the provisional verdict set out by the Canadian judge. 'The Cory Report is a damning indictment of British rule in Ireland...This is a scenario usually associated with repressive dictatorships,' crowed Gerry Kelly, a Sinn Féin representative who had himself served multiple jail sentences for his role in IRA bombing campaigns in London.

The SDLP leader, Mark Durkan, divined wider strategic reasons for the delay in the immediate convening of a public inquiry (as recommended by Cory) into the Finucane murder than those cited by the British government, namely the need to pass new legislation to ensure the protection of national security. Durkan stated: 'People will be cynical about their [the British government's] newly-found determination to secure prosecutions now. People are asking if this is the government's real reason for the delay or just an excuse.'[33]

The Democratic Unionist Party, still on an electoral war footing after its strong showing in the Assembly elections, astutely put forward its candidate in the forthcoming European campaign, to complain about further concessions to the IRA. 'It is outrageous,' Jim Allister fulminated, 'that the taxpayer is going for years to come to be subjected to a series of inquiries, costing further hundreds of millions.' The Ulster Unionist leader, David Trimble, however, captured the agenda with his barbed articulation of certainty. The Canadian judge, he maintained, had demonstrated 'astonishing naivety', but 'if as a result...the truth about Finucane and [Rosemary] Nelson comes into the public domain incontrovertibly then there will be some side-benefit.'[34] The comment had the effect — even if unintended — of reinforcing the campaign of innuendo insinuating complicity in terrorism waged from the instant that the lawyers were killed.

The dissembling involved in Trimble's response represented shrewd politics but bad history from the leader of the UUP.[35] It suggested that the activities of the lawyers made them susceptible to attack. While it may be a somewhat surprising intervention from an academic lawyer and Nobel peace prize-winner, who later maintained that it was an unfortunate reality that such difficult questions needed to be posed, it is a perspective that remains deeply embedded within large sections of the security forces.

A serving intelligence officer told the author recently that 'the murder of Finucane was worse than wrong: it was a mistake', stemming from 'flaws in strategic reasoning'.[36] According to this argument, which is based on a clinical calculation of expected utility, there were sound tactical reasons to believe that allowing the killing to proceed could have benefits for the intelligence community. The problem lay in not working out in advance how to combat the unintended consequences. Killing an officer of the court provided significant and ongoing traction for the subsequent unravelling of the intelligence network, considerations not calibrated at the time. In the dispassionate and calculated view of this officer, the killing was 'a tactical success and a strategic disaster'.

Within the higher echelons of the old RUC a much more atavistic approach is the norm. In the estimation of a former head of Special Branch, Finucane was 'involved'. This meant that he was vulnerable to assault, if not a legitimate target. These distinctions are more than semantic. They are crucial in parsing how the unified agenda governing different aspects of the security nexus, created in the 1980s and early 1990s, fell apart in response to the new dynamic created by the peace process. Metropolitan priorities changed and those most exposed were the locally recruited, whose remit was to provide material support for a previous policy. The ideological buttress fell apart as, in Tony Blair's memorable phrasing, 'the hand of history' caused unsustainable pressure. According to the Special Branch officer quoted above, the RUC in general and its security apparatus in particular were defenestrated for base political motives. This concern was captured in a hugely prescient intervention on the day of the first IRA ceasefire in August 1994. Jim Molyneaux, then leader of the Ulster Unionists, referred to it as the most destabilising event in the history of the party.

Back in 1989, when Sir John Stevens was first brought in to investigate allegations of collusion, a very different reality pertained. The Manichean script disseminated by the Northern Ireland Office posited the conflict as a terrorist assault on a fully functional democratic state. In the context of an ongoing war of attrition with the IRA, the security forces required the extra leverage provided by the deployment of agents within the ranks of paramilitaries. Even if it meant the tacit condoning of murder, the publicly sacrosanct legal and political processes were circumvented as a matter of operational policy.

In such circumstances, it was imperative that the ambiguities inherent in giving operational primacy to the security nexus be downplayed. The unanswered question is whether or not this circumvention was itself endorsed by the political establishment? If so, there needs to be a fundamental re-assessment of the initial purpose of the Stevens Inquiry. Notwithstanding the integrity of the Metropolitan Police Commissioner, was the establishment of the inquiry, and its later reconvention in response to the 1999 British Irish Rights Watch report, merely an act of 'symbolic reassurance'?[37] To what extent did its remit change since it began its investigations fifteen years ago? In this context what is particularly remarkable is that despite releasing a summary of his conclusions, even the terms of reference of the second Stevens inquiry have yet to be publicly disclosed.[38]

Either way, as noted above, whether sanctioned politically or not, serious allegations of collusion between the various nodes of the security nexus to frustrate the inquiry need to be resolved as a matter of urgency. Prior to Sir John Stevens' first arrival in Belfast in 1989, the top echelons of the RUC and the army decided to maintain a deliberate policy of obstruction against external scrutiny.[39] A document dated September 1990 was quoted in the Cory Report that raises the most profound questions of accountability or, more appropriately, the potential lack of it. Given its importance, the document and Cory's interpretation of it merit airing.

> I have reviewed a document which would appear to lend strong support to the allegation that the RUC SB and FRU consciously set out to withhold pertinent information from the Stevens Inquiries. It sets out the minutes of various meetings attended by senior officials, including the former GOC NI (General Officer Commanding, Northern Ireland). This document confirms that the GOC NI had discussed the Stevens Inquiry team with the Chief Constable of the RUC before the Inquiry team even arrived in the province. The document also states that: 'The CC (Chief Constable) had decided that the Stevens Inquiry would have no access to intelligence documents or information, nor the units supplying them.'[40]

The document also notes that the decision by the army not to hand over material to the inquiry that related to the intelligence it had recovered from Brian Nelson was taken 'under the instructions of the RUC', who, on paper, retained operational pre-eminence in the prosecution of the war. This state of affairs necessitates two comments at this stage. First, Sir Jack Hermon, who was Chief Constable at the time Nelson was operational, gave an interview to *Panorama* in 1992 in which he placed the blame for the fiasco on the army acting without due regard for the rules. He castigated the army for running agents in an irresponsible manner. 'I feel that what we are saying is that to a degree at least, the running of an agent went badly wrong, and that if it was seen or when it was seen, it should have been identified and immediate steps taken to correct anything that had happened that was not proper'.[41] There were obvious reasons why the former Chief Constable would wish to transfer the blame to the army, particularly given the fact that one of its agents had just been convicted of conspiracy to murder. What is difficult to reconcile is why the security nexus, including the RUC itself, refused to provide Stevens with the information that would allow for recommendations to put in place adequate controls.

Hermon intimated that he was sympathetic to the argument put forward by the commander of the unit handling Nelson that Home Office guidelines were 'more appropriate in dealing with the criminal fraternity in the East End of London rather than the terrorist organisations in Northern Ireland'. For Hermon, however, the problem was that what would be required would not necessarily be acceptable. 'They are very difficult to follow but they are guidelines and one could well say that they were inadequate. But the question would then be raised just of whether what was adequate could be acceptable within the law.'[42]

As a result of this worldview, the operation of the secret war against the IRA was destined to remain in the shadows, where its brutal reality would not publicly offend democratic sensibility. It was a question that Judge Cory found deeply disturbing. Cory remains neutral on whether causal responsibility lay with the Chief Constable under whose watch the abuse took place or with the failure of his replacement, Hugh Annesley, to challenge effectively the cultural environment in which information was deliberately withheld. Cory judged the existence of the document, however, to be:

further evidence of the unfortunate attitude that then persisted within RUC SB [Special Branch] and [British Army] FRU [Force Research Unit]. Namely, that they were not bound by the law and were above and beyond its reach. These documents reveal that government agencies (the Army and the RUC) were prepared to participate jointly in collusive acts in order to protect their perceived interest.[43]

Given the centrality of policing and criminal justice to contemporary debates over the future of devolution in Northern Ireland, the use or misuse of intelligence and covert policing remains an acutely sensitive political issue. This has been underscored by a war of attrition between the IRA and what the republicans term 'faceless securocrats' in which claim and counter-claim poison the political atmosphere. The restoration of devolution did little to quell the war. Recent skirmishes that have demonstrated an alarming propensity towards political implosion include allegations of gunrunning from Colombia, the controversial break-in at the Castlereagh headquarters of Special Branch on St Patrick's Day 2001, a heavy-handed police investigation into allegations that the IRA had orchestrated a spy-ring from within the devolved administration at Stormont, and the unmasking of Stakeknife, allegedly the army's most highly placed agent within the IRA.[44]

As this book was going to press, the Chief Constable of the PSNI publicly accused the IRA of carrying out a heist at the Northern Bank headquarters in Belfast, which saw the robbers escaping with a hoard of £26.5 million. Citing 'intelligence', Hugh Orde opined, 'The provisional IRA were responsible for this crime and all main lines of inquiry currently undertaken are in that direction.'[45] The announcement followed weeks of feverish speculation, fuelled by arrests of prominent republicans in Belfast. Orde claimed that the decision to attribute blame was made for 'operational reasons' and was not the result of political pressure.

In the background, however, it has become increasingly clear that the British government has not embarked on a fundamental change in strategy, a move that has led to the partial dismantling of the security apparatus.[46] Following the Patten Commission on the future of policing in 1999, there has been a sharp divergence of interests within the security nexus. The Police Service of Northern Ireland has replaced the RUC and the former power of Special Branch has been sharply delineated, at least in public.[47] It was notable that Sir John Stevens explicitly endorsed two controversial reports into how Special Branch had responded to the Real IRA bombing of Omagh in 1998 in which twenty-nine people and unborn twins died, the worst single atrocity of the Troubles.

While the break-in at Castlereagh was deeply embarrassing to the entire security nexus, the element most exposed was Special Branch, which saw its elite status and self-proclaimed professionalism left open to ridicule.

At a strategic level, the blame for the excesses of the past in relation to the 'Dirty War' has found tangible expression in a convenient scapegoat. But is this really the case? Can responsibility be so cleanly compartmentalised? In order to answer this question, one must excavate the grounds for the initial policy. Criminal investigations into the Finucane killing are now coming to an end and a moment of truth is approaching. Three of the leading figures within the UFF chain of command in west Belfast are now dead. Tommy 'Tucker' Lyttle died of a heart attack in 1995. His former colleagues killed William Stobie after his trial collapsed in 2002. Brian Nelson died in 2003 of natural causes in Florida. Ken Barrett, the self-implicated gunman, is now temporarily incarcerated. What is also on trial is the system that allowed Barrett to kill.

The question of accountability is at the heart of the heated debate over the reality of the Dirty War. Did the politicians know what was going on and condone it, or did they fail to police the state apparatus, leading to the potential charge of an alarming abdication of responsibility? We require a much more nuanced appreciation of the interlocking mechanisms that created the security nexus in order to ascertain the level of responsibility. Terrorism, like its mirror opposite, counter-terrorism, operates at an institutional as well as a personal level. While it is highly unlikely that a paper trail will ever emerge that points definitively to a political mandate for extrajudicial activities, it is important to examine what the policy priorities were at the time and how political rhetoric fed into that system. Within the Northern Ireland context, each of the security agencies, including Special Branch, MI5, the SAS and the FRU, sat on a Tactical Action Group. Overarching this was a Security Coordinator, who in turn sat on the Joint Intelligence Committee (JIC). Located in the Cabinet Office in Downing Street, the JIC was made up of the directors of each intelligence agency, including MI5 and MI6. The JIC's research output was discussed at regular weekly briefings with the Prime Minister. The level of political involvement in the process — as consumer of the output or as post-production editor for propaganda purposes — is a matter of intense debate. The same question lies at the centre of the controversy over the publication of two dossiers alleging the clear and present danger posed to Britain's vital interests by Saddam Hussein's chemical and biological weapons programmes, a key justification for the war against Iraq in the spring of 2003.

By its very nature, intelligence-gathering is a fallible pursuit requiring judgement calls based on incomplete, contradictory and sometimes erroneous information. As Northern Ireland attempts to rebuild confidence in policing, the unresolved issues surrounding how the intelligence community investigated, or, more accurately, failed to investigate because of wider security considerations, looms centre stage. The key issue facing a public inquiry into the Finucane killing is how to gain access to the contact records held by MI5, the one node in the network that had operatives stationed at every level in the horizontal and vertical web and who were ultimately responsible for the security briefings provided to the political establishment. At stake is not only ownership of the past but control over the future.

In order to frame that debate it is necessary first to examine how British security policy developed in response to IRA operations. This is followed by a detailed examination of the political environment pertaining in Northern Ireland in 1988 and 1989, providing important contextual details for the rationale behind the killing of Pat Finucane. Chapter Five details the way in which the criminal investigation into the murder was stymied and the implications of this for the integrity of the criminal justice system. Chapter Six places the inquiry in context.

Chapter 2
The Security Nexus

The Good Friday Agreement, sold as a moment of history, was designed to provide a template for Northern Ireland to move beyond conflict. Following five years of incomplete implementation, stalled negotiations, allegations of bad faith and spying, the British and Irish governments choreographed a revival. Underwritten by the apparent rapprochement of Sinn Féin and the Ulster Unionist Party, guarantees were sought from the IRA that its war was over. In return for the implementation of what amounted to the retrospective endorsement of partition, the Ulster Unionist Party would pledge to uphold the power-sharing executive. It promised an alluring and intriguing spectacle. The putative deal involved the devolution of policing and the criminal justice system for the first time since Stormont was prorogued in 1972. The momentous potential of the Agreement was underscored by the fact that it was now rendered conceivable that political representatives of the IRA (an organisation that had spent the conflict engaged in a war of attrition with the security forces) could, in theory, now direct the future of policing provision in a state it had pledged to destroy.

The trust involved in the rapprochement was all the more remarkable given the fact that the Assembly had collapsed over allegations of IRA involvement in a spying controversy at the heart of government the previous September. In the event, the Ulster Unionists balked at the last moment, citing a lack of transparency in the third act of IRA decommissioning carried out under the auspices of an international commission. The process was turned over to the adjudication of an electorate increasingly polarised and, from a unionist perspective, deeply sceptical of whether the process was advisable, let alone workable.[1] The resultant election confirmed that, contrary to the design blueprint, Northern Ireland was moving to the extremes, with the Democratic Unionist Party supplanting the Ulster Unionists and a more avuncular Sinn Féin reversing the traditional dominance of the SDLP. Attempts to resuscitate devolution at Leeds Castle in Kent in September 2004 proved unsuccessful. Despite briefings that suggested that the IRA was prepared to decommission itself, the DUP refused to countenance any return to devolution without greater transparency and the introduction of accountability structures within the governance of the Assembly, a strategy which suggested that for this particular branch of unionism, the ending of the IRA was not in itself sufficient. The transplantation of moderation with the politics of the extreme served only to verify mutual self-righteousness. The raid at the Northern Bank and the attribution of blame to the Provisionals has destroyed any short-term return to devolution.

Throughout the tortured negotiations that preceded the very public failure of politics, the issues of policing and the criminal justice system were the trump cards, used to threaten and entice depending on ideological perspective and circumstance.[2] As the peace process developed, the interlocking security nexus, created and finessed during the containment period of the Troubles, was dismantled in piecemeal fashion. Each change, from the Patten Commission on the future of policing to the, as yet unimplemented, Review of Criminal Justice, necessitated reassessments of previously sacrosanct core beliefs about the nature of the conflict and the causal responsibility of discrete sets of actors for the ensuing violence. In the process, the corrosive impact on the entire policing and criminal justice system of the institutionalisation of emergency legislation was progressively revealed.[3]

As with the disbandment of the B Specials in 1970 and the renaming of the Ulster Defence Regiment in the early 1990s following widespread evidence of interlocking membership and collusion between the regiment and loyalist paramilitaries, there was recognition in London that the core of the problem rested in the self-identification of one community with the forces of law and order. The cynicism of providing the Royal Ulster Constabulary as an institution with the St

George's Cross — the highest award for gallantry — while relegating it to the history books as a deeply flawed institution, served merely to heighten unionist distrust. It provided grist to the mill for those opposed to any change while tying the hands of pro-Agreement unionist negotiators, forced to labour under ultimately futile motions to retain the corporate identity of the RUC in the title deeds of the Police Service of Northern Ireland.

Changing the name without changing the structure, particularly with reference to Special Branch, was, however, equally problematic for sections of the nationalist community.[4] The relatively recent defenestration of Special Branch over its role in the prosecution of the war against terrorism was a shrewd political move by London. It placed the blame for excess on the locally recruited, while downplaying the reality of how Special Branch was just one part of a fully integrated security nexus set in place in the early 1980s.

In order to demonstrate how and why this nexus was established, it is first necessary to revisit the pivotal period of 1969–73, when the contours of the arena were shaped. Two further distinct phases are then tracked in order to demonstrate how structural changes in the security network mirrored and, on occasion, facilitated, political developments through the application of military pressure. In the second stage, profound changes to the criminal justice system were pushed through as all sides bunkered down for a long war of attrition. The policy was accompanied by the removal of the British army from frontline duties. By giving primacy to the police in managing confrontation on the streets, the British government sought to convince Northern Ireland and wider constituencies that significant progress was being made in the struggle against a mere criminal conspiracy. This containment strategy disintegrated as the IRA used the prisons as a key battleground, which culminated in the 1981 Hunger Strike. A third phase then opened up with an aggressive counter-insurgency strategy, beginning with the shoot-to-kill allegations of 1982 and continuing, with ever-increasing sophistication, until, and beyond, the murder of Pat Finucane in 1989.

THE DESCENT INTO VIOLENCE

Sectarianism has a long pedigree on the island of Ireland, the bedrock on which the competing unionist and nationalist discourses about the legitimacy or otherwise of the state is built. For the republican tradition, the mere existence of Northern Ireland is an affront to the nationalist creed. For Northern Ireland unionists, the indivisible nation state had an original British patent, modified by exigency and Protestant evangelicalism, with the predominantly Catholic nationalist community cast as heretic, accepted on sufferance. The civil rights movement in the late 1960s, driven by an agenda that agitated for change within the constitutional status quo, provided a crucial new dynamic. It forced the governance of Northern Ireland into the national and, sporadically, international spotlight. This increased scrutiny highlighted the extraordinary measures through which unionist dominance was maintained.

Protestant extremists depicted the demand for equality under the law as cover for an IRA campaign to destroy the state. Compromise and tolerance, never highly regarded concepts in the Manichean world of Northern Irish politics, became code for the actions of traitors. As the congregation of the Free Presbyterian Church, under Ian Kyle Paisley, grew both numerically and in political influence, the language of politics took on a distinctly biblical, apocalyptic tone. Stormont was forced to either live up to its democratic ideals or accept an uncomfortable alternative that it was, at root, a state founded — and sustained — on base sectarian principles of domination. In the maelstrom of August 1969, the entire structure buckled under the weight of its own contradictions. Caught in a vice between ideological certainty and the necessity of change that, by its very nature, weakened the underpinnings of government, the strain was unsustainable.

As Lord Cameron reported in his investigation into the reasons behind the descent into violence, one of the key determinants was 'a growing and powerful sense of resentment and frustration among the Catholic population at failure to achieve either acceptance on the part of the government of any need to investigate these complaints [housing allocation, gerrymandering and job discrimination] or to provide and enforce a remedy for them'.[5] As a consequence of political failure, interlinked but subtly differentiated imperatives were forced onto the agenda of the metropolitan centres uninterested in — and ignorant of — the volatile nature of events on the ground in Belfast.

As I have argued elsewhere, the outbreak of the Troubles revealed alarming intelligence gaps concerning both the agitators of change and the direction they were likely to take.[6] Stormont ministers relied on assessments that were based more on visceral belief than careful analysis, a myopia that intensified as the civil rights campaign progressed. The hidden hand of the IRA, divined wrongly by Unionist politicians and the police as the propelling force behind the Northern Ireland Civil Rights Association, became a self-fulfilling prophecy. This revelation occurred not necessarily because of the republican movement's strategic guile, but rather because of strategic flaws in the security response to the campaign of civil disobedience. As a consequence, from the baton charging of civil rights protestors at a pivotal march in Derry in October 1968 onwards, what the socialist agitator Eamon McCann referred to as a 'howl of elemental rage' was unleashed that none was capable of assuaging.[7]

By the time the Prime Minister, Sir Terence O'Neill, gave a television address warning that Ulster 'stood at the crossroads', the course to chaos had already been plotted. Little more than five years after the IRA was forced to call off an ineffective and futile border campaign, it reasserted its position as a necessary defender of Catholic communities within the working class ghettoes of Belfast and Derry, communities that played little or no role in the development of the political strategies guiding the civil rights movement. The very different demography of the two major cities played a crucial role in mediating their response to the escalating crisis. The overwhelmingly nationalist population of Derry, coupled with its proximity to the border, made the discrimination apparent and simultaneously allowed for contestation. Belfast, by contrast, was a much more volatile arena. In August 1969, fears of pogroms once again descended on the overcrowded streets on the western edge of the city centre. This process intensified as the marching season approached and erupted into sustained violence in August 1969. In the search for scapegoats, the IRA proved a useful target, as demonstrated by a tribunal of enquiry set up under Lord Scarman to establish the causes of the violence.

> It was considered that the civil rights movement [unknown to its leadership], though embracing many sincere and well-meaning people, had been successfully infiltrated by the IRA for purposes wholly unconnected with reform or the removal of injustice and that there existed a strategic plan which envisaged the ultimate destruction of the government and Stormont by the employment of guerrilla tactics under arms.[8]

This retrospective justification underpinned the entire RUC submission to the tribunal. In disputing allegations from the Catholic hierarchy and representatives of the community that the response to the events of 15 August 1969 demonstrated the partiality of police action as a driving force in fuelling the violence, counsel for the RUC made clear its own institutional bias.

> The events of the past two years, with their sorry catalogue of attacks on army and security personnel, must surely have convinced everyone that there are in Northern Ireland a number of people who regard murder as a legitimate means of achieving their political objectives. We submit that on the night of 14/15 August, such people were active in the disturbances in Belfast.[9]

The Provisional IRA, whose origins can be traced directly to the violence in Belfast on 15 August, was indeed the main beneficiary of rising Catholic alienation. It is important to emphasise, however, that this was contingent on shifting dynamics that no one was able to control rather than a pre-ordained reality.[10] The fatal flaw in the civil rights movement centred on its mistaken belief that the street protests it unleashed could be controlled. The moderates did not allow for the very different strategy followed by the radicals both in Derry and within the university-based People's Democracy, which saw the protests, in part, as an opportunity to grace the world stage of student protest. The radicals did not allow for the hidden agenda of the republican movement; and the IRA leadership did not allow for the way in which militarists south of the border within the organisation saw in the upheaval the possibility of a resurrection of the armed struggle. The ranks of the Belfast IRA, which could not even muster a minibus of volunteers to attend the fiftieth anniversary of the Easter Rising in 1966, swelled as the course of Irish history took a dangerous detour into uncharted terrain.

The first successful attempt to use intelligence agencies to control the direction of events in Northern Ireland came not from within the province, or from the British intelligence agencies, but rather from south of the border. Within the Irish Republic, the lurch towards violence was viewed with horror and amazement in equal measure. The implosion of the Nationalist Party, and, with it, the subservient position of Northern nationalism as a supplicant to be humoured rather than engaged with, challenged fundamental certainties south of the border, where the level of ignorance about what was actually going on within the Catholic community mirrored that in London and Belfast. The violence of 1969 altered the dynamics more quickly in the Irish capital because the ideological imperatives were more urgent. Crucially, the violence and its management became integral to the complex manoeuvrings for power within the governing party, Fianna Fáil.[11]

Two of the most senior politicians within Fianna Fáil — the Minister for Finance, Charles J. Haughey, and Neil Blaney, the avuncular Minister for Agriculture — controlled, with implicit sanction, a covert campaign to infiltrate the civil rights movement and pledge arms to defend, if necessary, Northern nationalists from threatened assault. Prior to their ignominious dismissal from office in May 1970, accused of an illicit attempted importation of arms into Dublin airport the previous month, the plotting ministers were given enormous leverage over the direction of events because of a panicked reaction by the Dublin cabinet to the largest population movement in Western Europe since the end of World War Two.

Days after the Taoiseach, Jack Lynch, gave a televised broadcast in which he concluded with the warning that the Irish government could not stand by while mobs ran amok in Belfast, the cabinet met to give tangible expression to how the Dublin administration would proceed. A cabinet directive mandated 'a sum of money — the amount and channel of disbursement of which would be determined by the Minister for Finance — should be made available from the exchequer to provide aid for the current victims of the current unrest in the Six Counties.'[12] The operation resulted in a charge to the Irish exchequer of £100,000 (more than £1,000,000 in today's prices). A subsequent investigation by the Dáil Committee of Public Accounts revealed that only a fraction was spent on humanitarian relief. The bulk of the money was used to finance weapons-buying operations in London, Europe and the United States. Funds were diverted through double-blind bank accounts for the financing of a propaganda *samizdat* called *The Voice of the North*; to broaden the membership of local committees of the NICRA through the careful nurturing of those amenable to Fianna Fáil leadership; and to finance a concerted attempt to deepen the schism within the Republican movement.

The case against Blaney was thrown out; Haughey and his co-defendants, who included a senior member of the Provisional IRA,

John Kelly, and a serving Irish army intelligence officer, Captain James Kelly, were acquitted in October, following two criminal trials. The machinations surrounding the extent of governmental involvement in nationalist politics in the pivotal period of 1969–70, authorised or not, however, provide important empirical evidence not only of the connection between elite political infighting and events on the ground, but also of how intelligence agencies could shape the ideological contours of the political arena in which violence occurred.

The covertly sponsored Irish government newspaper, *The Voice of the North*, was instrumental in recalibrating the terms of the debate about the causes of the conflict and its potential solution, backing a line of argument used by Neil Blaney in his public feud with the Taoiseach. The possibility that weapons could be made available, although unfulfilled, steeled the resolve of Northern republicans to split from the Official IRA and with it the policy of critical engagement with the Southern state.[13] In the aftermath of the initial crisis, Dublin moved quickly to provide secret backing for constitutional nationalism to counter the vacuum emerging as a consequence of the escalating violence. Crucially, the careful nurturing of what was to become the SDLP, and the time given to its leading voices by civil servants and the government, as a potential mechanism to shore up rather than further destabilise the Northern state, only occurred *after* the dismissal of Blaney and Haughey. It represented a defence mechanism within the Fianna Fáil leadership to the alternative, more destabilising perspective advocated publicly by the Donegal party boss throughout the Arms Crisis, but only by the more devious Minister for Finance in the immediate aftermath of the acquittals. There was much truth in the charge by the opposition, Fine Gael, following the extraordinary scenes outside the Four Courts that the 'picture which emerges is one of sordid intrigue combined with extreme incompetence and gross laxity in the handling of public business'.[14] The critical importance of the Arms Trial rests on the fact that it coincided with a decision to disengage from Northern adventurism, which, despite rhetorical flourishes associated with Haughey's sensational return to power in 1979, and the incidental timing of the 1981 election during the Hunger Strike, remained marginal to Southern politics, if not to the power struggle within Fianna Fáil itself.

For the British government such disengagement was, quite simply, not an option. It was forced to revisit the integrity of a sectarian quarrel. A long-term irritant, encapsulated in Winston Churchill's scathing reference to the dreary steeples of Fermanagh and Tyrone surviving intact despite global shifts in power, the contemporary violence also needed astute micro-management. It was a quality in short supply in a city where gunfire rang out and acrid smoke billowed from countless flashpoints.

Less than four days after the military were first deployed on the streets of Belfast, the General Officer Commanding of the army in Northern Ireland took control over the entire security apparatus.[15] The decision, taken through necessity rather than volition, represented a subversion of the relationship in a democratic society between the army and the police. It gave powerful witness to the extraordinary measures required to restore even a semblance of order. An early reliance on the worldview promulgated by increasingly fearful unionist ministers, civil servants and the police, particularly after the Conservatives took power in June 1970, proved counterproductive. The inability to restore calm was occasioned by rising and unrealisable expectations on both sides of the community concerning both the operational function of the troops and the wider political purpose of their deployment.

On his first visit to Northern Ireland in June 1970, the Conservative Home Secretary, William Whitelaw, spent less than forty-five minutes with nationalist representatives. A marked contrast in the security response to Catholic and Protestant demonstrations further tainted perceptions of bias, simultaneously reinforcing fears about the threats emanating from each and destroying the illusion that the army was neutral on the competing claims of each group as to who held causal responsibility for the deteriorating security situation.[16] Maintaining order without radical change to the governance structure itself was, despite protestations to the contrary, itself an overtly political act. Imprisoning civil rights leaders, such as Bernadette Devlin, for public order offences deprived the security forces of any moderating force on the ground. The decision by British army forces to 'stand idly by' as the St Mathew's Church in a Catholic enclave on the eastern edge of Belfast city centre came under sustained assault in June 1970 provided the nascent Provisional IRA with a tailor-made propaganda coup.

The battle was critical for the credibility of the Provisional leadership. It demonstrated to sceptical nationalists the inability of the British army to provide adequate defence. It also outlined the possibility of an alternative to the politics of cowed oppression; an alternative that met fire with fire. From the defence of St Mathew's onwards, there was to be no turning back. The authority of the Provisional IRA was further augmented by the introduction of what amounted to a parallel policing force in nationalist areas. The symbolic importance of a formal rejection of authority was reinforced by the explicit support of politicians for the initiative. By relinquishing their position as the official opposition at Stormont, the Nationalist Party had symbolically retreated behind the barricades to be protected by a paramilitary force that openly called for the destruction of the state.

The announcement that rioters would be shot on sight and the introduction of a mandatory six-month term of imprisonment for incitement through the Criminal Justice (Temporary Provisions) Act on 1 July 1970, gave powerful witness to the fact that military means alone would be used to gain leverage over what was essentially a political problem. Two days later this strategy was made manifest in the infamous Falls Road curfew.[17] Acting on information about a hidden cache of weapons, the British army launched its most aggressive policing action since its deployment in August 1969. As helicopters descended around the Lower Falls Road area, loudspeakers were used to proclaim that anyone on the streets after dark would be shot on sight. It was a pivotal miscalculation, the long-term consequences rendered more serious because of a decision to allow two unionist ministers to tour the area in an open-top armoured car. Increasingly nervous about the turn of events and with a potentially explosive trial involving the former Minister for Finance scheduled for the coming months, Dublin was forced again to intervene. The moderate Minister for Foreign Affairs, Patrick Hillery, visited the area and made clear in an edition of the BBC *Panorama* programme — deemed so sensitive that it was not broadcast in Northern Ireland itself — that it was 'totally wrong to think that in the modern world you can with force of arms, force of British money, keep a state there which is quite unusual and depends on tyranny at times'.[18]

Despite this outward show of unity with the self-diagnosed oppressed of the Belfast ghetto, a profound shift in the Irish government's diagnosis of the problem had occurred. From its perspective, the principal threat to stability emanated not from the heavy-handed response of the military or the blinkered worldview of the Stormont government, but rather from the self-proclaimed defenders of

Northern nationalism. In an impassioned address on the eve of the traditional Twelfth of July demonstrations, Jack Lynch reached out to both the unionist and British people and governments and appealed for calm.

> It is for political leaders to govern wisely and justly. I accept the guarantees of the British government that they will do so. My government is the second guarantor. Therefore, you, who have suffered distress and indignity in the North, are no longer unprotected victims.[19]

The appeal fell on deaf ears. Orange Order leaders saw opposition to their demonstrations as further evidence of a coordinated campaign to destroy the legitimacy of the state; a campaign in which they believed the British government had tacitly colluded through the findings of yet another eminent judge, Lord Hunt. In a controversial report that inflamed unionist perceptions that Britain could not be trusted and bolstered republican certainty that its cause was morally justified, Lord Hunt recommended that the B Specials be disbanded, with its membership subsumed within a new regiment of the British army, no longer under operation control of Stormont. Harry West, a hardliner with pretensions to assume the Ulster Unionist leadership, caught the mood with a speech at the main Orange demonstration in Belfast.

> Today we have a softly softly approach that has proved disastrous, no-go areas in two of our principal cities and with self-appointed defence forces, no Specials and no-nothing policy in our government. All this, together with the threat of an armed insurrection from the Republic, presents a very great threat to our country… [Ulster requires a] strong-armed security force under the control of the Northern Ireland government and under the command of an Ulsterman.[20]

The inability of the Stormont regime to manage that process, or the British government to force restraint, placed insurmountable burdens on an army with little or no experience of civil policing. Its credibility as an independent arbiter, already threatened as a consequence of the St Mathew's Church incident and the Falls Road curfew, was comprehensively undermined as the military swamped nationalist areas. Martial law, although not formally declared, was in effective place.[21] The strategy played into the hands of the Provisional IRA. It correctly calculated that an increase in bombings against commercial targets would lead to increased pressure for a policy of repression, which would, in turn, feed into a cycle of violence. Despite protestations that it was an honest broker, the introduction of the military had served to alter, irrevocably, the dynamics of civil disturbances, with the radicals determined that a further push would force the British to wash their hands of the entire mess, a view openly canvassed by the influential newspaper *The Economist.*

British revulsion and resolve were strengthened by the murder of three young soldiers in 1970, shot in the back of the head by an IRA murder gang who befriended them in a bar before killing them as they urinated by the side of the road on the outskirts of Belfast. Three days after the killing the political might of the shipyards was pressed into action as 4,000 workers demonstrated through the city centre demanding the introduction of internment. Outflanked by critics within the party, O'Neill's successor as Northern Ireland Prime Minister, Chichester Clark, was forced to resign, replaced by Brian Faulkner, for whom internment represented the only possibility of controlling the militant tendency.

Faulkner was caught in a trap of his own design. On the one hand, he came to power precisely because he advocated a stringent security policy; yet its deployment would lead to more instability, not less. He was to find, like O'Neill and Chichester Clark before him, that by its very exercise the grip on the levers of power weakened and with it the legitimacy of the state. An early indication of Faulkner's priorities was the fact that his first meeting after securing the premiership was with General Tuzo, the General Officer Commanding of the army in Northern Ireland, at which he claimed that the ineffectiveness of security policy was linked to the fact that the army was not deployed to 'seek out and destroy the terrorist'.[22]

As the security situation deteriorated, the interaction between the army and the political establishment was placed on a more calibrated footing with the establishment in 1970 of a Joint Security Committee, with a senior civil servant appointed to liaise between the Northern Ireland Cabinet Office and army headquarters in Lisburn. Despite apparent misgivings about the efficacy of internment, the military concurred, offering in a press conference an indication of the scale of the carnage unleashed. Between July 1970 and February 1971 '743 pounds of explosives, 8,070 yards of fuse, 2,618 detonators, 282 assorted weapons, and approximately 40,000 rounds of ammunition had been discovered and 171 people charged with unlawful possession.'[23] The stage was set for the introduction of administrative internment as a political necessity.

Operation Demetrius was launched in a pre-dawn raid on 9 August 1971. By the end of the day more than two-thirds of all republicans on whom the RUC had intelligence information had been incarcerated in makeshift prisons. The vast majority of those scooped up were Official IRA, not the Provisional faction, whose membership had either been largely inactive throughout the civil rights period or who had joined after the establishment of the barricades and on whom no credible information existed.

As the Provisional IRA's campaign intensified, the need for credible intelligence became an operational imperative, one that was facilitated by the use of what was euphemistically termed 'in-depth interrogation methods' on those who were interned. Degrading treatment, including the use of sleep deprivation, was designed to garner information. Allegations, later upheld by the European Court of Human Rights, of the blindfolding of internees and the staging of mock executions, along with the systematic removal of rights to legal representation, seeped into the public domain. The very fact that internment was exclusively deployed, in its initial stages, against the nationalist community further radicalised its membership and fuelled the perception that the state was now actively condoning torture as an acceptable instrument of security policy.

Designed to isolate the IRA from its latent support base, Operation Demetrius was a profound miscalculation. On the very day internment was introduced, fourteen people died in gunfights between the army and republicans, including a Catholic priest. In a graphic account marking the twenty-fifth anniversary of its introduction, Kevin Myers of the *Irish Times* recalled events of that day in Ardoyne: 'Insanity seized the city. Hundreds of vehicles were hijacked and factories burnt. Loyalist and IRA gunmen were everywhere…Ardoyne seemed as if it was going to provide the greatest horrors of all as Protestants fled the area, burning their homes before they left.'[24] The next day ten people died, then six, then four. By the end of the month thirty-five people had been killed.[25] The IRA demonstrated its ongoing capacity by significantly increasing the level of violence. As community relations plummeted and whole communities once again were on the move across the sectarian interfaces of Belfast, the IRA found its inchoate message receiving widespread political backing by default.

A consortium involving all Republican, Nationalist and SDLP politicians called for a withdrawal from public life, rent strikes and even toyed with the establishment of a People's Assembly in Dungiven in response to 'a course of repression...further proof of the total failure of the system of government in Northern Ireland'.[26] As the violence escalated in 1972, it became imperative to find a democratic legitimacy to the security response.

THE CHANGING LEGAL ENVIRONMENT

Throughout the civil rights era there had been repeated calls for the repeal of the Civil Authorities (Special Powers) Act (Northern Ireland), which gave draconian power to the police and owed its origin to the violent nature of partition. In 1971 the legislation was repealed. It was an indication, at surface level, that the authorities had belatedly given due cognizance to the deleterious effect the legislation's existence was having on the minority population, against whom its provisions — including administrative detention — had been traditionally disproportionately applied. As Ní Aolain has pointed out, the public policy implications of the SPA rested on the fact that 'when the state is faced with crisis (whether actual or perceived) the harnessing of law to manage the exigency is linked to, and affirmative of, broader political goals.'[27] The reintroduction of internment in 1971 destroyed any suggestion that lessons of past failure had been internalised and illustrated graphically that Northern Ireland could only be governed through exceptional means. The proroguing of Stormont in April 1972 merely made this reality manifest.

The political implications worsened as the criminal justice system was further recalibrated. Despite solidifying the legal basis of 'administrative detention' through the introduction of judicial hearings, the political effect was more, rather than less, alienation as a clear strategic imperative came into view. The entire criminal justice system was to be realigned in order to strip away any vestige of political legitimacy from the insurgency. The moral superiority of the state rested on its concomitant ability to demonstrate that the strategies used in containing the situation were beyond reproach, an inherent impossibility given the deployment and legitimising of anti-insurgency methods taught as best practice in the Sandhurst Military Academy and put into practice in military facilities at Long Kesh and on a naval warship moored in Belfast Lough.[28]

A case could be made that the extraordinary circumstances required extraordinary measures. Ceding the principles underpinning the democratic state for tactical advantage, however, carried its own destabilising dynamic.[29] The piecemeal nature of the changes occluded their significance. Taken together, they represented a serious assault on the liberal democratic order, an assault that the legal establishment actively condoned.[30]

The year 1972 had started badly, with the Bloody Sunday catastrophe — the killing of thirteen unarmed demonstrators at a banned civil rights march protesting against internment in Derry. The government was forced to cede a public inquiry as riots broke out in Belfast and the embassy in Dublin was burnt to the ground, fulfilling the British ambassador's premonition in 1969 that 'we are in for a hard time from the Irish. The embassy, though highly flammable, doesn't belong to us.' While the inquiry served to demonstrate that the circumstances would be carefully evaluated, nothing was left to chance. The government chose its ground and its investigating judge carefully. Two days after the killings, the Lord Chief Justice, Lord Widgery, attended a meeting with the Prime Minister, Ted Heath. Heath alerted the judge that 'it had to be remembered that we were in Northern Ireland fighting not only a military war but a propaganda war'. The confidential minutes, inadvertently made public in 1995, continued:

> The Lord Chief Justice said that he saw the exercise as a fact-finding exercise...It would help if the Inquiry could be restricted to what actually happened in those few minutes when men were shot and killed; this would enable the Tribunal to confine evidence to eye witnesses. The Lord Chancellor [Lord Hailsham] agreed that this should enable the Tribunal to deal with the main question, whether the Troops shot indiscriminately into a crowd or deliberately at particular targets in self-defence.[31]

This reasoning permeated the initial response to the killings, with army briefings indicating that all of those killed posed a clear and present danger to the troops, who, it was claimed, had been fired on first.[32] In a report now comprehensively discredited, Lord Widgery, while noting that the shooting 'bordered on the reckless', absolved the paratroopers involved in the killings at Bloody Sunday of criminal liability. Working from self-limited terms of reference and ignoring crucial witness statements, the Lord Chief Justice justified at least some of the killings through unsubstantiated 'guilt by association' reasoning:

> None of the deceased or wounded is proved to have been shot whilst handling a firearm or bomb. Some are wholly acquitted of complicity in such action; but there is a strong suspicion that some others had been firing weapons or handling bombs in the course of the afternoon and that yet others had been closely supporting them.[33]

While the Widgery findings served an immediate political purpose, a much longer-term erosion of judicial independence was orchestrated with the passage of legislation that had the effect of legitimising, on pragmatic and theoretical grounds, wholesale changes to the criminal justice system. Again, eminent members of the judiciary were pressed into service to provide a patina of legitimacy for overtly political decisions. In a report commissioned to investigate problems of intimidation in jury trials involving terrorist suspects, Lord Diplock recommended the abolition of jury trials. This formed the basis for the Emergency Provisions Act (1973), which enacted Diplock's conclusion by creating a list of proscribed organisations and a list of scheduled offences. Evidence could once again be collected without a warrant and the security forces had the right to question suspects about their movements without due cause. The Prevention of Terrorism Act (1974) marked a further deterioration of *habeas corpus*. Under Sections 14 and 15, suspects could be held for forty-eight hours before being charged and up to seven days with the authorisation of the Northern Ireland Secretary (a new cabinet level position established to provide the pro-counsel with democratic accountability).[34]

Limited rights to solicitors for suspects arrested under the legislation gave the authorities a powerful legally justified regimen for the recruitment of informers and collation of intelligence.[35] The notorious conditions in the major detention centres in Castlereagh in Belfast and Gough Barracks in Armagh added significantly to the pressure

detainees were placed under.[36] These operational realities were fundamental to the facilitation of changes to the legal status of prisoners.
This did not mean, however, that the limits of judicial manipulation
had been reached. On the contrary, Northern Ireland was to witness
more transgressions from the rule of law in response to a low-
intensity conflict that was very real, if not publicly admitted.

As the 1970s wore on, so too did the killings. Domestic killings
within Northern Ireland garnered indifference in the rest of the United
Kingdom. Local communities were devastated along the borderlands
as the IRA was accused, with justification, of engaging in a campaign of
ethnic cleansing. An acceptable level of violence had been reached.

The accession of Margaret Thatcher to the leadership of the
Conservative Party and her subsequent landslide victory in 1979
changed the dynamics. The murder of her Northern Ireland
spokesman, Airey Neave, whose escape from Colditz during World
War Two had made him a British icon, within the confines of the
Houses of Parliament in an INLA car bomb made matters personal.
(How personal was further demonstrated five years later when the IRA
tried to assassinate Mrs Thatcher and her entire cabinet as they
attended the Conservative Party annual conference in Brighton.)

The sense of anger and frustration within the United Kingdom
towards republican violence was heightened dramatically in August
1979, when in carefully co-ordinated attacks the IRA despoiled the
waters of both coasts. The Queen's uncle, Lord Louis Mountbatten,
was killed along with four others when their boat was blown up as it
passed the headland of the Mullaghmore peninsula in County Sligo.
Across the country, an IRA active unit detonated a remote-control
bomb carefully secreted at Narrow Water Castle on the coastal road
on the outskirts of Warrenpoint. A second bomb was timed to
explode as back-up troops arrived on the scene. Eighteen soldiers
were killed, the highest single loss of military life in the Troubles.
Margaret Thatcher travelled to Crossmaglen, a heavily fortified village
in the heart of South Armagh, to be photographed wearing army
fatigues, a very public validation of the symbiotic relationship
between the political and military establishment that had been
cemented by the Falklands Crisis two years later. While there, the local
army commander showed the Prime Minister the epaulets of a
lieutenant colonel killed in the Narrow Water attack, saying that that
was all that remained of one of his finest officers. The IRA issued a

statement through *An Phoblacht* which ratcheted up the rhetorical war. It described the Mountbatten attack not as a vile murder of a defenceless old man and his family as they enjoyed a boating trip, but rather as 'a discriminate operation to bring to the attention of the English people the continuing occupation of our country. We will tear out their sentimental imperialist heart.'[37] Mrs Thatcher put the IRA on notice that she intended to reply in kind.[38]

CRIMINALISATION AND THE HUNGER STRIKE

The opening of the Maze prison, ten miles west of Belfast, on the site of the Long Kesh camp, in 1976 gave tangible expression to the policy of criminalisation. Built in a distinctive series of modules, from an aerial perspective each block represented the letter H, giving rise to the eponymous protest movement. The phasing out of special category status coincided with the opening of the jail, ensuring that the prison structure became a pivotal battleground. A standard high-security prison regime was implemented, with segregation along paramilitary affiliation the only concession to the exceptional nature of the Northern Ireland conflict. From the moment the first IRA prisoner was transferred into the prison, the lines of conflict were sharply delineated. Kieran Nugent refused to wear prison issue clothing, sparking off a campaign of disobedience that escalated from the wearing only of blankets, to a refusal to dispose of excrement. The conditions during 'the Dirty Protest' were exceptionally difficult for prisoners and staff alike. Press visits were sporadically organised to push home the message that the deplorable conditions were self-inflicted; for its part, the Republican movement organised protests and rallies that failed to interest the wider nationalist community. As both sides hunkered down to a battle of wills, it was becoming increasingly clear to the inmates that the tactical advantage lay with the British. It was a view shared by the outside political and military leadership, who cautioned the inmates against escalating the dispute further to the weapon of last resort: the hunger strike.

Failure would further sap morale within the prison, where a large percentage of IRA personnel had already accepted prison rules rather than suffer the self-inflicted deplorable conditions. Crucially, for the wider movement, the possibility that the criminalisation policy would be retrospectively vindicated by the IRA backing down was regarded as an unacceptable risk. Danny Morrison, the key communications strategist for Sinn Féin in the early 1980s, recognised the danger. 'The British government was hoping to inflict a humiliating defeat and force the prisoners to accept criminal status with untold repercussions for the morale and of the struggle on the outside and the perceptions of the struggle on the outside.'[39]

Tommy McKearney, a prominent IRA bomber, was one of those who took part in the first hunger strike in the autumn of 1980. 'We did detect at that time that morale was flagging among Republican prisoners — not disappearing but somewhat flagging — and the decision was taken that we had to make a serious effort to break the impasse.'[40] When it became apparent that the prisoners were committed to the hunger strike, the command structures inside the jail and their counterparts on the outside hammered out a compromise, mediated through Sinn Féin, that inferred the restoration of special category, or political, status without giving the British government a hostage to fortune by rendering explicit an impossible claim. The protest was based on five key demands designed to differentiate the prisoners: the refusal to wear prison clothes or engage in work; the right to self-organise; free association with other prisoners; weekly family visits; and the restoration of remission lost as a consequence of the Dirty Protest.

The Irish government, now under the stewardship of Charles Haughey, sought to use political leverage on Mrs Thatcher to ensure that 'some adjustment could be made in the prison rules themselves or in their interpretation or their application'. The British Prime Minister rejected such sophistry out of hand. She made clear that a line had been drawn. As with her domestic economic agenda, there was to be no alternative. If the prisoners wanted to die, so be it. 'May I make one point about the hunger strike in the Maze prison. And I want this to be utterly clear. There can be no political justification for murder or any other crime. The Government will never concede political status to the hunger strikers or to any others convicted of criminal offences in the province.'[41]

As the British and Irish governments continued to fence over responsibility for the volatile situation developing in the prison, and the Sinn Féin leadership fretted over the implications of failure, everyone waited for the crisis point that would inevitably occur as a prisoner reached the point of no return. Brendan Hughes, the Officer Commanding of the prisoners in the Maze and one of those who participated in the first protest, recalled graphically in a television reassessment the harrowing reality:

> You lose the fat first. Then your muscles start to go and your mind eats off the muscles, the glucose in your muscles and you can feel yourself going. You can actually smell yourself rotting away. That was one of the most memorable things for me: the smell, the smell of almost death from my own body. We had long hair and long beards. We hadn't washed in years. Then your body starts to deteriorate. Your body starts to eat itself. I mean that's basically what happens during hunger strike, until the point where there's no fat left, no muscles left, your body then starts to eat off your brain. And that's when your senses start to go. Your eyesight goes, your hearing goes, all your senses start to go when the body starts to eat off the brain.[42]

Secret negotiations between MI6 and the Belfast leadership, conducted through two intermediaries in Derry, appeared to offer a settlement on 18 December, fifty-three days into the protest. The prison authorities had removed all of the prisoners on the critical list to the hospital wing and denied them access to either Bobby Sands, the new Officer Commanding in the jail, or to the outside political representatives. The prison governor and a civil servant outlined to the prisoners that a deal was imminent but refused to allow an outside witness to ratify the agreement. As Sean McKenna, one of the hunger strikers, slipped into unconsciousness, a prison doctor arrived into Hughes's room. 'Dr Ross came flying down to tell me that Sean was dying and that if I didn't intervene, Sean would be dead.' Hughes was placed in an impossible situation. He knew that a potential deal had been worked out yet he could not confer with or take advice from those responsible for negotiating its terms. Isolated and fearful, Hughes called off the protest.

Twenty years later, sitting in a decrepit flat on an upper floor of an apartment complex at Divis Tower in Belfast, Hughes recounted the events of that evening with emotion. 'About four hours later the priest arrived along with Bobby [Sands] into my cell with this large document. At that stage I couldn't see. I couldn't read it. But they were convinced that we had the deal. That night we were over the moon, everybody that is except for Sean. We didn't know whether Sean was going to survive or not. We really believed that we had the agreement.'[43] Despite attempts by the republican leadership in Belfast to present it as a victory, it was apparent that linguistic sophistry could not disguise the fact that the core demands had not been even partially ceded.[44]

A second hunger strike was then called to begin on 1 March 1981, timed to coincide with the fifth anniversary of the ending of special category status. Again, there was opposition outside the jail to the decision by the prisoners, who felt betrayed by the manner in which the authorities interpreted the offer made the previous December. The struggle for control of the prison issue became, this time, literally, a matter of life and death. Rather than the prisoners launching the campaign simultaneously, their strategy was carefully calibrated to ensure maximum impact and create an escalating sense of crisis. Candidates wishing to put themselves forward were vetted by the IRA leadership inside the jail to ensure that there was both personal commitment to stay the course and a geographical spread to ensure maximum penetration into the consciousness of the nationalist population. Bobby Sands and Brendan 'Bik' McFarlane drew up a list of candidates who were then subjected to external vetting. According to McFarlane, secret communications were smuggled into the prison from the Army Council. It ratcheted up the pressure by demanding of the volunteers for potential martyrdom a crucial question. McFarlane, as the intermediary of the IRA, needed the recruits to provide a positive response to his very calculated formulation: 'Did they understand fully in personal and political terms what it meant. Did they realise the position they were putting the struggle in?'

The Hunger Strike was never about simply prison reform. It was to do with the return of political status. On a wider field, the British had chosen the H Blocks. They had chosen the Diplock court system. They chose Castlereagh. They chose this whole conveyor belt system as a means of breaking the Republican struggle. And they thought that the soft underbelly to begin with would be the prisoners. People are less inclined to support a criminal conspiracy than they are a political struggle or a revolutionary struggle. The Hunger Strikes in essence were a battle between British forces and Republican forces as to who was going to have victory or defeat in pursuing struggle for liberation in Ireland.[45]

Despite attempts by the Irish government to mediate a solution, the actions of the British government made it clear that holding the line was regarded in London as more than merely a question of pride. The irony was that the failure of the putative deal agreed on 18 December and the subsequent preparations for a second strike coincided with one of the most important initiatives agreed between London and Dublin concerning the management of the conflict.

Just months after the British Foreign Secretary had concluded negotiations that led to the independence of Zimbabwe, a high-profile summit was arranged in Dublin Castle for 8 December 1980. It was the most high-powered gathering of Anglo-Irish ministers and diplomats since the beginning of the conflict. The communiqué issued at the end of the meeting spoke of a need over 'the coming year to special consideration of the totality of relationships within these islands'.[46] The problem was that the seeds of compromise could only bear fruit in stable soil. Within Northern Ireland the political land-scape was being churned relentlessly by unionist fears, whipped up by Ian Paisley in a series of freedom rallies staged across the province at which he warned darkly of a dagger aimed at Ulster's heart. That sense of impending doom was heightened by an extraordinarily maladroit radio interview by the Irish Minister of Foreign Affairs, Brian Lenihan, during which he argued that the concept of the 'totality of relations' opened the possibility of unity within a decade.

Each metropolitan government was forced to intercede for competing constituencies, their hands tied by the intransigence of their charges. The British government, which had already conceived of the usefulness of the summit only in terms of how increased cooperation could enhance security policy, was unwilling to countenance the possibility of a second front opening up. Haughey remains convinced that the communiqué offered a profound opportunity to transform the situation. In an interview with the author, he argued that it was 'a towering achievement that redefined the problem and pointed the only way to a solution'. A summit that had the potential to transform relations was fatally undermined by the dismal reality pertaining on the ground. When a delegation sent by Haughey to the Maze prison, in order to negotiate a settlement, travelled to London they were rebuffed unceremoniously. Mrs Thatcher publicly decried their efforts in a terse response: 'It is not my habit or custom to meet MPs of a foreign country to consider special category status for certain groups of people sentenced for crime. Crime is crime. It is not political.'[47]

This rhetoric could not be sustained, however, with the election of Bobby Sands in the constituency of Fermanagh/South Tyrone, following the serendipitous death of the sitting Nationalist MP. A general election in the Republic saw two hunger strikers elected and Haughey deprived of government office as a coalition administration gained temporary power. The IRA could no longer be viewed or presented for propaganda purposes credibly as an unrepresentative clique. This new reality was underscored as the coffins emerged from the Maze. Although the crowds thinned as the summer progressed, the strategic forward planning of the hunger strikers ensured that resentment fanned out through the province. No section of the community was untouched by the spectre of death. Monsignor Denis Faul remembers ruefully the implications of that long hot summer.

> We made the point repeatedly to the British government. We said: 'Do you think you are winning? But you're not winning. Go and look at the wakes, go and look at the funerals, look at all the young people queuing up to see these emaciated corpses. You're not winning. You're losing.' But of course they couldn't see it.[48]

By the time the dispute was called off in October 1981, ten men had died inside the prison and sixty people had been killed outside. The intervention of prisoner families, in a process mediated by Denis Faul, proved instrumental in breaking the stalemate. Although many of the demands were subsequently put in place, inside the prison the mood was one of despair. Faced with international pressure and increasing nationalist alienation, the British government had withstood the onslaught of negative publicity. A statement issued from the prison noted that the 'nationalist minority was politically inconsequential' and highlighted a visceral feeling that 'pacifism in the Northern Ireland context is energy-wasting, futile and unproductive in that it is a permanent guarantee of second-class citizenship and subservience to an alien and foreign government'.[49]

In his sober analysis of the prison conflict, Richard English notes that despite inflicting a technical defeat on the prisoners, the victory for Britain was a Pyrrhic one, bought at the cost of increased polarisation and nationalist alienation, sowing the seeds for a strategic change in direction for the republican movement, whose capacity to set the agenda was severely limited. For English, 'it would be wrong to see 1981 as *beginning* a process of republican politization; it would be more accurately understood as an unintended *accelerator* of a process already favoured by the leaders of the movement.'[50] Another consequence was the fact that each side became more aware of and sophisticated in media manipulation. Stories from prison about ill-treatment and spin from the outcomes of critical engagement between IRA personnel and the security forces were presented as evidence of duplicity. This was disseminated to a much more receptive audience within nationalist communities, now prepared to countenance the fact that the state was, in fact, capable, if not necessarily proven, of bending democratic mores in pursuit of policy objectives. The contours of the conflict were changing again as the key battleground moved back out of the prison and into the shadows.

INSTITUTIONALISING THE PRIMACY OF INTELLIGENCE POLICING

Significant upgrading of the RUC's intelligence prowess had begun with the appointment of Kenneth Newman as Chief Constable in 1976. As the capability of Special Branch grew, the force established Divisional Mobile Support Units, Headquarters Mobile Support Units and Special Support Units, all provided with military training in surveillance and ambush techniques. Inadequate, inefficient internal structures were comprehensively overhauled and a more sophisticated intelligence-handling regime was instituted within Special Branch, modelled on the army's 14th Intelligence Unit. The hierarchical structure was designed not only to mirror that of its educators, but more importantly to link Special Branch more effectively into a wider security nexus.

The process was formalised with the passing of internal guidelines, known as the Walker Report (see Appendix 1), which created a policing culture that centralised decision-making power in the hands of Special Branch. The sole function of policing was viewed through the prism of the war on terror. The guidelines made it clear that meeting the needs of the intelligence community trumped any pursuit of criminal activity. Under Walker, 'all proposals to effect planned arrests must be cleared with Regional Special Branch to ensure that no agents of either the RUC or the Army are involved'. The report also made it apparent that in the event of a dispute between the Criminal Investigation Department (CID) and Special Branch, the matter had to be referred to a higher level within the force. The reality of this referral process rested on an adjudication that privileged the Special Branch worldview.

The Walker Report states that 'the charging of an agent must be the result of a conscious decision by Special Branch and CID in which the balance of advantage has been carefully weighed'. The injunction did not necessarily apply only to serving agents but also to those identified as having potential use to the intelligence web. The Walker Report specifically mandated sufficient time to elapse between the charging of a suspect and a court appearance in order to ensure that Special Branch could ascertain potential worth. This was deemed necessary in order to 'ensure that information provided by the person so recruited is handled in such a way that his value as an agent is not put at risk at an early stage'. For the CID, this meant that its own source network had to be turned over to the intelligence community. The document states that 'an agent or a source reporting on subversive organisations should be handled by Special Branch, if not possible the agent should be handled and reported on jointly'. This formulation preserved the supremacy of a force within a force.

The existence of the Walker Report was publicised in an edition of the *Insight* series on UTV, broadcast in April 2001. Entitled 'Policing the Police', the programme focused on the distortions caused by the competing and conflicting dynamics underpinning the RUC in the Walker era. The force had to balance the need to attract and retain informers capable of providing information about future operations with the main purposes of policing laid down by parliament. Under the terms of the legislation, each constabulary is charged with four key functions: 'to protect life and property, to preserve order, to prevent the commission of offences and to take measures to bring offenders to justice'. The question was not necessarily whether the policy design conceived in Whitehall was appropriate to the circumstances pertaining in Northern Ireland, rather it was whether the primacy of intelligence gathering meant the de facto suspension of the rule of law.

In signed testimony to the programme, senior police officers spoke openly of how the primacy of the war on terror had fundamentally skewed the policing agenda, destroying in turn the credibility of the force. Frustration, resentment and anger at the primacy of the Special Branch came to the fore as the deceit at the centre of the intelligence web unravelled. Some of the most respected criminal detectives spoke of how investigations were curtailed, operations were hampered and crucial information that could have secured convictions was withheld. A former chief superintendent claimed that he 'feared Special Branch more than the Provisional IRA or the Real IRA'. A superintendent supplied testimony that defied belief: 'I remain fearful of my life even though I have retired.' A third senior officer controversially claimed that malign forces could engineer his death in a road accident.

The fact that such witness statements came from serving and retired members of the force gave added weight to the central allegations aired in the film. These surrounded attempts by Special Branch to pervert the course of justice in the investigation of the Finucane murder, specific matters dealt with more fully in the next two chapters. Here it is important to emphasise the moral ambiguities inherent in giving potential informers effective immunity from prosecution in the hope and expectation of potentially saving lives in the future.

For Brice Dickson, the Chairman of the Northern Ireland Human Rights Commission, there could be no justification for such a policy. 'I think to refuse to prosecute or to delay the prosecution of such an individual in the hope of getting other evidence from him is completely unjustified', he stated in an interview for the programme. When shown the Walker documentation, Professor Dickson, the director of a body established specifically as part of the Good Friday Agreement to reinforce a commitment by the state to international human rights standards, expressed distinct unease. He was 'somewhat alarmed by some parts of the report and in particular to those parts that give such extreme power to the Special Branch'. While acknowledging the caveat that it depended on how power was in fact exercised, Professor Dickson was convinced that a fundamental principle had been ceded for tactical gain. 'The potential for abuse is very great', he concluded.

Even those sympathetic to the RUC accepted the corrosive nature of the force under the Walker guidelines. Chris Ryder, a former member of the Policing Authority, accepted that 'there was always that inner core, that inner sanctum of Special Branch which was surrounded by excessive secrecy, excessive expulsion of outsiders and an excessive arrogance'.

The question of arrogance goes far beyond mere personality traits. In mapping the security nexus it is necessary to bear in mind that the Special Branch was only one of a number of key discrete but inter-locking nodes in the security network. The opaque nature of report-ing structures and incomplete information in the public domain makes it difficult to assess the culpability of individual nodes for transgressing the rule of law or failing to properly monitor operatives in the field. What is clear, however, is the central involvement of the domestic intelligence network, MI5, in both the formulation of the Walker Report and the wider design of how each node in the network collated and disseminated information. The significant changes to the RUC were accompanied by an overhaul of the entire intelligence network. On 2 October 1979, a Chief Security Co-ordinator was appointed to ensure that control was exercised over the chaotic intel-ligence community. The first appointee was a former head of MI6, Maurice Oldfield.[51]

The entire structure resembled a spider's web. At the periphery, agents and informers collected information, ranging from malicious gossip and hearsay to inside information at the heart of the paramil-itary planning operations. The agents had individual handlers, who then imparted the information to teams of collators at individual intelligence-gathering organisations. These included Special Branch, specialist communications and research units within the army, and MI5 itself. Each node then cross-referenced the material with existing databases in order to paint an accurate picture of paramilitary intent. The aim was ostensibly to make threat assessment judgements in order to prevent future attacks, in particular set piece 'spectaculars', such as the killing of the soldiers at Warrenpoint. In most cases, however, the decision as to which facet of the security response to deploy was not taken by an individual unit. Rather, the information was then forwarded to a higher-level Tasking and Co-ordinating Group (TCG), comprising unit directors and officials from the Northern Ireland Office.

It was the responsibility of the TCG to determine how to respond to the often incomplete and partial intelligence presented. As with most organisations, its hierarchical nature carried the risk that specific infor-mation may not necessarily be passed forward in order to protect sources or budgets. Organisational theory points to the pathological risk that bad news is filtered out at every stage of a hierarchical reporting model. Within the TCG the risks were compounded because of the existence of competing horizontal cleavages, in which the major actors had a vested interest in running their own agents. The result was that the TCG faced criticism if co-ordination policy worked and allegations of state-sponsored terrorism when it failed to prevent attacks.

WALKER IN OPERATION: THE 1982 SHOOT TO KILL ALLEGATIONS

At the core of the allegations over 'shoot to kill' has been the perception that the specialist units in the nexus were despatched with ruthless determination to meet fire with fire, irrespective of the consequences or the risk to innocent bystanders caught up in a maelstrom. The principal agencies used for these killings were two specialist divisions, the SAS and 14th Intelligence. A statistical analysis carried out by Fionnuala Ní Aolain found that 80 per cent of the killings involved people involved in paramilitary activity.[52] For Ní Aolain, a law professor at the University of Ulster, the deaths of innocent bystanders added to the perception that 'these operations have the singular aim of eliminating paramilitary threats at all costs and that no accommodation is made for any other unforeseen eventuality'.[53] If the use of the army was problematic, increasing the capacity of the civilian police force to engage in similar activity was extraordinary.

The aggressive use of counter-insurgency measures as state strategy became apparent in late 1982, with three incidents involving the killing of IRA personnel by members of E4A, a specialist unit attached to Special Branch. The first incident took place on 11 November, two weeks after three police officers had been killed when a bomb hidden in a culvert exploded as their armoured car passed the Kinnego Embankment on the shore of Lough Neagh. Forensic tests revealed that the bomb material had come from an arsenal stored in a hayshed under surveillance from both MI5 and the SAS, but that surveillance had been interrupted, leaving the RUC officers dangerously exposed. Intelligence further suggested the involvement of two IRA figures, Sean Burns and Eugene Toman, in the planning of the Kinnego operation, and the men were placed under sustained surveillance.

At 9.00 pm on 11 November, Burns and Toman, along with a third IRA member, Gervaise McKerr, approached a roadblock. In an instant, more than one hundred bullets were fired into their car. Pathology reports showed that Toman was hit in the heart as he attempted to get out of the car. Less than two weeks later, the same unit was involved in the killing of a seventeen-year-old youth, Michael Tighe, in the hayshed used to store the cache of IRA weapons used in the Kinnego bombing. His companion, Martin McCauley, was seriously injured.[54]

In a third incident, on 12 December 1982, the same E4A unit was involved in the killing of two members of the INLA, Seamus Grew and Rory Carroll. The INLA had been responsible for a firebomb that had ripped through the Dropping Well disco in Ballykelly, a frequent haunt for off-duty soldiers, earlier that month. Eleven of the seventeen killed in the explosion were members of the Cheshire Regiment. The INLA leader, Dominic McGlinchey, had been under surveillance by a detective from Special Branch who was collecting intelligence illicitly in the Irish Republic. Carroll and Grew were spotted in the INLA commander's company and a roadblock was established to intercept them. Just before Grew and Carroll passed, an off-duty soldier crashed into the roadblock, injuring one of the police officers. In the pandemonium, Grew and Carroll passed unimpeded.

The Special Branch detective, following the INLA suspects, alerted his colleagues, and one officer from the unit, John Robinson, got into the car to give chase. When the inspector cut off the Allegro carrying the suspects, Robinson, armed with a machine pistol and a pump action shotgun, opened fire. Both men were shot at point blank range. Amid calls for an inquiry, the Northern Ireland Secretary, James Prior, accepted that special anti-terrorist units had been established within the RUC, but he explicitly denied the dispensation of summary execution as policy.

The killings of the IRA and INLA personnel prompted a sustained investigation by the Deputy Chief Constable of Great Manchester, John Stalker. The investigation was mired in controversy from the beginning. In his autobiography, Stalker wrote 'the circumstances of those shootings pointed to a police inclination, if not a policy, to shoot suspects dead without warning rather than to arrest them'.[55] As with Sir John Stevens in a later period, Stalker was confronted with wilful obstruction in investigating the disputed circumstances of the 1982 killings.

The surveillance material in the hayshed, which could have shed light on the precise circumstances surrounding the Tighe killing, was withheld from his investigating team. Stalker was castigated for seeking information from the solicitor representing Gervaise McKerr. In 1987 the Mancunian officer was removed from office following an unconnected investigation into the English officer's relationship with a businessman who had alleged but later disproved links with crime. Despite the contentious issues surrounding the three sets of killings, the obstruction of both the original criminal investigation and Stalker's probe, and the revelations that intelligence agencies were aware of ongoing operations, the issue failed to gain significant on-going traction beyond the confines of the republican movement and its support base in Irish-America. John Robinson was tried and acquitted of murder in 1984.

The relevant statute under which the case was brought was the Criminal Law (Northern Ireland) Act of 1967, which states: 'A person may use such force as reasonable in the circumstances in the prevention of crime, or in effecting or assisting in the lawful arrest of offenders or suspected offenders or of persons unlawfully at large.' As Brendan O'Brien has pointed out in his history of the IRA, it effectively sanctioned 'a broad and imprecise legal framework which provided a considerably lower standard than [the absolute necessity provision of] the European Convention on Human Rights to which the UK is a signatory'.[56]

The question of whether or not the response of the RUC was disproportionate was immaterial to the police hierarchy, which viewed the conflict in terms of a war rather than criminal enterprise. Indicative of this mentality was the warning of the Chief Constable, Sir Jack Hermon, to Stalker at their first meeting that the first rule of law in Northern Ireland is survival. 'Remember, Mr Stalker, you are in a jungle now.'[57] At the trial of the three officers charged with the killing of Eugene Toman, the Deputy Chief Constable maintained that the purpose of the MSUs was to ensure the primacy of 'speed, fire-power and aggression'. The trial judge, Lord Gibson, concurred. In acquitting the three accused, he announced from the bench that 'I regard each of the accused as absolutely blameless in this matter. That finding should be put on their record along with my own commendation for their courage and determination in bringing the three deceased men to justice, in this case the final court of justice.' (Lord Gibson was later killed by the IRA in an ambush, minutes after leaving a Garda escort on his way back to the North from a holiday in the Republic. The IRA statement admitting responsibility, specifically cited the trial ruling in the shoot to kill case as justification for the murder of one of the most senior officers of the court. The killing of Gibson is one of the cases now the subject of an independent public inquiry following persistent allegations that rogue members of the Gardai leaked information on the judge's movements to the IRA.

A subsequent inquiry, run by Colin Sampson, the Chief Constable of West Yorkshire, was established following Stalker's removal from office. It recommended that no fewer than eleven police officers be charged in relation to perverting the course of justice during the investigation into the shoot to kill allegations of 1982. While the Director of Public Prosecutions was prepared to run the case, the Attorney General, Sir Patrick Mayhew, pronounced that such a course of action was contrary to the public interest. The negative publicity surrounding the case resulted in the RUC being displaced within the security network, ensuring that with the exception of intelligence gathering, the counter-insurgency 'set-pieces' would be left to the army.[58] By transferring operational responsibility to the military from the late 1980s onwards, without adequate supervision or accountability structures, the political authorities allowed, by default, loyalist paramilitaries to be recruited into the nexus, particularly in Belfast and in Mid-Ulster, where loyalist gangs murdered with impunity. In the so-called murder triangle, around Lurgan and Portadown, the heavily infiltrated Ulster Volunteer Force company (later to form the Loyalist Volunteer Force) were responsible for the killing of scores of innocent Catholics in a campaign of terror that mirrored the ethnic cleansing allegations faced by the IRA.[59]

As the security situation deteriorated, the authorities responded by lowering the standard of proof required in order to source a conviction. A further series of mass arrests was justified and convictions gathered through the dubious practice of relying on uncorroborated informers. It succeeded in temporarily filling the jails but represented such a serious assault on due process that the judiciary could not tolerate the risk that witness testimony could be tainted by self-preservation or coercion.[60] The eventual collapse of the supergrass system was, in turn, accompanied by an upsurge in allegations from human rights groups that summary execution became a de facto instrument of the state judicial arsenal. If the courts could not or would not convict suspects on uncorroborated evidence, the central question was whether justice would be dispensed on the street? In this context, as a direct consequence of maladroit legislative design, the republican movement gained significant traction for their belief that the legitimacy of the state could, and should, be contested. State failure had become self-sustaining and with it the circumstances that allowed for, indeed mandated, an assault on democracy from within.[61]

In the circumstances it became an imperative to find a political solution that could find support in Dublin and from there gain acceptance in the North. The primary vehicle for achieving this was the 1985 Anglo-Irish Agreement. It signified an articulation by the two governments that the arrested political development within Northern Ireland could be traced to the extremes, in particular the activities of the IRA. The combination of embroiling the Republic in the development of, but not control over, security policy and continued nationalist electoral support for the SDLP had the effect of blurring the political focus on the consequences of state policy in the prosecution of the war against terror. Behind the symbolism of investigations into past abuse, the structural environment that facilitated it remained not only intact but became an imperative as the decade progressed.

A huge arsenal of weapons being shipped from Libya to Ireland was seized by the French authorities onboard the *Eksund* on 1 November 1987. The indiscriminate violence that such a cache could have unleashed was made deadly apparent at the Remembrance Day bombing by the IRA in Enniskillen ten days later, in which eleven people were killed.[62]

Notwithstanding the horrific carnage of the atrocity in Enniskillen, within the republican movement itself a new dynamic developed from 1985 onwards in which military strategy was rendered subservient to political gain. This strategy eviscerated the movement's capacity to respond to a sustained ideological and material assault by constitutional nationalism, by the Republic, by the British state and by the loyalist paramilitaries heavily infiltrated and now partially directed by the security services.[63] Despite the undoubted success of the IRA hunger strike as a means to launch the Sinn Féin political machine, the maintenance of the military campaign capped the vote within nationalism, allegations of torture and state killing notwithstanding. In a scathing address to the SDLP annual conference, the SDLP leader, John Hume, referred to republicans as the self-proclaimed 'keepers of the grail of the nation. That deep-seated attitude, married to their method, has all the hallmarks of undiluted fascism.'[64]

In public pronouncements, the Sinn Féin leadership, particularly Gerry Adams and Martin McGuinness, remained committed to core beliefs throughout the early 1980s. McGuinness reassured republicans at a rally in June 1984: 'We recognise that only disciplined revolutionary armed struggle by the IRA will end British rule.'[65] In a defining interview, Adams reaffirmed: 'There can be no such thing as an Irish nationalist accepting the loyalist veto and partition. You cannot claim to be an Irish nationalist if you consent to an internal six-county settlement and if you are willing to negotiate the state of Irish society with a foreign government.'[66]

Behind the scenes, moves were afoot both secretly within the IRA and more publicly within Sinn Féin to respond to a changed political landscape as a consequence of antipathy in the North and the conclusion by Dublin and London, acting in concert, that security needed to be vouchsafed as a political imperative. The result was the ending of the policy of abstention from the Dáil. In a carefully choreographed move, the Provisional IRA had forsaken the very basis on which the split in 1969 originated, creating the dynamic for another schism and with it further allegations of sell-out and betrayal.

The killing of eight members of an East Tyrone Active Service Unit of the IRA in a carefully planned ambush in the Armagh village of Loughall on 8 May 1987 exemplified both the success of British agent penetration into the IRA, and the capacity of the security forces to change the dynamics of republican strategies. As the IRA unit crashed a digger with a huge bomb attached into the unmanned police station in the centre of the town, army and police personnel opened fire from at least four positions, discharging up to twelve hundred bullets. Four innocent civilians, Anthony and Oliver Hughes, along with a woman and her child, were caught up in the crossfire. In both cases, there was no attempt by the soldiers to ascertain who was in the cars or to calibrate the exact threat they posed. Anthony Hughes died of his injuries. The IRA unit had been compromised in advance; whether this was achieved through electronic eavesdropping or an informant is still a matter of intense debate.[67]

The penetration of the East Tyrone IRA led to what amounted to an open season on its operatives throughout the late 1980s that mirrored the recalibration of loyalist targeting in Belfast. Gerard Harte and his brother Martin, along with Brian Mullin, were ambushed and killed by the SAS in August 1988. The Harte brothers had been under electronic surveillance for at least a year and were involved in the hijacking of the digger used in the ill-fated Loughall attack. In October 1990 Dessie Grew and Martin McCaughey were killed in an ambush near the village and in June 1991 two further members were killed when the SAS used a rocket-propelled grenade to destroy their car. Four other members of the East Tyrone IRA were killed in February 1992 after a drive-by shooting at Coalisland police station. In all four ambushes, British intelligence was excellent.[68] By severely limiting the IRA's capacity to engage in offensive operations within the taciturn republican heartlands, the security forces effectively shaped the contours of the military conflict.

The need to keep up the pressure created and sustained the development of another front. Ostensibly aimed at limiting the capacity of loyalist paramilitaries, the strategy was to secure short-term gains at the expense of the moral authority of the state as an independent arbiter. In facilitating the direction of terrorism through a process of omission and commission, the state was about to cross a political rubicon.

Chapter 3
Crossing the Rubicon

The IRA entered 1988 a depleted and demoralised force. The killings at Loughall had wiped out a major component of its military capacity on domestic soil. Its supply of political capital had been squandered by the strategically maladroit and politically indefensible slaughter at the Memorial Day bombing in Enniskillen. In order to avenge its fallen and to justify its own logic, the IRA required a clean kill against the British army. The target chosen was the ceremonial changing of the guard in the relatively undefended British outpost of Gibraltar on the Iberian Peninsula. Given the dispute with Spain over sovereignty, the choice also played into the anti-colonialist rhetoric that defined the political trajectory of the republican movement.

From the beginning, the operation was compromised, although whether that was because of loose talk within the active service unit, or because of an informer within the wider ranks of the Belfast IRA or, simply because three of those chosen had either criminal convictions or were known to the security forces and thus under constant surveillance remains a matter of intense debate.[1] The ability of the security forces to engage in long-term surveillance outside the Northern Ireland arena was underscored by the operation. Military and intelligence advisors, including two contingents from the SAS, were dispatched to the colony on 2 March. Four days later, Mairéad Farrell, Daniel McCann and Sean Savage were left dying on the streets of the protectorate. The controversial denouement of the operation and the legal disputes it generated shed crucial light on the contours of a covert strategy that facilitated the elimination of the enemy rather than the bringing of its foot soldiers to the courts.

The killings fuelled the allegations, re-ignited after the Loughall ambush, that the security forces were again committed to a conscious shoot to kill policy. It was not merely the fact that the IRA personnel involved were unarmed that gave the issue such traction in sections of the British media. The controversy deepened because such executive action took place in the streets of a quiet colonial outpost rather than the rural heartland of Northern Ireland itself, where a de-sensitised British public regarded the methods deployed by the SAS as acceptable if distasteful.

Over the course of two weeks in March, the Northern Ireland conflict once again dominated international news. The Gibraltar killings opened what Richard English has termed a 'crescendo of retaliatory violence'.[2] The enduring symbolic power of the images generated by these and subsequent killings — the clinical dispatch of the IRA active service unit, the jerky, grainy film of a loyalist gunman launching an obscene and audacious gun and grenade attack at the Milltown funeral of those 'incapacitated' in the colony by the SAS, the horrendous reality of the abduction and murder of two soldiers whose unmarked car careered into the cortège of one of those murdered at Milltown — retain their potency even today. They fed into and intensified mutually exclusive perceptions of what some considered an outrage and others saw as a justifiable response to the reality of terrorism. The barbarism on the streets ensured public acceptance of much media and official discourse that only the firm application of all measures necessary could restore order to the anarchy unleashed on the streets.

The progressive unravelling of governmental dissembling by investigative journalists and lawyers to an inquest into the Gibraltar shootings that September, which operated at an acute informational disadvantage because of stated national security concerns, was accompanied by a strengthening of resolve in the highest echelons of the political, military and intelligence establishment that the Dirty War be intensified. Despite the opening of another front in the propaganda war, and the dangers it posed to the reputation of the state, the government pressed ahead with its justification for an active counter-insurgency strategy, with substantial levels of public support in the rest of the United Kingdom.

The broadcast media, in particular, accused of orchestrating trial by television, faced enormous political and commercial pressure to provide only surface level analysis. Those public service broadcasters such as the BBC and Thames Television, an anchor of the ITV network, who departed from the script found themselves on a collision course with government. It was a game played for the highest stakes: the independence of the BBC, the largest publicly funded television corporation in the world, and the commercial viability of one of its main commercial rivals. By raising questions about glaring deficiencies in the official account, they became actors in a fight that pitted the moral legitimacy of the state against resourceful republican terrorists, particularly adroit at manipulating the politics of moral hazard, while not themselves governed by it. The media war was also, in retrospect, a crucial form of crisis management. It skilfully diverted the discourse into an intellectual cul de sac.

As the dispute between the government and the main broadcasters intensified, the media itself became the story. The public policy implications of the use of SAS deployment were displaced by the media in favour of more narcissistic deliberation. This narrowing of the media prism had a profound impact. It severely limited the meticulous description of the institutional context in which controversial incidents occurred. In its place a more simplistic world was fashioned, governed by the manipulation of grotesque images that Northern Ireland appeared only too happy to produce.[3]

On the ground in Northern Ireland itself, the debate was carried out in more direct and brutal terms, increasingly away from sustained and rigorous gaze. The media's willingness and capacity to critically engage was severely limited both by the earlier bruising encounters with the government and by the introduction soon after the Gibraltar inquest of a ban on the appearance in the broadcast media of those associated with, or espousing the views of, the republican movement.[4]

As the shrill rhetoric took on an even more rebarbative tone, the middle ground disintegrated. The IRA stepped up its attacks on the British army; the SAS responded in kind, staging a number of carefully planned ambushes. Adjudication of terrorist guilt at times appeared to transfer inexorably from the courts to the barrel of a gun carried by elite military squads poorly trained in the demands of democratic policing. In such circumstances, it was inevitable that myopic justifications and rationalisations took root that allowed for the killing of an officer of the court.

The fact that Pat Finucane came from a staunch republican family, that one of his brothers had escaped from the Maze prison and another, who had served a prison sentence for an IRA offence, was romantically involved with one of those killed in Gibraltar, added to the intensity of an ill-informed debate largely carried out at the level of emotional instinct rather than rational analysis.

DEATH ON THE ROCK: THE KILLING MACHINE EXPOSED

Sean Savage, the youngest of the IRA unit dispatched to Gibraltar, had been charged with membership of the IRA but was released prior to trial. Danny McCann, one of the most experienced explosives experts within the IRA, had served a two-year prison sentence. His selection for the operation, conducted by the secretive General Headquarters Staff, was doubly surprising given the fact that he had walked away from the IRA two years previously. He was a close confidant of Ivor Bell, the former quartermaster in Belfast who had been forced out of the IRA because of his opposition to the political route taken by the leadership. McCann also favoured a military approach that was not necessarily in keeping with the Adams doctrine.

Mairéad Farrell, the third member of the team, was already a republican icon. Convicted of the 1976 bombing of the Conway Hotel in Dunmurray, she played a leading role in the orchestration of the 'dirty protest' in Armagh women's prison. On her release, she enrolled in a politics and economics course at Queen's University. She toured the country giving talks and interviews on the necessity for pursuing an armed struggle for which she herself had been sentenced to ten years imprisonment. She started a relationship with Pat Finucane's brother Seamus. 'We set up together the first home for either of us — we'd both spent our twenties in prison. She was very, very special and we spent a lot of that time together. Mairéad was very independent, very determined, a strong woman. She wanted children, she was like any other girl, she liked socialising, dancing, music, fashion and loved meeting people.'[5] This touching human portrait stands in stark contrast to the iconographic image fashioned by both sides after SAS soldiers felt compelled to shoot her five times in the face and a further three times in the back from a distance of less than three feet.

For the republican movement Farrell was a model freedom fighter, prepared to sacrifice everything for the cause of Ireland. For the SAS operative charged with preventing her plans, a fanatical and danger-ous terrorist who needed to be incapacitated was confronting him.

The tabloid media was even more blunt: she was a dog that needed to be put down. Farrell herself was stoical about her likely fate, telling an interviewer that pursuing the republican ideal was a Hobson's choice: 'You have to be realistic. You realise that ultimately you're going to be dead or end up in jail. It's either one or the other. You're not going to run forever.'[6]

Farrell and McCann's unscheduled disappearance from Belfast in November 1987 triggered the immediate interest of the intelligence agencies. Their photographic details were transmitted to European police, customs and security agencies. Observed entering southern Spain, the IRA cell became the target of a joint intelligence mission. It was deduced quickly that the ceremonial changing of the guard just across the border in Gibraltar was the likely target, and the parade ground was cordoned off as unscheduled building work began. This was a perfect example of how intelligence could be used effectively to foil an attack, while minimising the risk that the source would be exposed. It should have raised at least the suspicion within the IRA that the security of the operation had been jeopardised. Inexplicably, it pressed ahead, whether through arrogance or the pressing need to strike what the IRA perceived to be a legitimate target.

Throughout the winter of 1987–8, the IRA suspects were kept under close observation. The parade ground was scheduled to re-open on 8 March, and a major anti-terrorist operation was put in place. When the IRA unit re-emerged in southern Spain in early March, they were walking into a carefully planned trap. Contrary to evidence at the subsequent inquest that the Spanish police lost the suspects soon after their arrival at Malaga airport, the suspects were under sustained surveillance until they crossed the land border to the British protectorate.[7]

The Joint Intelligence Committee in London dispatched two specialist units to Gibraltar, which had separate but overlapping responsibilities. A sophisticated surveillance operation was overseen on the British-controlled side of the border by the Secret Intelligence Service (MI6), which also provided a security briefing to the Gibraltar police. Rather than bringing over counter-terrorism officers from either the Metropolitan Police or the RUC, Whitehall ordered two SAS contingents to enter the protectorate. The first was a bomb disposal unit, the second comprised undercover operatives. This second SAS unit had been tasked specifically 'to assist the Gibraltar police to arrest the IRA active service unit should the police request such military intervention'.[8] This, in legal terms, was not problematic, despite the reality of the regiment's deployment in Northern Ireland. As the inquest and the ruling of the European Court of Human Rights found, the deployment of the SAS did not amount to evidence that the killing was premeditated. It was not the acts of individual soldiers, acting in good faith on information provided to them by their handlers, that placed the operation in legal jeopardy. Rather, the legality of individual actions needed to be viewed in the context of 'whether the anti-terrorist operation as a whole was controlled and organised in a manner which respected the requirements of Article 2 and whether the information and instructions given to the soldiers, which, in effect, rendered inevitable the use of lethal force, took adequately into consideration the right to life of the three suspects'.[9]

In the interregnum before the IRA unit crossed the border, the SAS practised arrest procedure with the Gibraltar constabulary and even helped identify a suitable secure holding position once the suspects were apprehended. At an operational briefing, the outlines of the containment strategy were made clear and pointed to the need to effect an arrest rather than 'incapacitate', a military euphemism for killing. According to the intelligence briefing, the IRA active service unit's most likely target was to be the ceremonial changing of the guard two days later. Photographs of the suspects were displayed and it was made clear to those in attendance that it was a distinct probability that lethal force would have to be deployed in order to minimise the threat to wider public safety. Again and again throughout the briefing and in subsequent assessments provided to sub-committees, the suspects were branded as 'dangerous terrorists who would almost certainly be armed and who, if confronted by the security forces, would be likely to use their weapons'.

Given the criminal records of the three IRA members, it was expected that a car bomb would be the preferred choice of weapon. After the adverse publicity occasioned by the atrocity in Enniskillen, it was speculated that the bomb would most likely be detonated by remote control, thereby minimising the risk of civilian casualties. According to evidence provided to the inquest, all military personnel discounted, with varying degrees of certainty, the suggestion that a timing device could be used. By contrast, the civilian personnel at the briefing recalled that both options were discussed, with neither possibility being ruled out. Members of the SAS units further testified that they had been briefed that each suspect should be assumed to have the capacity to secrete a device capable of exploding a bomb from within a radius of one and a half miles. This was to provide a crucial rationale for taking all necessary measures.

Following the briefing, the Police Commissioner in Gibraltar issued an operational order setting out formally the aims and objectives: to protect life; to foil the attempt; to arrest the prisoners using the minimum amount of force; and to ensure the accurate gathering of evidence for a subsequent court trial. The rules of engagement also made clear that force could not be used unless requested by a senior member of the Gibraltar police 'or unless it is necessary to do so in order to protect life. You and your men are not then to use more force than is necessary in order to protect life.' Crucially the rules continued:

6. You and your men may fire without warning if the giving of a warning or any delay in firing could lead to death or injury to you, or them or any other person, or if the warning is clearly impracticable.

7. If the circumstances in paragraph 6 do not apply, a warning is necessary before firing. The warning is to be as clear as possible and is to include a direction to surrender and a clear warning that fire will be opened if the direction is not obeyed.[10]

The next morning the operation went into effect. Despite the surveillance operation at the border, Sean Savage passed through undetected. At 12.45 local time a white Renault car driven by Savage was parked in the square where the changing of the guard was to occur. Surveillance officers reported that the suspect, whom at this stage they could not positively identify, seemed to spend some time fiddling between the seats. This intelligence was communicated through a secure telecommunications channel to two teams of plain-clothes SAS soldiers patrolling the town centre. The officers tracking Savage reported that he appeared to be taking anti-surveillance measures, stopping at the end of side streets, constantly checking to see if he was being followed. An hour and fifteen minutes later, McCann and Farrell were spotted crossing the border by foot. Again, the reports by the surveillance officers that both suspects were acting suspiciously were disseminated through secure channels.

At 14.50 the three suspects were observed examining the parked

Renault. Within the operations room, the possibility of executing an immediate arrest was discussed and then rejected for two interlinked reasons — there remained a lack of certainty on identification and a concern that not enough evidence had been collected to secure a conviction. The intelligence on its own was not admissible in court and, if the suspects were merely on a reconnaissance mission, guilt could not be established. Over the next few minutes, the military advisors vied for operational control. Once the suspects had moved away from the car, a member of the bomb surveillance unit conducted a cursory examination. Noting that its rusting aerial was 'out of place' for the age of the vehicle, he reported back to the operational command that they were dealing with a '*suspect* car bomb'.

According to the Police Commissioner, the judgement in the command centre was that the Renault should be regarded as a '*possible* car bomb'. Crucially, this caveat was not passed on through the surveillance channels to the military operatives on the ground. The 'expert' opinion of Soldier G (who had examined the car and who was identified as a bomb disposal expert but who, in reality, had little experience dealing with either radio communications or explosives), was to play a crucial role in the risk assessment formulated by the undercover SAS soldiers in position around central Gibraltar. Despite the lack of hard evidence that the suspects presented a clear and present danger and the less than expert estimation of the bomb disposal member, operational control was handed over to the military according to a pre-arranged script signed off by the Police Commissioner.

> I, Joseph Luis Canepa, Commissioner of Police, having considered the terrorist situation in Gibraltar and having been fully briefed on the military plan with firearms, request that you proceed with the military option, which may include the use of legal force for the preservation of life.

With the military now in control, the arrest procedures practised with the Gibraltar police were no longer an operational priority. The fact that the military had provided the Police Commissioner with a pre-printed statement ceding temporary control suggests that the 'military option' was never designed to place the SAS merely in a supporting role. Rather, it served to provide a further layer of legal justification.

As the suspects approached the Landport tunnel with Spain, the SAS units began a pincer movement. When Savage broke away from Farrell and McCann, one group of soldiers followed Savage; the others kept their eyes trained on the two more experienced suspects. Under the rules of engagement the SAS could only open fire if there was a clear and present threat of a loss of life to either the individual soldier or to the general public. The need to provide a warning no longer applied if the soldier believed that in doing so he heightened the threat.[11] In his evidence to the inquest, the SAS operative with primary responsibility for targeting McCann, identified only as Soldier A, hedged his bets:

> I was just about to shout a warning to stop, and at the same time I was drawing my pistol, and the effect overtook the warning. He looked straight at me, we literally had eye-to-eye contact and the smile went off his face. It's as though McCann had a realisation of who I was, as though I was a threat to him. The look was of alertness, very aware. All of a sudden his right elbow moved aggressively across his body. It looked as though he was definitely going for the button.[12]

This certainty contrasted with evidence that McCann was initially shot in the back. The second shot discharged was aimed at Farrell's back; the next three into McCann — once more in the back and then twice in the head. Forensic tests showed that Soldier A was less than three feet away as he opened fire on both terrorists. A second operative, Soldier B, testified that he shot in the opposite formation, targeting Farrell first before incapacitating McCann and then reverting to the female terrorist. Both soldiers testified that such force was necessary in order to ensure that neither could detonate a bomb. Eyewitness testimony from residents in a nearby apartment block claimed that neither terrorist was in a position to detonate anything after the first shots and that the shots to the head were carried out while the suspects were lying prone on the ground. The European Court of Human Rights, which held that there was no evidence to substantiate the charge that the final shots were fired while the suspects were lying prostrate, discounted this controversial testimony.

A similar rationale was used for the apprehension of Sean Savage, who was shot nine times by Solider C, the last two in the head, as his body was inches away from the ground. His colleague, Soldier D, fired a total of six shots, two of which were aimed at the neck and head. At the inquest both officers made clear that their training equated incapacitation with death. This was the only way to ensure that the threat was eradicated, a view endorsed by the attack commander.

At 16.06 the military handed back control to the civil authority, which disregarded the earlier admonishment to the military that the preservation of evidence was an overriding imperative. Shell cartridges and cases were picked up without marking their position and the bodies of McCann and Farrell were moved without forensic examination. Following their removal to the morgue, their clothing was removed prior to examination, thereby destroying crucial evidence that could indicate the exact trajectories of the bullet entries. A less cavalier approach was taken at the Savage crime scene, where the position of the body was outlined in chalk, along with three strike marks indicating bullet wounds to the head. Crucially, both groups of soldiers were brought to the Gibraltar police only to hand in their weapons. An army lawyer, who made clear that the soldiers would not be made available immediately for questioning, accompanied them. Instead, they were immediately flown out of Gibraltar for debriefing at regimental headquarters in England. Gibraltar police were not given access to them for forty-eight hours.

In the House of Commons, the Foreign Secretary, Geoffrey Howe, gave a blithe rationale that raised more questions than it answered:

> When challenged, they [the IRA suspects] made movements which made the military personnel operating in support of the Gibraltar police to conclude that their own lives and the lives of others were under threat. In the light of this response, they were shot. Those killed were subsequently found not to have been carrying arms.[13]

The official version of events was suspect from the beginning, and this rapidly became apparent through a series of controversial television programmes broadcast in the months after the killings, the inquest procedure and two separate investigations by the European Commission and the European Court of Human Rights. Six weeks after the Gibraltar shootings, on 28 April 1988, Thames Television broadcast 'Death on the Rock', which was to become one of the most controversial documentaries screened in the history of the Troubles. The programme provided the first concrete evidence that the killings were avoidable, but, more explosively, in a domestic British audience context, it was mired in controversy because it repeated the allegation that the coup de grace shots to the heads of each of the suspects were fired from point blank range.

The producer of the programme, Roger Bolton, had long experience dealing with sensitive issues relating to Northern Ireland. He had been sacked as editor of *Panorama* in 1979 as a consequence of a deeply embarrassing documentary in which the flagship current affairs programme filmed the IRA as it effectively took over the republican town of Carrickmore. In the House of Commons, the leader of the Ulster Unionist Party, Jim Molyneaux, condemned that film as potentially treasonous. The programme was never shown and the BBC's offices were raided to seize the material. While the Director of Public Prosecutions found there was sufficient evidence to answer charges relating to the Prevention of Terrorism Act, the government contented itself with a warning that any further breaches would entail a prosecution.[14] Bolton was to find himself in even more trouble following his decision to commission 'Death on the Rock'.

Denounced as trial by television, the importance of the programme rested less on the sensational but discredited claims that the suspects had been shot when on the ground, than on its questioning as to whether lethal force was necessary at all given the fact that the IRA personnel had been under such sustained surveillance from the moment they arrived in southern Spain. As noted above, it was precisely this point that tipped the judgement of the European Court of Human Rights. And it was precisely this point that the defence solicitor, P.J. McGrory, laboured, unsuccessfully, at the Gibraltar inquest.

In its final adjudication in 1995, the European Court raised a number of deeply embarrassing questions for the British state. Why were the suspects not prevented from entering Gibraltar? Why were they not arrested immediately on arrival? The Court found that 'the danger to the population of Gibraltar — which is at the heart of the government's submission in this case — in not preventing their entry must be considered to outweigh the possible consequences of having insufficient evidence to warrant their detention and trial. In its view, either the authorities knew that there was no bomb in the car — or there was a serious miscalculation by those responsible for controlling the operation. As a result, the scene was set in which the fatal shoot-ing, given the intelligence assessments which had been made, was a foreseeable possibility, if not a likelihood.'[15]

THE MILLTOWN KILLINGS

In Northern Ireland itself, the IRA released a statement rich in irony. It condemned state-sponsored execution while admitting that those killed were on a military operation. As the Gibraltar soldiers were being debriefed, the republican movement planned a show of defiance at the funerals of those killed by the SAS at Milltown Cemetery. It was to be the biggest spectacle seen in west Belfast since the Hunger Strike funerals in 1981. Thousands of people followed the cortèges as they converged at the gates of the cemetery. The security that day was unusually light for such a high-profile event, particularly given the fact that full paramilitary funerals were to be provided, carefully choreographed by the republican movement to provide symbolic reassurance to the faithful, and stunning visuals for the international media, now ensconced in Belfast.

With the entire republican leadership gathered around the open graves, a solitary gunman ran towards the mourners, hurling grenades and firing from a Browning automatic pistol and a heavy-duty Ruger .357 Magnum. The audacity of the attack and its capture on videotape gave it instant notoriety. The gunman, Michael Stone, was instant-aneously transformed into one of the most iconic figures within loyalism. Stone claimed that his intention was 'to kill killers' and maintained that his intention was to target Gerry Adams and Martin McGuinness. This claim is hard to justify. While he was patient enough to wait until the coffins had been lowered into the graves, Stone was still too far away from the epicentre of proceedings to target any specific individual.

As panic broke out and mourners dived for cover among the grave-stones, the initial threat to the alleged target, the republican leader-ship, further dissipated. Stone did not abort his mission. Rather he continued to fire, sporadically reloading the speed clip on the Browning as he retreated towards the motorway. Pursued by groups of young men, the loyalist zigzagged through the graveyard. In an interview for the *Insight* television programme 'Portrait of a Killer', Stone recalled that 'it was literally a dance of death. They were hiding behind the headstones and if a target presented itself I shot it.'[16]

Three men were killed, one of whom was an IRA volunteer. Seventy were wounded, mainly from shrapnel and the shards of marble dislodged from the gravestones. Stone made it to the motorway where he tried unsuccessfully to hijack a car. He was by then out of ammunition, and the crowd closed in, beating him unconscious before the police arrived. Without their intervention it is questionable whether Stone could have survived.

Despite the poor quality of the television footage, there could be no mistaking either its enduring power or its capacity to engender very differing responses. For the loyalist community, Stone was a hero, prepared to risk almost certain death in order to avenge the dead of Enniskillen. For many in the republican movement and beyond, bravery was an adjective reserved for those who pursued the killer.[17] Such primordial responses, coupled with Stone's capture and carefully phrased responses to questions posed by detectives, pushed the issue of collusion off centre stage.

Following his arrest, Stone made a number of statements to police claiming that he was a freelance loyalist operator. This stoical response was accompanied by the UDA's denial that Stone was acting on its authority. The UDA's unequivocal denial of Stone has to be discounted as a consequence of the organisation's acceptance of him as a fellow traveller both in remand and in prison. His status within the organisation was further underscored by the decision of the Northern Ireland Secretary of State, Mo Mowlam, to conduct face-to-face negotiations with a delegation including Stone in the lead-up to the reconstitution of the loyalist ceasefire in 1998.

Stone also admitted his role in a number of other killings, each designed to foster his self-perception as a dedicated soldier, not a psychotic gunman with a pathological hatred of Catholics. In each case, Stone alleged that he targeted only those about whom he had been given accurate information. These included Patrick Brady, a fringe member of Sinn Féin who was shot as he arrived for work at the Kennedy Dairy on the outskirts of west Belfast in November 1984. Brady was killed on the spurious grounds that he used his delivery round to scout loyalist areas. Stone alleged that he had received intelligence material showing his target at a Sinn Féin Ard Fheis. In the febrile atmosphere of 1984, it was enough justification for the killing of a milkman.

In a prison interview, Stone maintained his position that the killing of Brady was justified. He saw the tactical execution of the operation as a sign of his expertise, boasting that 'because of Brady's size — twenty-two stone — I chose the shotgun. I reckoned he was so big that if I only got shots off from a pistol, and they were only body shots, he might survive. I was intending to do it quickly. I planned to immobilise him with one road to the body and then shoot him in the head as he was going down. The shotgun from the car at close range was the best weapon.'[18]

Stone also admitted the murder of two other Catholics. Dermot Hackett was a bread deliveryman in west Tyrone. In a statement to the court, Stone alleged that his intelligence officers told him that Hackett was an IRA man. In a third incident, Stone admitted killing a joiner as he renovated sheltered housing for the elderly in the Old Warren Estate, a predominantly loyalist public housing complex in Lisburn. Again, Stone alleged that his target was using his day job as a cover for gathering intelligence for the IRA. Stone also remained wedded to his self-justification as a loyalist volunteer forced by circumstance to defend his community. In his worldview, no blame could be attached to him as an operator if the targets had no or only tangential connections with the republican movement. Nor, he claimed, should blame necessarily be attached to the intelligence officers within the UDA/UFF who, in turn, received the information from the security forces.

> Anything I got was from UFF intelligence officers. They collated all the information ... granted some of it looked very professional ... I've no comment to make on that but as I said, the intelligence officers, that's their job — to gather intelligence from wherever and whatever means they can to get that intelligence — I've never actually seen anything with an official stamp on it. I was just shown stuff and told that's the target.

In his first major broadcast interview since his release from prison as part of the Good Friday Agreement, Stone dramatically refashioned the story of his most notorious killings at Milltown Cemetery. Expressing no remorse for his actions, the iconic loyalist now claimed that the Milltown attack had the express sanction of the UFF leadership.

Stone's main point of contact was John McMichael, the political face of the UDA. McMichael is revered within loyalism for his attempts to inject a political dynamic to the paramilitary organisation, a mythology that discounts his simultaneous role as the director of its terrorist capacity. It was McMichael who provided Stone with the intelligence material and who had scouted a number of operations, including an abortive attempt to assassinate Martin McGuinness in Derry, in the months prior to the Milltown killings.

The links between Stone and McMichael were well known by at least two nodes in the security apparatus. The RUC Special Branch had photographed the two loyalists meeting on a number of occasions. The Force Research Unit also knew of and tacitly condoned the role played by McMichael. Its most important undercover agent, Brian Nelson, had been promoted to the position of Director of Intelligence within the UFF on the explicit orders of the UFF leader, as a consequence of his role in the importation of an arms cache from South Africa in 1986.[19] Most of the weapons were subsequently seized but a shadowy grouping called Ulster Resistance, which had tenuous links to senior figures within the Democratic Unionist Party, had secreted a sizeable proportion. Stone was to claim that the weapons used in the graveyard attack on the Gibraltar mourners came from this cache. In his autobiography, Stone gave a detailed account of the preparations for the Milltown attack. He claimed that not only had a serving RUC officer accompanied him to collect the weapons and transported him safely back to Belfast, but that he had been given aerial photographs of the area pinpointing the location of lookout posts and had been told in advance that there would be no army or RUC presence at the funerals.[20] Stone's changed account was designed in part to further justify his actions as a disciplined soldier and in part to rescue the UDA from allegations that it was merely a gangsters' cartel, operating with the tacit approval of the security forces. For Stone, the UFF's operations represented an extension of the army's capability.

SETTING THE AGENDA: THE PROPAGANDA FRONT

By accident rather than design, one of those killed by Stone at the Milltown funerals, Kevin Brady, was a member of the IRA. At Brady's funeral, two days later, the carnival of death once more returned to the streets of Belfast. Two plain-clothes British soldiers travelling in an unmarked car came across the Brady cortège. It has never been established definitively whether the soldiers were undercover operatives or naïve off-duty youngsters who took an unfathomable risk in venturing into west Belfast amid such high tension. Fearful that they would be surrounded, the soldiers calculated that it was better to execute an emergency procedure, turning the car at high speed and driving directly into the mourners. When the car stalled, one of the soldiers withdrew his weapon, further escalating an already danger-ously volatile situation.

The crowd, angry, nervous and convinced that another murder plot was unfolding, set upon them. The discovery of identity cards on the soldiers linking them to the Signals Regiment fuelled suspicions that they were part of a covert plot to unleash carnage. Following the Gibraltar killings and the Stone attack at Milltown earlier in the week it was an understandable reaction. The response, however, demon-strated the gruesome reality that Northern Ireland was in the midst of a war, in which inhumane and degrading treatment was an acceptable modus operandi. Beneath the outward veneer of political justifi-cation, tribal passions were unleashed that yet again none was able to control. On the streets of west Belfast that afternoon, there was no restraint, a demonstration of how fatally undermined the leviathan of the state had become. The soldiers were beaten, stripped and bundled into a black taxi, the grisly scenes relayed once again across the world by the presence of the international media. Taken to wasteland, they were shot: the first seven times, the second, six. Mark Devenport, a BBC reporter who arrived at the scene moments later, recalled being approached by a group of what he termed 'urchins' who remarked with glee that the soldiers 'got what they deserved. We should have burned them.'[21]

One of the most iconic photographs of the Troubles depicted Father Alex Reid, who was later to become a key broker of the IRA ceasefire, giving the last rites to the dying soldiers. As the mob dis-pensed street justice, an entire community, not merely a small clique, became instantaneously criminalised. The barbarity of the attack and the culture of silence that protected the killers reinforced negative stereotypes. Again the media agenda itself was distorted by the government's decision to demand that the BBC hand over crucial videotape evidence, a request the corporation rejected on the grounds that such action would jeopardise the security of its camera crews. The pressure was not one-sided; sinister threats were made to the BBC by the IRA that if any of its personnel gave evidence they would, in turn, become legitimate targets.[22]

The killers were never found, but a number of senior IRA figures were charged with organising the murder. One of those was accused was Patrick McGeown. His lawyer was Patrick Finucane. In November 1988, McGeown was acquitted of all charges before the case passed even its preliminary stages. Finucane argued successfully that the Crown provided insufficient evidence to proceed. It was a cause of acute embarrassment that the state was forced to drop such a high-profile prosecution. The lawyer was photographed outside with McGeown, where, with remarkable understatement, he further humiliated the state: 'I thought we had merit in our submissions to the court.'[23] In an interview in 1992, McGeown told American lawyers that his acquittal irked police officers. He reported being stopped by an officer who told him, 'Don't think you got away with that. We intend to make sure that you won't be about too long. And your mate Pat, we'll fix him too.'[24]

It was an image that further conflated for some in the security establishment the professional duty of the advocate with the cause of the republican movement. In November 1988 the RUC Chief Constable and his deputy travelled to London to brief the junior Northern Ireland Office Minister, Douglas Hogg. Hogg subsequently reported that at the meeting the RUC intimated that the authorities faced a serious problem because of the fact that at least six solicitors were 'effectively in the pockets of terrorists', by which they meant that the lawyers should be construed as 'defending the organisation rather than the individual'.[25]

In the Special Branch documentation, according to the Cory Report, a common theme 'permeates' the files, which date back to 1979. 'What is most striking is that Patrick Finucane is repeatedly identified as a "republican sympathiser; an extreme republican sympathiser [who] represents PIRA members who face terrorist charges" and an individual who "comes from a staunch republican family".'[26]

Finucane had been identified as a target for loyalists from as early as 1981. At the height of the Hunger Strike, a Security Service agent reported 'one target stood out above the others. This was Patrick Finucane, a solicitor with strong republican connections who was closely involved with Bobby Sands at the time of the latter's election campaign.'[27] The Cory Report reveals damning evidence that the security network viewed the threat to the lawyer's life as 'very real and imminent'. A joint meeting was held with representatives of Special Branch on 24 August 1981 in which it was decided that 'no action would be taken [to warn Finucane] because intervention would compromise the security of the agent'. Crucially, Cory views this not as a failure of Special Branch but a collective one. 'In documents very recently made available to me, it is apparent that all parties agreed to comply with this decision. Indeed the decision was referred to by an officer of the joint Security Service/Secret Intelligence Service as "courageous".'[28] Cory views this as 'an indication that both the Security Service and RUC SB [Special Branch] saw agent security as taking precedence over the need to warn a targeted individual that his life was at risk' and sufficient in itself to warrant a public inquiry.[29] A similar dynamic governed decisions taken in the autumn and winter of 1988, leading inexorably to Finucane's death three months later. From the moment that a copy of the photograph was made available to loyalist gunmen by Brian Nelson, a serving agent of the British army, the die was cast and Pat Finucane's demise was a chronicle of death foretold.[30]

CALIBRATING TARGETING

The threats to Finucane escalated further in the autumn of 1988. His media profile increased dramatically following his success in gaining damages for one of the most senior members of the IRA, Brian Gillen, in a case involving maltreatment in the Castlereagh holding station in the 1970s. It was the first time that a defence lawyer had succeeded in a *habeas corpus* application, which charged that the detention of a prisoner under the emergency laws was rendered unlawful because of mistreatment.[31] The award of damages did not stop detectives routinely picking Gillen up for questioning. The sense of anger and frustration at Finucane's insouciance infuriated Special Branch officers, who made no secret of their antipathy.[32] Loyalist paramilitaries reported a similar dynamic. In 1998 the BBC journalist John Ware published an account of an interview he had conducted with Tommy Lyttle, the commander of the UDA in west Belfast. According to Lyttle, two officers suggested during routine questioning that Finucane should be targeted. Ware wrote that in the interview with him,

> Lyttle said he was so astonished at this suggestion that he informed a regular contact in the RUC Special Branch. 'I told him: What the hell is going on in Castlereagh? Why is Finucane being pushed?' The officer said it would be 'a bad blow for the Provos to have

Finucane removed'. Did that amount to approval that he should be shot? 'Put it this way,' said Lyttle, 'He didn't discourage the idea that he should be shot.'[33]

In secret filming carried out by the *Panorama* programme 'A Licence to Murder', one of those subsequently charged with the solicitor's murder placed the blame firmly at the door of Special Branch for inculcating the idea that he should be targeted. Ken Barrett alleged: 'To be honest, Finucane would be alive today if the peelers hadn't interfered.'[34] To buttress his story, Barrett made an extraordinary claim that transforms the allegation of state collusion from omission to commission.

According to Barrett, a Special Branch officer, whom he described as a 'fucking cool customer', attended a meeting with loyalist paramilitaries, which left the killer with little doubt as to what was required. Asked specifically what was said, Barrett continued:

> Just that Pat was one of their men who was an IRA man like. And he was dealing with finances and stuff for them, and he was a bad boy and if he was out, like, they'd have a lot of trouble replacing him, stuff like this. He says: 'He'll have to go.' He said: 'He's a thorn in everyone's side. He'll have to go.' He was determined in pursuing that. That's the one he wanted. They didn't want any fucking about. They didn't want to wait months. They wanted it done.[35]

There is no independent evidence to back up Barrett's claim. Even if true, there is no linkage between the individual police officer and the wider security nexus. Curiously, in the report into the third investigation into collusion released by Sir John Stevens, this point is addressed and pointedly left unanswered. The report notes that the question of RUC involvement in the incitement of loyalist paramilitaries was investigated by the team, but it fails to deliver judgement. Instead the report skips on to a tangential point relating to the fact that investigators 'attempted to establish whether loyalist paramilitaries or RUC officers had threatened Mr Finucane, and whether he had made any formal complaint. The absence of any record means that this criminal allegation cannot be substantiated against any RUC officer.' This formulation spectacularly misses the point addressed but not answered in the preceding paragraph relating to the allegation of incitement.[36]

What is apparent is that the Security Service itself knew that Finucane was again at risk. In a report obtained just before Christmas 1988, a source reported to MI5 that a meeting of UDA commanders was planned to 'discuss plans to kill the three solicitors who have represented republicans at recent hearings'. Finucane was identified only as the solicitor involved in the shoot to kill allegations surrounding the killing of Gervaise McKerr in 1982, which was again before the European Courts and therefore in the media spotlight. According to Cory, 'a reasonable person could well consider that such an agency did indeed know that Finucane was the "shoot to kill" solicitor at the time the report came in. The report, received just two months before the murder, did not apparently trigger any action on the part of the Security Service.'[37]

Cory notes that no documentation exists which would suggest that information was again deliberately withheld to protect their agent. There is no question, however, that other nodes in the security network were also informed and failed to act on the risk faced by Finucane and two other solicitors through the activities of other key agents, among them Brian Nelson, the chief intelligence officer of the UDA,[38] and William Stobie, its quartermaster in the cockpit of west Belfast.[39] In this context, it is particularly striking that no mention is made of Finucane in the threat assessment book held by Special Branch or evidence of any information entered into Tactical and Coordinating Groups, which brought together agents from all sections of the security nexus and was designed to cross-reference partial snippets of gossip, hearsay and informants' reports in order to generate credible intelligence. If the system was set up to save lives, it operated sporadically. Finucane slipped through the radar. Whether this was by accident or design is a question that can only be answered by an independent inquiry. What is clear, however, from both the conclusions of Cory and Stevens, is that an analysis of RUC records demonstrated that both sides of the community were not dealt with in equal measure when it came to threat assessment.[40] In a crucial conclusion, Stevens states baldly that 'nationalists were known to be targeted but were not properly warned or protected', indicating a systemic pattern of behaviour that extended beyond the Finucane case and involved giving agents carte blanche to engage in criminal behaviour up to and including murder.

It will be recalled that MI5 had processed the specific threats facing

Finucane from the UDA on 19 December 1988. Yet on 6 January, the RUC Special Branch forwarded to Douglas Hogg the specific dossier which explicitly highlighted the assertion that 'Finucane has continued to support the Republican cause using his expertise in an advisory capacity, and associating closely with PIRA/SF personnel'.[41] The dossier was forwarded on Hogg's explicit request for concrete details.

Again the timing of the request demonstrates the acute importance of managing the political environment. The information was to be used as the government faced determined if diffuse opposition to the renewal of the Prevention of Terrorism Act, not just from republicans but also from a panoply of legal experts, including the European Court of Human Rights, which had ruled that detention for seven days without a legal appearance was a violation of the European Convention. The abolition of the right to silence, the broadcasting ban and the government's decision to derogate from the European Convention on Human Rights, rather than amend the Act's provision on seven-day detention on the grounds that it was facing a public emergency threatening the life of the nation, were highly contested and contributed to a volatile debate within and outside the corridors of Westminster.

There was no question that Finucane's high-profile role in orchestrating challenges to the legal provisions adopted by annual legislation such as the Prevention of Terrorism Act added dramatically to his own personal risk. It was Finucane who had taken the initial case to the European Court on Human Rights, challenging both the legality of the seven-day detention of terrorist subjects and the broadcasting ban. He had also proved highly successful in reopening the controversy over the shoot to kill allegations in 1982 by securing a High Court judgement that forced the RUC personnel involved in the killing of Gervaise McKerr to give evidence.

In such a feverish atmosphere, it is implausible that there was no co-ordination between the government and the Security Service on such a sensitive matter at such a sensitive time. Yet eleven days later, four days after a paper trail began noting dissatisfaction within the FRU about the lack of credible information emanating from its agent within the UFF, Brian Nelson, Douglas Hogg told the Select Committee examining the Prevention of Terrorism Bill in the House of Commons: 'I have to state as a fact, but with great regret, that there are in Northern Ireland a number of solicitors who are unduly sympathetic to the cause of the IRA.'

The assertion prompted an angry response by the SDLP Deputy Leader, Seamus Mallon, who was flabbergasted at the crassness of the intervention, an intervention in direct contravention of the UN Basic Principles on the Role of Lawyers, which state: 'Lawyers shall never be identified with their clients or their clients' causes as a result of discharging their functions.'[42] Mallon launched a devastating attack in the House of Commons:

> That is a remarkable statement for a minister to make about members of the legal profession who have borne much of the heat in a traumatic and abnormal situation. Such words should not be said without the courage to support them. I find it appalling that the minister should make such an accusation with such emphasis, and without, it seems, the intention of substantiating it….I have no doubt that there are lawyers walking the streets or driving the roads of the North of Ireland who have become targets for assassins' bullets as a result of the statement that has been made tonight. Following the minister's statements, people's lives are in grave danger. People who have brought cases to the European Court against this legislation will be suspected. People accused of IRA membership and other activities will be suspected. We have thrown a blanket over many lawyers in the North of Ireland and it will be on the head of this minister and government if the assassin's bullet decides to do, by lead, what this minister has done by word.[43]

Attempts by both Mallon and the Law Society to force the government to clarify whether either the Secretary of State for Northern Ireland or the Attorney General had given Hogg an imprimatur failed to elicit a response. The Secretary of the Law Society, Michael Davey, wrote to Hogg claiming 'disbelief' at the maladroit nature of the minister's interventions, which he added 'though extremely damaging are glaringly non-specific'. The Law Society called for clarification, adding that it could not believe that Hogg was 'suggesting that because people who have been charged are from time to time successfully defended, that in itself is a cause for alarm'.[44]

Despite his high profile, Finucane stayed silent. One of the other lawyers known to be a target of loyalist intentions, P.J. McGrory, released a statement championing the political right to have aspirations for a United Ireland. 'If he [Hogg] is saying there are solicitors acting in these cases who are sympathetic in another sense — approving of the methods of the IRA and that they would assist them in carrying out their various enterprises — then that is a very very grave accusation indeed.'[45]

It was telling that the furore over Hogg's comments coincided with the publication of a report by the Standing Advisory Commission on Human Rights, which was established by the Northern Ireland Secretary of State as a formal advisory body. The chairman of the commission, Oliver Napier, decried the manner in which the government had decided to enact legislative change under the renewal of the Prevention of Terrorism Act, precisely because it undercut 'the consultative process which in a democratic society is absolutely vital'.[46] The Secretary of State rejected this criticism with a statement in which he claimed that the 'measures we are currently taking are necessary and fully justified on their individual merits. That is why the government has invited parliament to approve each of them at the earliest opportunity.'[47]

The removal of the right to silence, through the Criminal Evidence Order, claimed the Secretary of State, was not derogation from the rule of law, but rather a prudent attempt to remove what the terrorists saw as a valuable weapon — their ability to exploit the incapacity of the courts to draw an inference from their decision not to incriminate themselves. Despite the nod towards parliamentary sovereignty, the government guillotined the debate on national security grounds. Frank Dobson, the shadow leader of the House, viewed the decision with disdain. 'Whatever the benefits the supporters of the Prevention of Terrorism Act claim for it, there is no doubt this law does reduce the openness of our society, does undermine our normal democratic procedures…That price is too high a price to pay.'[48]

With members of the Labour Party accused of being 'soft on terrorism', the leader of the House, John Wakeham, maintained that it was vital that the Security Service had the power to use the Act's detention and exclusion powers. Otherwise, 'it would enormously weaken our ability to defeat terrorism. This is simply unacceptable.'[49] For Seamus Mallon this was merely confirming evidence that 'the people who are ruling Northern Ireland now are the military and the police authorities, not the Northern Ireland Office'. Complaining of Stalinist tactics, Mallon argued that 'the reality is that if the Home Secretary introduced a judicial factor to the detention rule he will have to give a reason why a suspect is being detained. I know that the army and the police have made it clear that they do not want that.'[50]

The tension further intensified with the release of the official report by Lord Windelsham into the 'Death on the Rock' documentary, which vindicated the programme, once again drawing attention to the role played by lawyers in exposing the official version of events in controversial murders. The stage was set for the most controversial murder of the Troubles.

Chapter 4
Killing Finucane

On 12 February 1989 Pat Finucane was sitting down for dinner with his family in his house on Fortwilliam Drive, a comfortable middle-class area of north Belfast. At 7.25 p.m. two masked men dressed in black with military-style camouflage jackets burst through the unlocked front door. They shouted out that they were Provos, 'here to take the car'. Finucane shouted back, 'No, you are here to take me out.'[1] As the solicitor approached the glass door separating the kitchen from the hall, the first shots were fired, leaving him prostrate on the floor with bullet wounds to the stomach and chest. The gunmen then entered the kitchen before dispatching a further eleven bullets, mainly at the face and neck, fired in a 'very slow and deliberate' manner.[2] At the inquest into the killing, the Chief Investigating Officer in the case, Detective Superintendent Alan Simpson, testified that the murder was 'unusual both in its ferocity and the fact that he was struck by all fourteen shots fired'.[3] The forensic pathologist testified that at least one of the bullets was fired from a distance of 15 inches.[4] One gunman, using a Browning semi-automatic pistol, which had been stolen by a member of the UDA from the Palace Army Barracks in Holywood in 1987, discharged eleven shots. A second gunman, using a .38 revolver, the provenance of which was never established, fired the other three shots.

As the loyalist killers ruthlessly murdered her husband in front of his sons and daughter, Geraldine Finucane moved towards an entrance to the dining room and covered her head with her arms. A ricocheting bullet wounded her in the ankle; the children were physically unharmed but severely traumatised by the targeted killing, among them Michael, now himself a solicitor practising in Dublin. 'I still remember it clearly. It is an image seared into my mind. The thing I remember most vividly is the noise; the reports of each bullet reverberating in the kitchen, how my grip on my younger brother and sister tightened with every shot. It's not a memory I care to visit very often, but it's there. I expect it always will be.'[5]

The UDA issued a statement claiming that it had targeted 'Pat Finucane the Provisional IRA member not Pat Finucane the solicitor. While the Provisional IRA threaten and shoot loyalist construction workers, removal men and those who simply share their lunchboxes, the inevitable retaliation will take place.'[6] Despite residual anger at his father's death, Michael Finucane has repeatedly and publicly expressed the family's preference for an immediate inquiry, even if the holding of it endangers subsequent criminal prosecutions.[7]

> If I could be satisfied that an inquiry process was thorough enough to get to the truth, to get to the bottom of this — who was responsible, who set it up, who ordered it, who maintained it, who funded it, who resourced it, who covered it up for so many years — if a public inquiry answered all of those questions, I would forego the prosecutions of the triggermen.[8]

At a hearing of the Helsinki Committee of the Commission of Security and Co-operation in Europe in May 2004, Geraldine Finucane once more came to a witness stand to ask for disclosure. Her evidence was cognisant that political imperatives, which have made her husband's murder so difficult to definitively resolve, retain their potency.

> The evidence in my husband's case shows clearly that the British State pursued a policy of state-sponsored assassination, using loyalist paramilitaries as the killers. In pursuing this policy, the British were no better than many despotic regimes around the world that are condemned and even invaded for their appalling human rights record. In seeking to cover up what they did for so many years, the government continues its policy of state-sponsored

murder. Those responsible were rewarded at the time and are protected now in the aftermath.[9]

Fifteen years after the events of that fateful night, the Finucane family
received a partial answer when Ken Barrett, one of the two gunmen,
arrived in Court 12 at the Laganside court complex in September
2004. Wearing a bleached denim jacket and jeans, Barrett, who had
claimed he was a victim of a state vendetta, was contesting charges of
murder, attempted murder, membership of a proscribed organisation
and possession of weapons. He looked tense as he changed his plea to
guilty. As a result, the trial of the only person charged with direct
responsibility for one of the most controversial murders in the history of the Troubles lasted less than a morning. The decision to plead
guilty not only shortened the trial, it also obviated the ostensible reason for a delay in ceding a public inquiry into the events that led to
the killing of Finucane, an inquiry that was being demanded by a
plethora of international legal groups, the United Nations and an
independent judge appointed by the British government.

In court were two of the detectives most centrally involved in the
investigation into Barrett's role in the killing. The first was Johnston
Brown, a CID officer who had first recorded Barrett's confession eighteen months after the killing when the loyalist was stripped of his
position as a UDA commander because of a dispute over the proceeds
of racketeering. Incredibly, Brown's inquiries were stymied by the RUC
Special Branch and his own superiors within CID. It was a vindication
for Brown that the court recognised publicly that he had first sourced
the confession, a formulation that raises questions as to why this
avenue was not explored then.[10]

The second policeman observing proceedings was Commander
David Cox, the officer in day-to-day control of the Stevens investigation, which verified the Johnston Brown account after an unprece-
dented eavesdropping operation across southern England in 2002–3.[11]
Parsing the interlinked stories of how and why the investigations were
corrupted is the focus of the next two chapters. They reveal disturbing
evidence of how the entire criminal justice system had been corroded
by the invidious compact that elevated the protection of informants
over the prosecution of serial murderers.

Sir John Stevens, the Metropolitan Police Commissioner, released a
statement that seemed deliberately designed to raise as many questions

as it answered, questions that could only be answered by the government making good on its promise to open a public inquiry.

> We hope this result will bring some comfort to the family of Pat Finucane. We know Mrs Finucane wants a public inquiry — that is a matter for government, but I personally hope that today's outcome will give some sense of peace and closure to her. The killing of Pat Finucane was cold-blooded and brutal in the extreme. Gathering evidence to bring this man to justice is a credit to the dedication and hard work of the officers on my team.[12]

The Stevens Inquiry team, despite lodging a number of files with the Director of Public Prosecutions, appeared from the statement, broadcast interviews and off-the-record briefings to see its work as substantially complete.[13] In a private meeting between the team and the Finucane family in February 2004, according to notes transcribed by the director of the British Irish Rights Watch, Jane Winter, and entered into argument for leave to a judicial appeal of the Secretary of State's decision not to immediately proceed with a public inquiry, John Stevens stated that 'so far as Pat Finucane's murder was concerned, Barrett was the end of live lines of inquiry'.[14]

At the same meeting, Commander David Cox told the family that 'the only case that impinges on a public inquiry into Pat Finucane's case is the Barrett trial'. He further stated, according to the note, that the Stevens team needed 'to be seen as impartial, but that did not mean that they were the family enemy.' Commander Cox is alleged to have claimed that 'they [the Stevens team] had felt they were being encouraged to say there was a whole string of prosecutions in the pipeline and that they were being used to try to block a public inquiry and they wanted to make sure that did not happen.'[15]

The Sinn Féin president, Gerry Adams, publicly questioned the change of heart by Barrett, who had previously claimed that he was a victim of state terrorism. Speaking just days before the beginning of pivotal talks at Leeds Castle in Kent, Adams claimed that the guilty plea 'came about as the result of the sordid deal brokered by the British system to ensure that the collusion cover-up continues'.[16] While there is no doubt that the Sinn Féin leader was making political capital out of the discomfiture faced by the British establishment, it is an inescapable fact that Barrett's change of plea ensured that even more embarrassing information about the true extent of collusion was not aired in court.

The Northern Ireland Office was forced to release a holding statement that was devoid of credibility: 'We will be establishing whether there are any other prosecutions that could be affected by a public inquiry and will make a further announcement as soon as possible.'[17] The murdered solicitor's wife and son once again took to the airwaves, where they repeated in restrained tones the need for a full inquiry. Michael Finucane spoke for many who are concerned about the public policy implications of the operation of intelligence networks:

> My focus a long time ago shifted from individual perpetrators to the system that made it possible. You can take Ken Barrett or Billy Stobie out of the equation and there's any number of Kens or Billy's to plug back in. However, the system makes it possible for these guys to kill with impunity. They get the means to do it, the resources and protection afterwards. That system needs to be analysed and investigated so you can resolve it and put it behind you. This to me isn't a resolution.[18]

The contours of that dispute were apparent within minutes of the shooting in 1989. As Geraldine Finucane and her family were transferred to hospital and the Criminal Investigation Unit of the police began a detailed forensic investigation, one of the most prominent solicitors in Northern Ireland, Paschal O'Hare, arrived at the Fortwilliam Drive crime scene to decry British government felonsetting. 'Maybe this dastardly act tonight will lead to some people in Britain curbing their tongue', he said in a reference to Douglas Hogg's carefully, if ambiguously, phrased comments the previous month during the parliamentary debate on the renewal of the Prevention of Terrorism Act.[19]

This view was endorsed by the Irish government and in editorials carried by the *Irish News* and the *Irish Times*, both of which decried the tenor of Hogg's insinuations for creating the dynamic that led to the killing of Pat Finucane. The former spoke of 'Mr Hogg's irresponsibility', which 'may very well have provided certain warped minds with a justification for murder, and in the process has delivered another serious body-blow to the rule of law in Northern Ireland'.[20] South of the border, the *Irish Times* noted sardonically that 'murder gangs do not, as a rule, consult political oracles. But to present them with excuses or endorsements or what can be taken for either is at least an act of folly; and at worst hideous irresponsibility.'[21]

The British government denied publicly that there was any link between Hogg's statement and the killing of Finucane, a formulation that its counterpart in Dublin publicly rejected. At the time of the initial Hogg statement, Fianna Fáil had raised the issue privately with the British government through the Anglo-Irish secretariat at Maryfield precisely because Hogg had been perceived to be articulating Home Office rather than simply personal bias. Now Dublin went public with its concerns. In a formal statement, Charles Haughey noted that 'the need for the greatest care to be given to any statements which might have tragic consequences in Northern Ireland has once again been underlined and I expect that this aspect will be urgently and fully considered.'[22] The Secretary of State, Tom King, politely rebuffed the calls for Hogg's resignation because of what Geraldine Finucane termed in comments released to the media from her hospital bed, the 'instrumentality' of the statement to her husband's death. King said:

> I don't see that connection. I have just made clear that everyone knows the very high profile that Mr Finucane had in recent times, and there is no question that there are some people — some of the sicker members of this society — to whom somebody who has a high profile becomes the sort of target that they fix on, they resent very strongly.[23]

Finucane was the victim of a loyalist gang which had been heavily infiltrated and whose actions were tracked, if not impeded, from the moment that the loyalist leader Jim Spence asked the army's most prolific agent, Brian Nelson, for a photograph that included the solicitor three months before his killing. In June 2003, the UTV *Insight* series, which has spent considerable resources covering this story, alleged that Spence himself was an RUC Special Branch agent.[24] Cory is silent on this allegation but the information provided through UTV's work on the wider issue of the management of the Dirty War, coupled with the Stevens Report released in April 2003 and the related information published by Cory, when taken together, represent a damning indictment of the security network's management of the threat faced by Pat

Finucane immediately prior to his death and its subsequent efforts to impede the criminal investigation, precisely because the exposure would serve to compromise that network.

Nowhere was this more apparent than in the case of William Stobie, whose trial on charges of conspiracy to murder Pat Finucane collapsed spectacularly in 2001. Stobie was a respected quartermaster of the UDA; he was also a respected agent. Stobie had served in the British army from 1969 to 1975 and re-enlisted in the Territorial Army from November 1983 to March 1985. He also rose up the ranks of the UDA and its military wing, the UFF. In 1987 he received a suspended jail sentence for possession of weapons and explosives, a criminal record that forced his removal from the formal ranks of the army. This conviction did not deter him from continuing his work as a quartermaster for the UDA, operating from his base in the Highfield Estate off the Springfield Road.

In an interview with *Insight* conducted just before his murder in 2001, days after he called for an independent inquiry into the events leading to the killing of Pat Finucane — a killing he was intimately involved in — Stobie addressed, in rather inarticulate fashion, an abiding question: 'I didn't join the UDA to be part of a gang or anything like that there, I joined them because I felt there was a bit of a war on so there was you know... Being in the UDA, when you start think back on it so you do, you know, what was it all about, I mean it was senseless at the end of the day you know, actually senseless.'[25]

Just how senseless can be illustrated from Stobie's involvement in the murder of Adam Lambert, a Protestant teenager killed while working on a building site on 10 November 1987, the day after the Enniskillen bombing, by a drink-fuelled UDA unit. As quartermaster for the area, Stobie was responsible for sourcing the weapons to be used. According to accounts given to a Belfast-based journalist in 1990, he also provided the vehicle.[26] Lambert, a student on work placement, was an unfortunate victim of an attack driven by alcohol and adrenalin. It was a telling indication of the volatility of those the security forces would later use to pursue its war against the republicans. The loyalists first targeted a bus driving down the Springfield Road but the gun jammed. Whether the passengers escaped injury because of mechanical failure or drunken incompetence has never been established. In their desire to find a republican, any target would do, so they scoured the area looking for likely victims. They eventually

Pat Finucane was one of the most adroit defence solicitors operating in Northern Ireland. Prior to his killing on 12 February 1989, at least three wings of the intelligence community had advance knowledge that he was being actively targeted. No warning was passed to him. (*Pacemaker Press*)

The funeral of three members of an IRA Active Service Unit killed in Gibraltar in March 1988 by undercover SAS operatives. Their funeral at Milltown Cemetery on 16 March was attacked by a loyalist gunman, sparking a spiral of retaliatory violence. (*Pacemaker Press*)

Fr Alex Reid of Clonard Monastery gives the last rites to one of two British soldiers, beaten, stripped naked and shot at the funeral of one of the mourners killed at the Milltown cemetery during the Gibraltar interment ceremony. (*Pacemaker Press*)

Pat McGeown leaves Belfast courthouse with Pat Finucane after being cleared on charges relating to the murder of British soldiers on waste ground in March 1988. McGeown later claimed that senior police officers warned him, 'Don't think you got away with that. We intend to make sure that you won't be along for too long. And your mate Pat, we'll fix him too.' (*Pacemaker Press*)

Police outside the home of Pat Finucane following his murder by the UDA on 12 February 1989. The organisation put out a statement claiming it had targeted 'Pat Finucane the Provisional IRA member not Pat Finucane the solicitor'. (*Pacemaker Press*)

The investigation into the killing of Pat Finucane has been one of the most extensive in British policing. It has been at the centre of three separate investigations headed by Sir John Stevens. When he released his interim report in June 2003, the former Commissioner of the Metropolitan Police argued that his 'inquiries have highlighted collusion, the wilful failure to keep records, the absence of accountability, the withholding of intelligence and evidence and the extreme of agents being involved in murder'. (*Reuters*)

Over the course of its investigation, the Stevens team collected 9,256 statements, recorded 10,391 documents involving more than 1,000,000 pages, and seized 16,191 exhibits. (*Pacemaker Press*)

In its initial stages, the Stevens team was housed in the headquarters of the Police Authority of Northern Ireland at Seapark, Carrickfergus. Stevens claimed that, throughout, his investigation faced deliberate stonewalling. 'This obstruction was cultural in its nature and widespread within parts of the army and the RUC.' (*Pacemaker Press*)

The offices used by the Stevens team were gutted by fire on 11 January 1990. Sir John claimed in his third report that the blaze in a secure police installation was 'a deliberate act of arson'. (*Pacemaker Press*)

Brian Nelson was one of the army's most senior agents operating within the ranks of the UDA. At his trial in 1992, the commanding officer of the Force Research Unit provided a character witness statement. Colonel Gordon Kerr claimed Nelson 'put country before family and to that extent he was very loyal to the system and it embarrasses me, personally, that the system has been unable to recognise the real difficulties of running agents within a terrorist organisation'. (*Pacemaker Press*)

William Stobie was quartermaster for the UDA unit involved in the killing of Pat Finucane. He was also an agent for Special Branch and had alerted his handlers of an impending attack. This information was not acted upon, neither were his warnings on weapons transfers after the killing. (*Reuters*)

In December 2001, Stobie was eventually tried for conspiracy in the killing of Pat Finucane. He rejected the charges, claiming that he was an agent of the state. After the trial collapsed, Stobie supported calls for a public inquiry. He was killed shortly afterwards by former colleagues. His killers have not been brought to justice. (*PA/Empics*)

Naming Names. A defaced mural on a sectarian interface in south Belfast encapsulates the public policy implications of the Finucane murder. (*PA/Empics*)

On 17 April 2003, Sir John Stevens handed over his brief report to the Chief Constable of the PSNI, Hugh Orde. For many years, Orde was the most senior officer involved in the management of the Stevens Inquiry. He has refused to publish the findings in full. (*Reuters*)

Justice Peter Cory, the Canadian jurist called on by the British and Irish governments to establish whether the grounds exist for public inquiries into six controversial killings, four of which occurred within Northern Ireland. The judge concluded that inquiries should be held in all cases. (*Irish Times*)

Rosemary Nelson, a prominent defence solicitor, who also suffered accusation of guilt by association because of a conflation of a lawyer and her client base. She was murdered by loyalist paramilitaries in 1999. (*Pacemaker Press*)

The scene of the car bomb which exploded as Rosemary Nelson drove to work on 15 March 1999. (*Reuters*)

Protestors at Stormont on the fifteenth anniversary of the Finucane murder. The British government refused to publish the Cory report, citing continued legal problems. When it was eventually published, more than ten pages were redacted on national security grounds. (*PA/Empics*)

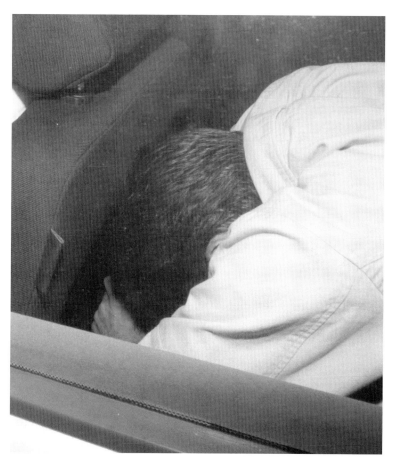

Ken Barrett arrives at Belfast Magistrates Court on 30 May 2003 to deny murder charges relating to the Finucane killing. In September 2004, just as his trial was about to begin, Barrett changed his plea. The decision meant that only the barest of outlines relating to his involvement were entered into the public record. (*PA/Empics*)

Sinn Féin has used the unanswered questions surrounding collusion to provide significant leverage in its negotiations with the British government. (*PA/Empics*)

The Finucane family visit 10 Downing Street on 2 November 2004 to press for a full public inquiry. (*Reuters*)

The self-perception of the UDA. (*Reuters*)

settled on Adam Lambert, chosen merely because he was an outsider who happened to be available.[27] At their subsequent trial, the loyalists involved claimed they were 'gutted' when they found out that Lambert was a Protestant, leaving the obvious question of whether they would have expressed the same conditional remorse if the teenager had been, as intended, Catholic.

In the aftermath of the shooting Stobie was arrested and brought for questioning to Castlereagh. Although the Criminal Investigation Department had grounds to suspect Stobie's involvement, there was not enough evidence to charge him. As he was leaving the station, Stobie became ensnared by Special Branch, who viewed his position as quartermaster integral to the continued success of its intelligence-gathering operation.

> I was going down the hallway and two other policemen asked me to go into an interview room and when I went into that interview room they started to ask me questions. They gave me a telephone number so they did and told me they would contact me and they asked me certain questions, so they did, did I know people in the estate. They were looking for information on guns, if they were hidden, where they were hidden and all this here. Who handled the guns and all that there.

Stobie's decision to co-operate brought him within the ambit of the Walker guidelines governing the handling of informers. It also meant that despite his involvement in the Lambert killing, no future arrest could be sanctioned without the authorisation of Special Branch.

> All proposals to effect planned arrests must be cleared with Regional Special Branch to ensure that no agents of either RUC or army are involved.
>
> A decision to arrest an agent must only be taken after discussion between Special Branch and CID. If agreement is not possible the matter will be referred to Assistant Chief Constable level.
>
> The charging of an agent must be the result of a conscious decision by Special Branch and CID in which the balance of advantage has been carefully weighed.[28]

Over the next three years, from 1987 to 1990, Stobie was to provide his handlers with information about the weapons movements of one of the most active loyalist groupings in the city. He was to receive '£20 a week with bonuses for good information'.[29] For the Special Branch, the information was regarded as credible, a view endorsed by Judge Cory as evidenced by the publication of a partial log in his report into collusion.[30]

The recruitment of a quartermaster as an agent was exceptionally problematic. It gave the police unique insight into when operations were likely to take place, who was involved in the transportation and handover of weapons and their recovery. It also gave them the capacity to render the weapons inoperable. While early or repeated intervention ran the risk of compromising the agent, the failure to act on that information also opened the appalling vista of a tacit acceptance on the part of Special Branch and the other agencies that not bringing perpetrators to justice in order to maintain the integrity of the system could be justified. In this context, the handling of William Stobie represents a talismanic example of the moral hazard involved and the incapacity of the state to minimise its distorting effect.

According to the log, Stobie did not limit the information he gave to his handlers to weapons movements (25 July 1988). He also provided information about the command structure of 'A' company and the general direction of targeting, when fuelled by rationale rather than alcohol. As an example, on 14 September 1988, Stobie 'informs handlers that the UDA in the Highfield area of Belfast are actively targeting INLA/IPLO members in west Belfast with a view to carrying out murder attempts in the near future'.[31] He passed over information on past killings, naming those responsible for the killing of Terence McDaid three weeks after his murder in a case of mistaken identity (31 May 1988), a murder that was to expose the loyalist killing machine. Stobie later admitted in interviews conducted with two journalists in 1990 that he had in fact driven the getaway car. These interviews were only published in 1999, just before he was belatedly charged with the murder.[32]

Stobie alerted his handlers in the week before Finucane's death that moves were afoot for an impending hit on what he termed 'a top Provie'. According to the pattern identified by Cory and Stevens, warnings were not issued nor were serious attempts made to intervene. Events were simply allowed to unfold, a situation that Stevens concludes resulted from the fact that 'the co-ordination, dissemination and sharing of intelligence was poor'.[33]

This appears a stunted theory of causation, which underplays the integrated nature of the security nexus and the manner in which it operated. Likewise, Justice Cory identifies the absence of credible information in the threat books held by the RUC as a primary cause for concern. However, given the wider febrile political context in which the murder took place and the warnings that had already been collected by MI5, this seems to place the blame inordinately on individual case handlers and on an institutionalised bias within a section of the RUC which has long been recognised as a 'force within a force'.[34] There is therefore a requirement to adopt a more granular reading of the interdependent nature of the security network than either Stevens or the linear structure of the Cory Report allows.

Stobie himself was more direct. The man who provided the weapons for Finucane's murder and was then protected by Special Branch in order to preserve its intelligence network before a belated prosecution, called for a full independent inquiry. Stobie had been on trial in 2001 for his role in the Finucane murder, based on evidence provided to the RUC CID in 1990 by a Belfast journalist to whom Stobie had confided. This evidence was not acted upon at the time, but it formed the basis of the charges brought through the Stevens investigation. Following the extraordinary collapse of the trial because of the failure of the journalist to testify, the loyalist paramilitary gave an equally extraordinary impromptu press conference.

> This was never about getting to the real truth about these killings. It was a PR exercise to make it look as if something was being done when in actual fact nothing was being done. This has cost the taxpayers millions of pounds and they knew it was a smokescreen all along. This was all about avoiding having to set up an independent inquiry, it was as simple and as cynical as that. I back that call for an inquiry and with this case now at an end I can see no reason why that cannot happen immediately.[35]

Stobie had signed his own death warrant. A week later he was killed as he left his house in the early morning. A statement from the Red Hand Defenders, a cover name for the UDA, admitted responsibility. John White, a political figurehead for the UDA in Belfast, claimed that Stobie's call for an inquiry had angered a lot of people in the loyalist community and further contended that the case was being used to undermine both the RUC and the Northern Irish state.[36] Stobie's killers have never been found. While Justice Cory has been careful to allow the facts of his report to speak for themselves in order to justify the holding of an inquiry, when asked to explain why all of those named in association with the Finucane killing featured in intelligence reports, he gave this pointed response to the *Insight* programme:

> That's something for a public inquiry. All those names are referred to in documents, which are referred to in the report. It's there. Now it's for someone or some group or three or whatever it is to look at that and to call the witnesses before them — with any luck, before they're all dead.[37]

It is therefore necessary to disentangle the complex history of the Stobie case and the prosecution of Barrett before reaching adjudication on Geraldine Finucane's testimony to the Helsinki Committee of the Commission on Security and Co-operation in Europe.

There is no question that Stobie was afforded considerable protection prior to and in the immediate aftermath of the Finucane killing for, as yet, undisclosed reasons. In September 1990, after the 'balance of advantage' which prevented the charging of a serving agent tipped decisively against Stobie, the loyalist paramilitary was 'burned' by his former protectors and he faced seven days of intensive questions by CID. It was precisely because he lived in fear of such a situation developing that Stobie had already taken out an insurance policy by confiding in two journalists, Neil Mulholland of the *Sunday Life* and Ed Maloney of the *Sunday Tribune*. There was only one proviso: the information was not be published unless anything happened to him.[38] Although there are differences in the degree of complicity in the specifics of the Finucane murder, both accounts, along with Stobie's subsequent interview with the *Insight* programme, contain the central allegation that his handlers had been informed twice that there was a danger of an imminent attack.

Many of the source contact forms published by Cory back up Stobie's version of events; Cory's conclusions on the matter, which are crucial in determining the credibility of Stobie's other claims and the reasons for not proceeding with a prosecution in 1990, have been redacted from the final report on the grounds of national security.[39] What is clear, however, is that not only do Stevens and Cory concur that Stobie's account has the ring of authenticity; both also express serious misgivings about the use of a quartermaster as an agent. As Steven concludes, 'his [Stobie's] activities, whilst an agent, clearly indicate his central role in the commission of serious offences from at least July 1988 onwards.'[40] This will be a central question at the public inquiry and it is the wider consequences of the policy rather than the specific questions of causality in the Finucane murder that puts the British state in the dock. The questions are even more profound when framed against the background of Barrett's recruitment as an agent for Special Branch in 1991 after he admitted his involvement in the killing of Finucane. While a credible rationale could be made, using the logic of counter-terrorism for protecting Stobie, no such 'duty of care' pertained to Barrett, who was simply allowed to murder with impunity. Excavating how this process was justified is key to understanding how the intelligence community operated in Northern Ireland and the consequences of institutionalising a culture of impunity.

ENDGAME: THE (MIS)HANDLING OF THE SOURCE MATERIAL

The partial records now in the public domain indicate that on 7 February 1989 Stobie rang his handlers to alert them of an imminent UDA assassination attempt. He had been asked specifically to supply a '9mm Browning pistol' by one of the most senior UDA commanders in the area. According to the source report, 'He has said it is for a hit on a top PIRA man for either 9 or 10 February.' According to the same report, Stobie was asked by his handlers to find a pretext for delaying the handover, which Cory surmises it appears he was successful in doing. On 9 February, the source unit recorded a telephone message from Stobie saying that 'the parcel was not delivered tonight, ask the boys [his handlers] to ring me at midnight'.

In Stobie's 1990 statement to Mulholland, published in part in the Cory Report, the police informer 'further advised that the target was almost certainly Patrick Finucane. Moreover, he stated that he had told them (SB) that an arrangement was made to collect the gun at noon the following day at a specific address in the Shankill Road area.'[41] Although there is no documentary evidence in the police files to back up this assertion, the intelligence records do reveal that two calls were made.

Stobie delivered the guns to the assassination team at the Highfield

Glasgow Rangers Supporters Club, where he watched the team depart.[42] He claimed to both Maloney and to the *Insight* team that he immediately informed Special Branch. According to Maloney, when Stobie asked his handlers subsequent to the murder of the solicitor why no attempt was made to intervene, he was given two reasons. First, by stopping the operation at such a late stage, Stobie's cover would have been compromised. Secondly he was told that there was not enough time and that 'anyway, Finucane was just an IRA man.'[43]

Three days after the killing, a source report notes 'S [Stobie] reports that he has been told to collect a 9mm Browning pistol from Loyalist K at 9pm and hide it.' As Cory concludes, 'it must be noted that this information, obtained just three days following the murder, was never passed along to the Senior Investigating Officer on the Patrick Finucane case. Further, there does not appear to have been a serious effort made to retrieve the weapon to examine and test it.'[44]

Stobie claimed that the collusion was more obvious. In his interview with *Insight*, he claimed that 'they [the RUC Special Branch] sent a Land Rover into the estate so they did just to watch but I ended up with another person and was away with the gun. The Special Branch had told me that it was too close to me. They probably think [sic] that if they went and got it the UDA would have knew that I had told them.' It is necessary to transcend the inarticulate nature of Stobie's responses in his interviews with police and journalists alike. Behind the incoherent grammar is a very clearly enunciated and politically subversive claim: The Special Branch had comprehensively failed to act on intelligence prior to the murder to intercept the murder gang. They again failed to intervene in the immediate aftermath of a murder that was generating national and international controversy, thus destroying the possibility of getting evidence, which could, at the very least, result in a conspiracy charge. According to Stobie: 'They could have done something, so they could have, you know.'[45]

It was his opinion that in effect the handlers were just as culpable as the paramilitaries. Justice Cory gives great weight to these allegations, observing that 'it is sufficient to note the significance of the evidence relating to SB's knowledge of Stobie's activities as Quartermaster, the facilitation of that role played by SB, SB's failure to recover a firearm that might have been used in the Finucane murder, and of course, SB's advance knowledge that there was going to be a hit on a "top PIRA man" in early February 1989.'[46]

In 1999, ten years after the killing, Stobie was charged with conspiracy to murder Pat Finucane. He had a ready-made defence, which had been prepared but not called for nine years earlier at proceedings in Crumlin Road Courthouse, where he faced gun possession charges. He claimed then that the guns had been planted by Special Branch in an attempt to silence him. In interviews with CID officers prior to his court appearance in 1991, the following exchange was recorded:

OFFICER	Do you expect us to believe that someone has planted these guns and left these guns behind in your house?
STOBIE	Yes.
OFFICER	Do you not think that is ridiculous?
STOBIE	I don't think it is ridiculous.[47]

Stobie had told the lawyers that if the case proceeded he would disclose the fact that he was a police agent. Furthermore, he would inform the court that he had informed his handlers of germane information that could have, if acted upon, stopped or led to the successful prosecution of those responsible for the Pat Finucane murder. Moments later, a prosecuting witness disclosed that Stobie had a prior conviction, which led to the collapse of the trial. The Crown subsequently announced that it was withdrawing all charges, leaving unanswered crucial questions, not least of which was Stobie's own admission to CID that he was, in fact, a UDA quartermaster and that he had informed Special Branch of the request from his commander for the Browning pistol.

The possibility that the truth of Stobie's involvement in both wider terrorism and in the specifics of the Finucane murder would emerge receded with the withdrawal of the Crown's case. They only came to the fore again in 1999, when the evidential trail uncovered by Stevens once again led back to the loyalist quartermaster through a re-examination of all documents held in relation to the Finucane case.

Stobie, in need of his insurance policy, released Maloney from the embargo. It was a belated, and ultimately futile, attempt to stave off charges. The political dynamics had changed and not only was the Stevens team prepared to sacrifice an agent of the Crown but also a crucial component of the wider security nexus. When arraigned, Stobie released what would have been explosive allegations but now only served as confirming evidence of what had seeped into the public domain: 'Not guilty of the charge you have put to me tonight. At the time I was police informer for Special Branch. On the night of the death of Patrick Finucane I informed Special Branch on two occasions by telephone of a person who was to be shot. I did not know at the time of the person who was to be shot.'[48] The prosecution did serve, however, to force a process of discovery that reopened the controversy surrounding the failure to investigate properly the Finucane murder and cast a withering spotlight on the behaviour of both the police and the operation of the wider criminal justice system in 1990 and 1991.

Here the incomplete nature of the surviving documents serves to muddy the water. The former investigating officer, Alan Simpson, has gone on record to claim that the information provided by Stobie was not passed to his investigating team.[49] This has been backed up by Justice Cory, who records that this failure, along with the failure to provide any of the information relating to the advance knowledge of Brian Nelson, 'did much to frustrate his investigation. RUC SB knew, or certainly ought to have known, that this information was necessary if a proper investigation of the murder were to be conducted.'[50]

The fragmentary nature of the information may provide a defence based on incomplete knowledge but in the immediate aftermath of the murder it is inconceivable that there was not a policing and public policy priority to sift through what information did exist in order to ensure that all possible leads could be investigated. Yet, not only was the source material protected from the investigating officers, but intelligence provided by Stobie on the transfer of weapons in the days after the shooting was not acted upon. Thus, an important evidential opportunity, which at the very least could have led to a conspiracy charge, was lost.

This was far from an isolated case of failure. It was an institutionalised consequence of allowing the primacy of intelligence-based policing.[51] This is made manifest by the way in which the authorities handled the claims made by the mentally fragile journalist Neil Mulholland. Following an appeal for information that could lead to the conviction of those responsible for the Finucane murder, Mulholland had approached the RUC. As noted above, Stobie had gone to Mulholland and Ed Maloney not because of a fit of conscience about the modus operandi of Special Branch, but rather because he feared that he was being set up to take the fall for the murder. It was the politically sensitive nature of the solicitor's killing that provided him with a degree of leverage. According to Stobie, the Branch knew that 'Finucane was away for his tea' and did nothing to prevent it.

As the political pressure mounted throughout 1990, Stobie wanted to protect himself, hence his conversation with the journalist.[52] However, by the time Stobie was arrested and questioned by CID investigating the weapons charges, it was clear that they did, in fact, have at least partial access to the Special Branch files. Consistent with the partial log released by Cory, Stobie had claimed to the CID that he had delayed handing over the Browning pistol according to the instructions of his handlers and had informed them that 'the parcel had not been delivered'. Stobie then claimed to the CID that he had, in fact, never handed over the weapon. Here it should be noted that the initial source reports suggested that Stobie had had a Browning in his possession, which was unaccounted for in the inventory handed over to the police in 1990.

The CID officers surmised that he had provided the weapon, and the discrepancy emerged because Stobie had not informed Special Branch. This was consistent with the facts in the documents on file. On this reading, the passage of the Stobie files to CID and the retention of only a limited amount of written detail served a dual advantage for Special Branch. It provided the grounds for a con-spiracy charge against Stobie, while protecting the intelligence agency from suggestions that it had failed to act on information that could have prevented the murder. It is clear from the interview notes that Stobie himself was convinced he would be prosecuted for his part in the Finucane killing: 'Stated that he thought he was being left to fry. Said that he meant that they [Special Branch] had obviously fallen out with him and he was going to have to take the rap for it. Stated that he had given them all the information he could and he never held back on anything.'[53]

The interviews between CID and Stobie assume strategic impor-tance in the management of the case for a number of reasons. At the Finucane inquest, on 14 September 1989, D/S Alan Simpson alleged that the police had interviewed fourteen people in connection with the murder but had found that, although their suspicions were not assuaged, and they remained reasonably certain that the main perpetrators of the murder were among the suspects, there was insufficient evidence to sustain a charge of murder. D/S Simpson further stated that none of the suspects had any connection with the security services.[54]

A central theme underpinning CID aversion to the activities of Special Branch has been its alleged failure to share information. The exchange between CID and Stobie reveals, however, that the officers involved in the Stobie arms possession charges had at least some of the files and were using them to extract statements from Stobie in which he would admit guilt of involvement in the Finucane murder. He did admit his position as a quartermaster and conspiracy to murder someone, but throughout the interviews remained adamant that he was ignorant of the precise target. It is therefore clear that sufficient evidence emerged to charge Stobie (indeed, as noted, the interview notes suggest that Stobie himself was expecting an indictment) with conspiracy to murder. The paper trail in 1990 on which the CID detectives based their questioning did not lead directly to Special Branch complicity, suggesting that either the documents were a full record or that if they manipulated, they were manipulated at the time that it was decided to 'fry' Stobie.

There is no indication at all that the notes were passed over to the RUC CID team directly investigating the Finucane case. This suggests either serious structural problems within CID itself, in which inquiry teams either did not overlap or share information likely to be of common concern, or that the Walker guidelines once again came into play with the CID unable to proceed with wider charges beyond the possession charges against Stobie. The political environment of the time certainly made it an operational imperative for Special Branch to adopt a dual strategy. First it had to protect itself against possible exposure from present or future allegations of collusion. Second, it had to ensure that if prosecution was a proffered option, the damage to the wider system of agent handling would be minimised. This, in turn, suggests a motive for ensuring that the documentary evidence corresponded to the Branch's argument that it was not cognisant of damaging material facts. Adjudication of this has to await a full judicial inquiry, but other examples of Special Branch mishandling of intelligence relating to the Finucane case suggest that this was a common occurrence.

Those questions re-emerged with chilling consequences in October 1991, when Ken Barrett, one of those involved in the killing, got into a car to discuss a potential informant arrangement with Detective Constable Johnston Brown. Brown had carved out a reputation as a straight-talking police officer with an uncanny capacity to put loyalist terrorists at ease, while at the same time working up their verbal indiscretions into an evidential trail that could lead to the proffering of criminal charges if not prosecution. Brown was later to prove pivotal in the successful prosecution of Johnny Adair for directing terrorism, a case based largely on secret recordings of the loyalist boasting of his involvement in terrorist activity, which could be cross-checked with the meticulous notes kept by the CID officer. It was this methodological thoroughness that placed Brown in jeopardy with colleagues in Special Branch.

Brown's account of attempts to stymie the prosecution of the killers of Pat Finucane featured in a specially extended edition of *Insight* in April 2001. It was one of the most important contributions to the debate about what the police did or did not know about the murder of the solicitor, and when they knew. Even more importantly, the way in which attempts were made to distort Brown's evidence indicate the lengths to which the documentary record at the time was manipulated in order to produce a credible intelligence gap that justified inaction. This would tend to lend critical weight to the claims made by Stobie to the CID officers during his interrogation that he had been set up. In both the Barrett and the Stobie cases, crucial source material was shorn of its importance. This indicates that intelligence gaps were not the result of incomplete information, which form a clear pattern only with the benefit of hindsight. Rather, they suggest that the picture was purposefully distorted from the outset. Speaking publicly for the first time, Detective Brown told an alarming story of how attempts were made in 1991 to protect the killer rather than bring him to justice.

> I don't have the ability to argue with people from headquarters. There could have been a hundred reasons why at that time they didn't want to move. They might have wanted to move a month or two down the line on it. It might have made more sense evidentially. They could be sitting there with the other nine-tenths of the picture. I don't know. Are you asking me did I expect them to bring him to book for the murder of Pat Finucane? Absolutely.[55]

Ken Barrett approached Brown after he had run into problems with his former colleagues over the theft of racketeering proceeds. The UFF gunman had serious gambling debts and thought he could trade information for financial reward, not knowing that CID had much shallower pockets than their colleagues within the security network. In order to prove his potential worth, Barrett claimed that he could provide vital information on some of the most high-profile and unsolved murders carried out by the UDA. This he claimed was from a position of personal knowledge. When prompted to name specific operations and his role in them, Barrett claimed that 'hypothetically speaking' he had killed Pat Finucane. Johnston, who had long experience dealing with loyalist and republican operatives, was immediately struck by the coldness of his informant. 'I was responsible for running some very dangerous people, some really bad, evil people. But none of them frightened me the way that Barrett frightened me. When you have been in the presence of Barrett you would compare him with [Michael] Stone [the UDA killer responsible for the Milltown attack] or Peter Sutcliffe [the Yorkshire Ripper]. This man is a serial killer.'[56] In evidence read into the court record, Barrett related to Brown how he repeatedly fired into Pat Finucane's head, telling the CID officer, 'You never tire of doing this Jonty.'[57]

As Barrett was providing information on paramilitary organisations, Brown had no alternative but to inform Special Branch of the potential value of the source. Under the Walker guidelines, 'an agent or source reporting on subversive organisations should be handled by Special Branch.'[58] Brown reported the content of his initial conversation with Barrett and it was decided that Special Branch should become actively involved in the management of the loyalist gunman.

The Special Branch officer tasked to accompany the CID team was one of those responsible for handling William Stobie, the quartermaster who had supplied the weapons for the killing, although this was not disclosed to Brown at the time.[59] It was decided that Brown and his new colleague from Special Branch arrange a meeting on 3 October in a car which was fitted with a recording device. Brown explained to *Insight* that he was optimistic:

> They provided the car complete with audiotape which was agreed. I mean it wasn't surreptitious as far as I was concerned. But it was certainly surreptitious as far as the informant was concerned.

He explained how he'd stood over Mr Finucane and had emptied this gun into Mr Finucane's face. And he wasn't just admitting the murder. He was boasting and gloating over the fact that he'd murdered this man. And he'd related how the bullets had gone into the floor and then because of the heavy stone floor, they were actually coming up past him and he had almost shot himself in error. So he relates this and I asked him well, what happened next. He said I think she got onto the road and she was shot and I don't know whether he shot her or whether his colleague but they left the house and got outside. And the man in the car, he said he was a young man and he couldn't drive off, he said what's that shooting, what was that about. Apparently the driver didn't know there was going to be a shooting. And he told him drive or I'll shoot you and I'll drive, and in terror the lad drove off.

As seasoned detectives, the CID officers checked the murder files held by CID to ascertain whether what Barrett was claiming was merely the result of hearsay picked up in the drinking clubs of north and west Belfast, or whether only someone intimately connected with the murder could have provided the information. For Brown, the key was Barrett's claim that he had 'forked' the solicitor.

The photographs and the video of the murder of Mr Finucane were a very closely guarded matter because it was really important that it didn't enter the public domain. Now, we did get access following this confession to the tapes and the next time I met him was on the 10th of October. But in the meantime my colleague had stuck the video into the machine and he called me over and says come and see this. And there was Mr Finucane lying with this fork. So yes, it was at that stage I realised we had what was a very, very important admission.

Brown was aware — as was Barrett when he made the claims — that the information provided could not be used in a criminal prosecution. As the statements were not taken under caution, they would not be admissible in court. Nevertheless, Brown surmised that the information offered an important starting point, offering new leads in a case that had gone cold. Barrett's revelations could unlock the unusual degree of silence that governed the loyalist paramilitaries involved in the operation. Special Branch, however, had a very different agenda. It wanted to recruit Barrett as a key informer.

To this day Brown cannot comprehend the logic. 'There's no doubt that the man's potential as an informant was profound, his ability to save life. I mean I've to agree that yes, it was profound. But how do you balance that against the clearance of crime which is being slapped against the face of the Royal Ulster Constabulary every turn of the road?' Despite his remonstrations to both CID and to the Special Branch officers involved in the handling of the case, Brown was told to 'move on', a euphemism he understood to mean that he was to forget about Barrett's allegations.

> I was told it had been discussed at a high level, a very senior level in the police and I have to accept that. The next meeting was scheduled for a week later and things were going along. I didn't expect that meeting to take place to be quite honest with you. I didn't expect the meeting on the 10th. I expected the senior police to come down totally on going this way and I didn't know of any reason not to. And I still don't know and I'm as at odds with what happened today as I was in 1991.

On the way to the meeting, the CID officers were told that a new strategic decision on how to handle Barrett had been made. The Special Branch officer claimed that it was necessary to repeat the interview and cautioned his CID colleagues to remain silent, particularly about the one issue in which the criminal investors were most interested, the murder of the solicitor. Johnston was perplexed. 'Here it is repeated like a child would want a toy, you mustn't mention, you mustn't mention, you mustn't mention.' After picking up Barrett, the Special Branch officer took out a folded piece of A4 paper containing a list of questions, which echoed the first interview in every respect save one. There was no mention of the Finucane murder.

> So really in this second meeting we were taking a back seat and I'm listening to this and the informant is complaining about going over the same ground that we went over on the 3rd of the 10th. He's getting as bad as the Special Branch officer. He's keeping asking me why are we going over this and over this and over this. It doesn't make sense.

Under the constraints placed on the operational independence of the CID under the Walker Report, Brown and his colleague were effectively neutralised. Special Branch officers told Brown that there was nothing new in the confession. Furthermore they maintained that they already knew from other sources of Barrett's direct complicity. There is no record in any public file that the RUC Special Branch passed this information on to the CID officers directly investigating the case. More seriously, the officers were told not to pursue the investigation. In a separate interview with the New York Lawyers' Committee investigating the case, Brown claimed that 'he had made his disgust at the decision widely known'.[60]

As the dispute between Brown and Special Branch intensified, he found himself under investigation for allegedly disclosing the names of informants on the Shankill Road — damaging allegations for a career investigator. According to Brown, these allegations were deliberately concocted falsehoods, designed to undermine his credibility with his superior officers and to warn him of the deleterious career consequences of his continued interest in the Finucane murder. As a tactic it worked. Brown was ordered to cease any future contact with Barrett, who remained a Special Branch asset. Any potential to use the confession was rendered subservient to a much more complex and morally questionable strategy, which was enshrined in the documentation provided to all serving police officers.

From the manner in which Johnston Brown's concerns were brushed off, it is clear that the protection offered to agents extended even to those who were guilty of murder. Brown is not naïve. He is deeply respectful of the need for a functioning and well-resourced intelligence wing. He simply wanted that force to be accountable. In the circumstances of the late 1980s and early 1990s, the wider intelligence network was quite simply out of control, willing to act as judge, jury, and, arguably, executioner. It was a moral compromise that was not publicly debated either within the wider community or within the police force itself. In our investigations into the wider operation of Special Branch under the Walker guidelines, the *Insight* team was provided with numerous documented cases in which officers claimed that they felt at considerable physical risk from their colleagues within Special Branch.

In those circumstances, it was understandable that Brown and his colleague reluctantly accepted the advice to 'move on'. There the matter rested until John Stevens returned to Northern Ireland in 1999 to conduct a third investigation into collusion, this time into the specific questions arising out of the Finucane killing. The Stevens detectives were loath to rely on the notebooks of an RUC officer, even one with the credibility of Johnston Brown.

Instead they focused their energies on securing a prosecution against William Stobie. The detective involved in running the case was Hugh Orde (who was later to secure the position of Chief Constable of the Police Service of Northern Ireland). In his interview with *Insight*, Orde claimed that the Mulholland interview was sufficient grounds to charge Stobie: 'Our decision was to follow the evidence and the evidence took us to Stobie.'[61] The policy importance of this statement cannot be overestimated.

If the Stevens team were not in possession of any more evidence than that provided to CID in 1990 by Mulholland and its examination of RUC Special Branch records at the time, this begs the question as to why the authorities did not proceed in 1991. As noted above, the recent attempts to bring Stobie to trial using the Mulholland evidence back-fired when the former journalist, then on extended sick leave from his employers in the Northern Ireland Office, petitioned the court that he was medically unfit to attend the trial. Stobie's solicitor, Joe Rice, encapsulated the conflicting and conflating dynamics with a measured statement issued after Stobie walked free:

> It's unusual that the Crown, some ten years later, decide to unmask the Crown agent and to bring these serious criminal charges against him. While William Stobie has nothing to hide, he would like to find out much more information about the role of the various different prosecuting authorities, the police authorities, the military intelligence, the Special Branch, the workings of the Stevens team and of course he would like much more information about the role of the office of the Director of Public Prosecutions in his prosecution.[62]

The release was an embarrassment to the Stevens Inquiry but fatal for Stobie, who was murdered within weeks for having the temerity to call for a public inquiry into these precise questions. From the moment that Stevens had caused Stobie to be charged, nerves began to fray within the loyalist cell that had carried out the Finucane killing. As we have seen, Barrett graphically displayed the extent of that unease in his comments to reporters involved in the making of the *Panorama* programme and recorded secretly during the summer of 2001. Then the gunman claimed that Stobie was a dead man walking, with Jim Spence demanding that 'something had to be done'. It was a clear intimation that Stobie would not make his trial. Immediately after the Stobie killing, Barrett saw the writing on the walls. Graffiti started emerging on gable ends in north and west Belfast alleging that Barrett was touting information to Special Branch. One proclaimed the legend 'Ken Barrett, Big Nose, Big Mouth, Tout.' In the volatile world of loyalist paramilitarism, it amounted to the advance delivery of a death notice. It was clear that any insurance policy held by Barrett with either his UFF colleagues or the Special Branch no longer had any value. Barrett was left with no alternative but to fly to England and into one of the most sophisticated bugging operations designed by the British police, the outlines of which were used to justify prosecution in September 2004.

While in England, Barrett continued his conversations with the *Panorama* team. At each meeting he further incriminated himself on the discreet recording devices, which captured the damning boasts of a paramilitary who defined his life through a demonstrable capacity to commit murder. Unlike his interviews in 1991, these tapes were not going to disappear. Without knowing it, Barrett was being filleted skilfully by John Ware, one of the most experienced and accomplished investigative journalists ever to have covered the reality of the Dirty War. In interview after interview, Barrett spoke about inner feuds and pathological hatreds. 'The killing of Pat Finucane was organised by the police. The dogs in the street know that. Everybody knows that. They wanted Finucane dead.'[63]

Aware that the net was closing in around him, Barrett, rather pathetically, turned to the BBC reporter for counselling. 'There are no heroes at this fucking game. You're buried on the Monday, you're talked about on til Wednesday and the drinking stops on Friday. What would you do, John, honestly....They'll [The Stevens team] charge me. They'll charge me and they'll stand by them ones [Special Branch and Spence]. Believe me, John.'[64]

When the programme was broadcast in June 2002, the admissions by Barrett served to obviate the evidential shortfall occasioned by the loss of the tape recorded by Special Branch. Even more damning evidence was collected under Operation Satiety, one of the most sophisticated surveillance operations ever mounted. Barrett had moved to Eastbourne on the southern coast of England, under the witness protection programme, where his every movement was tracked. Barrett's home was bugged by an elite section of the National Crime Squad, which broke into the bungalow after the killer and his partner and her daughter were provided with a week-long holiday, courtesy of the taxpayer, at the Centre Parc Resort. Within the confines of the house, Barrett was unguarded about his role in the Finucane killing. In one particularly chilling exchange the gunman reminisces with his partner about the beginning of their relationship.

> BARRETT: It was '88 when I met you.
> BEVERLEY: It wasn't, it was '89. I didn't know you when you
>   killed Pat Finucane.
> BARRETT: You did, because I went to jail shortly after Pat
>   Finucane [on unrelated charges].[65]

The tapes provided the police with key insights into the relationship and with it the means to execute their trap. Cooped up in the house with limited money, Beverley constantly urged Barrett to try to get a job. The Stevens team set up a front limousine company and advertised regularly in the local media for a chauffeur. Barrett, facing constant criticism from his partner, eventually spotted the advertisement and applied for a job. Unknown to the loyalist paramilitary, the directors of this firm were undercover police officers. Over a period of six months Barrett chauffeured a range of clients across the southern coast and engaged in drinking sessions with the two directors, who confided in their employee that the micro business was a front for their real source of wealth: an international drug smuggling operation. They asked him if he could help in a delicate operation: the killing of an associate. On 28 April, the officer captured on tape Barrett's admission of involvement in the killing of Pat Finucane. According to the tape, Barrett claimed: 'I mean, it wasn't the first time I done it. He was an IRA man and all that. He thought he couldn't be touched. He got fucking massacred. Twenty-two times he got hit…I lose no sleep over it, you know. I have to be honest, I whacked a few people in the past…People say, "Ken, how do you sleep?" I say: "I sleep fine".'[66]

On handing out Barrett's sentence, Justice Weir condemned what he called 'a terrorist killing, carefully planned and meticulously executed'. In an implicit rebuttal of the policy decisions to recruit known murderers as informers, Justice Weir argued that 'it could in no way mitigate the seriousness of your own admitted actions in the despicable events of that evening... I have searched in vain for any semblance of genuine remorse in your various accounts of your participation in this crime contained in the court papers and have found on the contrary only boastful expressions of self-satisfaction.'

The reason for Barrett changing his plea to guilty at such a late stage also raises acute suspicion. When the *Sunday Times* published partial transcripts of the surveillance operation, Barrett's solicitor, Joe Rice, outlined the basis of the defence strategy. According to Rice, 'among the many points we will be making is a challenge to the legality of the alleged admissions'.[67] Granted, Barrett had made essentially the same admissions to Johnston Brown (and Special Branch) in 1991 and to the *Panorama* team ten years later. Furthermore, he was damned by his own admission in the casual way he referred to the murder to his partner and her young daughter in their home in Eastbourne. Nevertheless, there was a strong legal argument that the admissions to *Panorama* could be dismissed as bragging to journalists who had paid him expenses totalling over one thousand pounds, a substantial sum for a down-at-heel gunman with limited life skills. In the event, less than a month later, Barrett issued diametrically opposed instructions to his legal team with his admission of guilt.

Barrett was taken away to begin his life sentence, leaving behind a number of unanswered questions, not least the suggestion by a defence counsel that there was insufficient evidence to link Barrett directly to the shooting. Barrett chose not to instruct his barrister, Andrew Harvey, to plead mitigating circumstances, although the lawyer did open a new line of unexplored questioning with his comments that 'there is a substantial body of evidence that other persons have confessed to police officers and journalists on different occasions that they fulfilled that role'.[68] When asked by Justice Weir if this meant that Barrett did not fire the fatal shots, Harvey replied: 'He feels any statements made by him in this court in relation to these charges may and indeed will place him in further danger over and above that which he is already under, as testified by the arrangement made to bring him here to court.'[69] Barrett was not going to make the same mistake as Stobie. Self-preservation rather than principle necessitated silence.

Cory makes no mention in his report of the possibility that his review of the secret source reports held by Special Branch provides any evidence that could endorse the first contention by Barrett that police held incriminating evidence against named assassins not yet brought before the courts. There remains, however, the possibility that sections of the report, redacted on the grounds that their publication could compromise the Barrett trial, address this issue. Set against this, as noted above, the Stevens team has intimated to both the Finucane family and the government that no other active lines of inquiry relating directly to the murder are being pursued.

Barrett's decision not to contest the charges has meant that these issues remain unexplored, leaving open the possibility that other members of the murder gang continue to be protected — if not actively, then certainly because of a refusal or inability to turn intelligence information into an evidential trail. The Stevens Inquiry, from its public pronouncements, has maintained that it has achieved substantial help from the current leadership of the Police Service of Northern Ireland, as might be expected following the elevation of Hugh Orde as the Chief Constable. In a statement released after Barrett pleaded guilty, John Stevens noted:

> I have investigated collusion between the security services and paramilitary groups and faced obstruction in the past. That was certainly not the case in our evidence gathering on the prosecution of Ken Barrett — we have had the full cooperation of the authorities in Northern Ireland. I hope today's result [the guilty plea] sends out a strong message — we do not give up.

This degree of certainty is hard to reconcile with the deliberate obstruction involved in the handling of the allegations by Johnston Brown and the manner in which the Special Branch provided the Stevens team with documentary evidence that provided *prima facie* evidence of an attempt to pervert the course of justice. As Brown complained when Barrett received his murder conviction, with justifiable anger and frustration: 'This should have taken place fifteen years ago.'

The premature foreclosure of the trial has meant that these destabilising questions were not tackled. Judge Weir maintained that 'this court has no means of assessing the correctness or otherwise' of collusion, 'nor has it any part of its function to do so.' Nevertheless he did see in the Finucane killing an attempt to cow the legal profession.

> I have no doubt that an object of this brutal crime was to intimidate and thereby deter other members of the legal profession from carrying out their duty to represent without fear or favour all those, including terrorists such as you, who come to them for professional advice and assistance. It is greatly to the credit of the profession that it has not allowed itself to be intimidated or deterred by this or other outrages carried out for the same purpose.[70]

That wider purpose was beyond the political sophistication of Ken Barrett and the other members of the gang. In this sense, there is considerable merit in the argument put forward by the Finucane family that the policy framework, which allowed the killing of an officer of the court, is really what is on trial. On this reading, the Barrett trial does not lift the lid on collusion. In fact it does the opposite. It is an argument that has received powerful endorsement from consortia of human rights groups including Amnesty International, British Irish Rights Watch, the Committee on the Administration of Justice and Human Rights First. On 16 September 2004 these organisations issued a joint press release in which they argued: 'Criminal proceedings have been insufficient in getting at the full truth of the Finucane case…Successive governments have aided and abetted the cover-up in this most sinister of murders, which involved collusion by several agents and agencies of the state, including the police and the army.'[71]

As Barrett was led away, it is necessary to reflect on the quality of the leadership provided by the Steven team. This is not the first time that Sir John Stevens has won a tactical battle in securing a scapegoat but lost the strategic advantage. A similar dynamic governed the guilty plea entered by Brian Nelson in January 1992. In order to understand why this killing has proved impossible to penetrate, it is necessary to revisit not only the obstruction that has bedevilled Sir John Stevens' previous investigations but also the subsequent prosecutorial strategies adopted by the Director of Public Prosecutions and the Attorney General.

Chapter 5
Tactical Successes and Strategic Failures

The UFF assassination squads kept up the pressure on the Catholic community throughout the summer of 1989. There is little to suggest that those responsible for running agents within loyalist paramilitary organisations did anything to rein in their charges. The political embarrassment caused by the UFF intensified following the killing of Loughlin Maginn, a 28-year-old Catholic, in his home in the village of Rathfriland, thirty miles from Belfast. As with the Finucane killing, the assassination team appeared to be practised killers, firing the first shots through the window, pursuing their victim as he staggered up the stairs, before delivering three coup de grace shots from point blank range on the landing. When the dead man's family forcefully rejected any suggestion that the killing was anything more than a sectarian assault designed to terrorise rather than serve a proto-military cause, the manner in which the UDA responded was to transform the reality of the Dirty War.

Determined to prove to a sceptical media that the UFF only targeted those with connections to the republican movement, the UDA leaked its intelligence files material. Montages were plastered across loyalist areas, montages that could only have originated within RUC stations or army bases. Featured on one was a picture of Loughlin Maginn. The issue of collusion was now firmly at the centre of the political

agenda and could not be ignored. In order to prevent any further slip-
page of support within the nationalist community, the RUC, under
the control of Hugh Annesley, had no alternative but to bow to the
political pressure and cede an external investigation. Yet again, a
senior English police officer was brought over to investigate. The man
chosen was John Stevens, then Deputy Chief Constable of Cambridge.
He had the benefit of a detailed account written by John Stalker, head
of a previous investigation, of how local and national elements
within the security nexus could conspire to undermine the stated
purposes of the probe. So too had the public.

Stalker, the Deputy Chief Constable of Manchester, who had been
unceremoniously sacked from his investigation into the 'shoot to kill'
allegations of 1982, had published his autobiography. Stalker's wry
conclusion that obstruction carried a valuable premium merits airing, as this dynamic not only informed the Stevens probe but also the
judicial review carried out by Peter Cory.

> In Northern Ireland time has a different rhythm. It can govern
> political as well as physical survival, and is traded and exploited in
> ways that are incomprehensible for those of us that live on the
> mainland. My investigation and the haste with which my team and
> I pursued it, threatened a delicate balance…I was no doubt seen as
> a mainland careerist who did not comprehend their world, and an
> important part of the RUC set out to *make* [emphasis in original] me
> understand that in Northern Ireland the survival and strength of the
> police is paramount. If the police fails, then government fails.[1]

For Stalker the fight between himself and Sir Jack Hermon, the RUC
Chief Constable at the time, was not personal, but rather a clash of
fundamental principles. It centred on what the English officer termed
the 'balancing [of] broad responsibilities in an imperfect world, and
of pursuing truth because it is an imperfect world'.[2] In the complex
world governing Northern Irish policing the simple inescapable truth
was that Stalker was expendable but the RUC was not, a truth that con-
ditioned the marshalling of forces and the outcome of the battle.
Stalker's recommendation that no less than eleven officers should
face disciplinary charges and criminal prosecution was a political
impossibility because of its repercussions not only in Northern
Ireland but also in London.

The discovery that the national security service, MI5, had been in possession of an audiotape that could comprehensively and definitively ascertain whether the killing of Michael Tighe in a hayshed outside Lurgan was justifiable or demonstrated the actions of what Stalker angrily denounced as akin to a 'Central American assassination squad — truly of a police force out of control' raised important questions of accountability and the subversion of the rule of law for political purposes.[3]

In the course of the investigation Stalker was refused permission to access the secret recording made by MI5 or the informant source reports from RUC agents on which the decision to deploy the unit against Tighe and his colleagues were based. Stalker was incredulous: 'The department I was investigating, the Special Branch, had the clear power to decide whether I should be given access to evidence that might or might not prove that some of their members had committed murder.'[4] Stalker's request for the tape, which was in the possession of Special Branch, and which could definitively answer the question of whether shoot to kill did exist as official policy, posed an appalling dilemma. Ownership of the tape belonged to MI5, which suggested to Stalker that the tape no longer existed. Even the transcript was withheld.

For the Chief Constable, Jack Hermon, it was a political impossibility to compromise the security in which his undercover operatives worked. According to Stalker, 'Sir John spelled out for me that it was his duty to protect them and that he did so as Chief Constable in the best interests of the public. The Chief Constable could not have been clearer. Policemen acting undercover in anti-terrorist operations were fully protected. They were not to be exposed to external investigation. The Chief Constable was the judge of the public interest.'[5]

The official version of events had been discounted at the trial of Martin McCauley in 1985 for weapons possession as it became clear that the cover story had been invented to protect informants. The RUC had not only connived in the presentation of false evidence to the Director of Public Prosecutions, but, more seriously, it had attempted to pervert the course of justice by failing to disclose material information. MI5 had actively colluded in this strategy by not disclosing the existence of its secret recording. Irrespective of McCauley's guilt or otherwise, the behaviour of the intelligence agencies suggested a systematic contempt for the legal system which the counter-terrorist campaign was pledged to uphold from terrorist assault. It was precisely this question that made Stalker's discovery and public demand for the use of the tape as an evidential tool to prosecute serving members of the intelligence community so explosive. What was at issue was not the actions of rogue units, or indeed a rogue force, but rather the manner in which the security nexus itself coalesced to protect mutual interests, irrespective of the cost. Despite the furore occasioned by the publication of the Stalker autobiography, the RUC Chief Constable had survived the political storm, retiring quietly just as the political pressure for a renewed investigation into the operation of the Dirty War once again became inexorable.

John Stevens began the first of his inquiries in 1989. Sixteen years on he is still trying to unravel the moral compromises inherent in agent handling in the Northern Ireland theatre and the complexities of cultural and institutionalised collusion. In the course of his investigations, the English policeman has changed his view from arguing that collusion was 'restricted to a small number of members of the security forces'[6] to a more nuanced appreciation of how the security nexus actually operated and the reasons why his investigations were viewed with suspicion and animosity.

Each investigation had followed separate lines of inquiry. The first focused only on the loyalists that received the documentation from police and army facilities; the second (which has never been published, even in summary form) centred on the true extent of Brian Nelson's involvement in murder, including that of Pat Finucane, and the degree of Military Intelligence and Special Branch complicity in protecting their charges. In an interview with the New York Lawyers' Committee for Human Rights in 1995, Stevens stated that he was not at liberty to discuss either his findings or even his terms of reference. 'He did indicate, however, that he knew "absolutely" who Finucane's killers were.'[7]

Four years later, on the tenth anniversary of the Finucane killing, British Irish Rights Watch forwarded a copy of its confidential report on the murder to the British and Irish governments with a view to forcing the convening of a public inquiry. Much to its chagrin, the British government forwarded the report to the RUC instead, as a potential evidential device for use in a criminal investigation. The Chief Constable, Ronnie Flanagan, in a move that gave ownership of the report (and therefore the capacity to publish or withhold its

content) to the RUC, invited Stevens back to Belfast. Far from becoming the vehicle through which an independent inquiry could be held,
the British Irish Rights Watch Report itself became victim of the
'rhythm' of Northern Ireland political imperatives.[8]

The Stevens team has always been aware of the political sensitivities
involved in its investigation. Turning the spotlight on the security
services themselves in the midst of the prosecution of a conflict in
which the IRA repeatedly demonstrated its determination to violate
democratic principles, including the attempted assassination of the
entire Conservative cabinet in 1984 and an attack on Downing Street
in 1991, was viewed with derision and anger within large components
of the security nexus. As Stevens noted in his short public summary
released in 2003: 'Throughout my three Enquiries, I recognised that
I was being obstructed. This obstruction was cultural in its nature and
widespread within parts of the army and the RUC.'[9] More damaging
perhaps was the insertion into the summary of a strongly worded
conclusion, which inferred that the withholding of documents
amounted to a deliberate attempt to pervert the course of justice.

> During my first Enquiry I asked to examine particular documents
> but received written statements that they did not exist. My latest
> Enquiry team has now recovered all these documents. The dates
> recorded on them show that they all existed at the time of my first
> request. Much of the effort of this Enquiry has had, yet again, to be
> spent building up its own intelligence database and in so doing dis-
> covering that it had not been given a full and proper disclosure.
>
> Following three recent, major disclosures by the army and the
> Ministry of Defence I am investigating whether the concealment of
> documents and information was sanctioned and if so at what
> levels of the organisations holding them. It has been necessary to
> interview the same witnesses a number of times because of the fail-
> ure to provide complete information at the first time of asking.[10]

From the very beginning a policy decision had been taken to limit the
supply of information, an operational reality that also applied to
Justice Cory.[11] This obstruction also involved a fire in the Seapark
police facility in Carrickfergus at a pivotal stage in the investigation.
The findings of the police investigation into the causes of the fire were
never made public. A change in government from Conservative to

Labour did little to improve the amount of information entering into the public domain. In 1998 the British government still clung to the official line that no sinister motive could be adduced. In a written response, the Minister of State with responsibility for the security brief, Adam Ingram, noted that 'the intensity of the fire and the resultant damage meant that the cause…could not be categorically established. However, the investigation concluded that the blaze had been started accidentally.'[12] Pointedly, Ingram did not reply to the request for the publication of John Stevens' assessment or clarify whether the investigation on which he based his brief was that of the RUC or an independent outside source.

The benign view of the fire has been comprehensively falsified by John Stevens himself in his public summary. Stevens even went as far as to suggest a linkage between the blaze and a warning received soon after his arrival in Northern Ireland that his operation was under sustained threat.[13] According to Stevens' summary:

> There was a clear breach of security before the planned arrest of Nelson and other senior loyalists. Information was leaked to the loyalist paramilitaries and the press. This resulted in the operation being aborted. Nelson was advised by his FRU handlers to leave home the night before. A new date was set for the operation on account of the leak. The night before the new operation my Incident Room was destroyed by fire. This incident, in my opinion, has never been deliberately investigated and I believe it was a deliberate act of arson.[14]

Although not stated explicitly, the phrasing implies that only those elements in the security nexus who were running agents, including the military and Special Branch, had both motive and opportunity. Nelson's fingerprints had been discovered on a cache of documents recovered by the Stevens team. They did not know the degree of complicity between the agent and his handlers in the plotting of a campaign of murder and its subsequent cover-up.

Taken together the three Stevens investigations amount to the most extensive criminal probe in the history of the UK. Advances in technology led to more detailed forensic investigation of documents and allowed for the arrest and subsequent charging of six people for having documents likely to be of use to terrorists, the charging of

William Stobie for aiding and abetting murder and the recently concluded trial of Ken Barrett, both of whom were serving Special Branch
agents and were afforded remarkable protection from prosecution
under the terms of the Walker Report.

For Kevin McNamara, one of the most dogged campaigners for a
public inquiry into the operation of the security nexus in Northern
Ireland, the moral implications for the legitimacy of the state were
profound:

> The Stevens Report's stark message is that successive British
> governments have sanctioned murder — that they have employed
> agents and given them a licence to kill. Agents have acted above the
> law, without the law and with impunity....If it is tacitly understood
> that intelligence agencies may operate outside the rule of law, or
> that such behaviour is given an informal legitimacy through the
> failure to set lawful parameters, it is not structurally possible to
> hold the agencies or their employees and agents accountable with-
> out the intervention of an outside independent body. It now seems
> evident that the intelligence agencies have been engaged in running
> agents inside both loyalist and republican paramilitary groups and
> promoting, planning and participating in terrorist activities in
> order to achieve internally defined goals.[15]

It was a bad-tempered debate, with Lady Hermon, the wife of the
former RUC Chief Constable at the time of the shoot-to-kill controversy in 1982, rather ungraciously pointing out that Mrs Finucane had
not cooperated with the Stevens team, a formulation which inferred
that the obstruction was a two-way process. Many of the politicians in
the chamber saw the premises of the debate itself as morally suspect.
Recommending definitive closure by issuing public interest certificates
to prevent criminal proceedings, John Taylor outlined the political
costs of not availing of this option:

> It would be wholly wrong to put on trial past or serving members
> of the security forces, the army or the RUC, for their part in the fight
> against terrorism at a time when more than 440 terrorists have
> benefited from the early release scheme established by the Belfast
> Agreement; nor, however, do we believe that members of the
> security forces should benefit from arrangements of the type put in

place for terrorists. That would introduce the concept of equivalence between the legitimate forces of the Crown and illegal terrorist organisations. That is morally repugnant to us and would rightly be resisted by the armed forces and members of the police.[16]

Patrick Mercer, a Conservative MP who had served two tours of duty in Northern Ireland, first as a former platoon commander with the Sherwood Foresters in the early 1970s and then, in what he ambiguously referred to as 'another capacity', suggested that neither politicians nor English policemen appeared to appreciate the complexities of having to run intelligence networks.

> The fact that they did not wish to leave the water in which they swam made it extraordinarily difficult for either a born and bred policeman or someone like myself from the mainland to penetrate those deeply violent, thug-like organisations where an outsider, even an outsider from a different housing estate, stood no chance of survival. That is why we used agents.[17]

For Mercer, it had become an imperative to reach a more granular understanding of the dynamics involved.

> Someone must defend the people who defend our democracy. Clearly, things have gone wrong. Policemen, soldiers and ministers have got it wrong; they must be accountable. I ask honourable members to bear in mind that the peace process is not where it is today because of some benign intent, some benign understanding by thugs and terrorists, some conversion, some sudden ray of light falling into their lives revealing to them that they are wrong and evil. The peace process is where it is today because the IRA and Protestant paramilitary organisations have been shown that they will be militarily defeated if they continue down the road on which they are travelling. Let us be in no doubt about that. There has been a campaign, and a campaign is about killing people if necessary and deterring people because it has to be done. That is not the sort of campaign that we have just seen in Iraq; it is by definition a dirty campaign.[18]

Responding on behalf of the government, the Security Minister, Jane Kennedy, reiterated the official conviction that the murder of

Finucane was both a tragedy for his family but also for 'the legal profession and the wider community in Northern Ireland'.[19] She continued that it was a 'matter of enormous regret' that the murder could have been prevented. After praising Kevin McNamara for his tenacity in investigating the issues central to the running of covert human intelligence agencies, she explicitly rejected his moral argument. 'Sir John Stevens does not conclude that successive governments have sanctioned murder. The report voices many concerns and I accept that its findings must be acknowledged, but the allegation that governments have sanctioned murder is not one of its findings. It is important that I state that for the record.'[20]

For Kennedy the importance of the Stevens process lay in its grounding as a criminal investigation, which was designed to result in prosecutions being brought before the court system. The government accepted that it was inevitable in the messy world of agent handling that the line between acceptable and accountable behaviour would, on occasion, be accidentally crossed, an inevitable by-product of the murky world in which the agents and their handlers operated. If that was deliberate, it was a consequence of flawed actors, who in turn, would and should be prosecuted. This logic underpinned the government strategy in 2003.

Just as limited disclosure has crossed the political divide in British politics, so too has the determination to blame the malaise on corrupted actors rather than a faulty design that rendered the state susceptible to corruption. The Labour response bears remarkable similarity to the response of successive Conservative ministers who were responsible for planning and responding to military operations and their moral consequences at the height of the executions of the Dirty War.

In part, however, the failure to elucidate these issues can be tracked to the operational priorities of the Stevens investigation itself. In each of the prosecutions, Stevens has focused less on those running the agents, preferring instead to highlight the criminality of their charges, including Ken Barrett, William Stobie and, most controversially of all, Brian Nelson. In none of the cases has the legal process been instrumental in bringing to the public domain information about how the intelligence network actually operated. As we have seen, the Stobie trial collapsed before the loyalist could give evidence. Barrett's decision to plead guilty mirrored the strategy adopted by Brian Nelson in

1992, ensuring that only the broadest of outlines involving murder was sketched. Through the Cory Report we now have a much more detailed appreciation of the extent of military knowledge of Nelson's activities. This allows an opportunity to measure the competing weights of the arguments over the degree of political responsibility for the execution of policy.

Nelson put the computer training provided by the British intelligence agencies to good use. In early 1987, soon after Nelson's re-insertion into Belfast, John McMichael, the overall leader of the UFF, provided him with over 1,000 files, many of which originated from the security forces. Much of the information was out of date and the FRU arranged for it to be transported to the secure army base at Thiepval, just outside Lisburn, where it was carefully checked and cross-referenced. Old files were discarded and a new system instituted.[21] Nelson's first priority was to provide a more effective targeting network. This was achieved through the creation of a series of 'P' or personality cards, which allowed Nelson to record personal details, including physical descriptions and addresses. Contemporaneous records reviewed by Justice Cory confirm the veracity of his account.[22] Following his elevation to Senior Intelligence Officer, Nelson was given specific instructions 'to build up an efficient intelligence network that would allow the organisation to target known Republicans for possible attack', which over time transmogrified into 'an index system of intelligence on all Republican personalities'.[23]

In a crucial passage, Justice Cory revealed that 'to maintain the system, Nelson relied upon various items of information, including radio transmissions, electoral registers and republican newspapers. However, his primary source material consisted of photo-montages and handwritten information acquired from either the military or the RUC. In his 1990 statement, Nelson estimated that approximately 90% of the material he worked with had come from the Ulster Defence Regiment.[24] Later in the report, Cory notes that Nelson's handlers within the FRU did in fact help calibrate his targeting by conducting vehicle checks and scouting locations for photo surveillance. He further notes that Nelson himself, in a document dated 1990 and recovered in Stormont, was given help in weeding out old information in the UDA intelligence files. As noted above, Nelson inherited a cache of over 1,000 documents from John McMichael when he took over the position of Director of Intelligence (Targeting). This leads then to four related questions: does quantity relate to quality; who else was receiving information; was this material filtered in turn by the FRU; and was the source of the leaks adequately investigated?[25]

Nelson's involvement in the murder of Gerald Slane in 1988 provides a telling indication of the consequences of allowing extra-judicial executions to take place. Unconvinced that the police could conduct a satisfactory investigation into the murder of UDA gangster Billy Quee, Nelson provided photographs of suspected IPLO members as eyewitnesses to the Quee shooting. According to the contact forms, eyewitnesses positively identified Slane as the gunman. This line of questioning was discounted by the RUC. At Slane's inquest, an RUC detective testified that there was no evidence whatsoever to link Slane to paramilitarism. The contact sheets reveal that Nelson then suggested Slane as a potential target and provided the killers with a photograph and checked the electoral roll for his address.[26] The contact sheets show that Nelson was in daily contact with his handlers about the planning of the Slane execution. Nelson then went on holiday and telephoned in the following day. In evidence at Nelson's subsequent trial, at which he pleaded guilty to collecting information likely to be of use to a terrorist organisation in relation to the murder of Slane, Colonel Kerr claimed 'he knew that Slane was, I think, one of about four targets that were being considered and he passed that to us, and we in turn passed it on.'[27] The records uncovered by Stevens reveal that the information passed on amounted to a vague summary that loyalists wanted three attacks to be carried out before the end of October. An officer interviewed by *Panorama* described this course of events as 'collusion by omission', a conclusion shared by Cory.[28] Yet Special Branch also knew from Stobie that anyone suspected of involvement in the IPLO itself was a likely target. If the system was design to save lives, it had significant systemic faults. Here we have two nodes of the security nexus who were aware that there was an impending attack, one of which knew precisely who was being targeted because its agent was doing the targeting, and no-one in authority was doing anything to stop it.[29]

The killing of Terence McDaid in May 1988 was also facilitated by Brian Nelson, who had been responsible for providing the loyalist gang with documents that owed their origin to security forces. Three years after her husband's death, Maura McDaid gave a chilling account of his murder. 'There was this horrendous thundering noise.

Terry and I just sat and stared at one another. At that the living room door flew back to the wall. Two men were standing at the door, they were completely clothed, there was no flesh to be seen. They ran in and just started firing. They just kept shooting around the room.'[30] Mrs McDaid sued the British government for damages. Just before the case came to trial, she was provided with a £50,000 settlement, more than would have been received should the case have come to trial. Both the army and the RUC, which had denied any knowledge beforehand of the plan to attack McDaid, made the payments.[31] Both had reason to prevent the case going to court or the disclosure of records relating to the murder.

Nelson had confused McDaid's address with that of his brother, Declan, who had been the subject of sustained targeting by the UFF from as early as September 1987.[32] Nelson had created a personality card for McDaid and provided the picture to a well-known loyalist assassin.[33] As part of the targeting, he had checked the electoral register at the local library. One of the addresses he gathered from his search was for Maura McDaid, Terence McDaid's wife. As Cory states, 'Nelson inadvertently began to target Terence as a result of the error in the address. Nelson then gave the particulars of the home address of Terence McDaid to Loyalist F of the UFF with the result that the hit team sent to assassinate Declan McDaid killed Terence on 10 May 1988. Although Declan McDaid was known to be a target as early as September 1987 he was never given any warning by the RUC and certainly his brother Terence received no warning.'[34]

This stands in stark contrast to the justification used by the Force Research Unit for its reliance on protecting Nelson. In evidence at Nelson's trial in January 1992, the commander of the unit, Gordon Kerr, blithely dismissed the killing of McDaid as a case of 'mistaken identity', glossing over Nelson's role in the creation of the P card on Declan and the insertion of Terence's home address. He further claimed: 'Although there were occasions when loyalist attacks did take place, when murders did take place, he was not privy to advance information about these activities, but he did produce a tremendous amount of information referring to their plans for assassination and this was, of course, life saving potential.'[35] The reality was very different.

McDaid's death prompted a barrage of calls from Nelson to his handlers in the Force Research Unit. Brian Nelson made no less than four telephone calls to his handlers on the night of the murder.

Inexplicably, there is no record of any of the calls, a situation that one of the detectives involved in the Stevens investigation rated as 'highly suspicious.'[36] In his final report Stevens asserts that this in itself could constitute collusion.

> The failure to keep records or the existence of contradictory accounts can often be perceived as evidence of concealment or malpractice. It limits the opportunity to rebut serious allegations. The absence of accountability allows the acts or omissions of individuals to go undetected. The withholding of information impedes the prevention of crime and the arrest of suspects. The unlawful involvement of agents in murder implies that the security forces sanction killings.[37]

It is in this context that a discovery by the Stevens team of a paper trail within secret military records, which appeared to suggest that traces of evidence existed to implicate Terence McDaid in IRA activity, should be viewed.[38] This information was passed over to Nelson to assuage any pangs of moral conscience. According to the Stevens detective, this was 'a story put together to appease Nelson. He would feel better if there was a connection between the deceased and the Provisional IRA.' The detective, who served on the Stevens team for five years, was staggered at the level of arrogance.

> When something's gone as badly wrong, as happened in the case of Terence McDaid where an innocent man has been murdered, I would have thought they would have sat back and thought about what they were doing, or what they were doing wrong and made some changes. But that never seemed to occur. I think it is a dreadful situation. He's [Nelson] passing it [his intelligence files] to other groups of killers who are completely outside his control and his handlers are just following on and letting him do it. It's a recipe for absolute disaster.[39]

This lengthy summary of failure by either Special Branch or the FRU to act to stop murder is crucial in providing the context in which the killing of Pat Finucane took place. Despite the obvious failure to intercede, there was no internal investigation, no review of how the handling process was being undertaken. The killing was allowed to go on. This was not just a failure at the outer edges. It was a failure at the very heart of Whitehall.

Far from scaling back his activities after the McDaid murder, Nelson was given even more latitude as he sought to develop his intelligence network with the help of his handlers from the Force Research Unit. This involved conducting surveillance operations and conducting vehicle registration checks on Nelson's behalf. Although no evidence exists which suggests that explicit information was passed relating to the Finucane murder, Cory concludes that 'the breach of policy [relating to the passing of information generally] is relevant in that it could be taken to reveal either tacit encouragement, or even active facilitation of UDA operations and the targeting that so often led to murder.'[40]

The Cory Report details that from January 1989 onwards, the Force Research Unit was increasingly unhappy about Nelson's performance. However, another interpretation is that despite the testimonials from Colonel Kerr and the Commanding Officer of the TSG at the subsequent trial, the unit was beginning the process of distancing itself from its star agent.[41] On 10 January 1989 a plan of action was hatched by the FRU:

> The time has come for Nelson to be hit by the facts. At the next meeting handler will challenge Nelson to explain what he does with the spare £887 he has each month. Nelson will also be asked to tell handlers what he believes he does for this office and his motivation for doing it.[42]

The warning had an effect. By early February the handler notes:

> Nelson initiates most of the targeting, although it is often unclear when the targeting has been completed and an attack is about to take place. Of late, Nelson has been more organised and he is currently running an operation against selected Republican personalities.[43]

In his statement made after his arrest in 1990, Nelson relates how he had been informed by a senior loyalist, 'I would really love to get that bastard Finucane…I have been told by someone that if I want to get someone really big, get Finucane, he is the brains behind the PIRA. Forget about Adams.'[44] While Nelson's 1990 statement suggests that he had passed over all of the information to his handlers, no records exist. Yet given the events that led to the killing of Slane the previous September, it is perplexing that no lessons appear to have been learned about the need to warn citizens who came under the sustained interest of Nelson, irrespective of their alleged background.

In his interviews, Nelson sought to differentiate between Finucane and Pat McGeown, with the latter described as a genuine target. He said that he was under the impression that the UDA was more interested in targeting McGeown, who was in the photograph with Finucane leaving the courthouse, and that the first he knew of the attack was when he tuned into the police scanner on the night of the murder. A subsequent document recently recovered by the Stevens team and written by Nelson himself appears to suggest that he was more involved than he claimed and that the targeting of Finucane had begun long before the photograph was passed over.

> Some two months before the actual shoot took place, I was asked by Loyalist J to see what I could dig up on Finucane. At this time I was informed by handlers that Loyalist J was showing interest in this solicitor. A few weeks later I enquired from Loyalist J if he still wanted to check on him as I was busy on other things. I was told by Loyalist J that he had found out what he needed to know.[45]

As Cory concludes, the documents recovered by Stevens, including Nelson's own written admission, raise serious and perplexing questions regarding the extent to which the FRU had advance knowledge of the targeting of Finucane. The inference could certainly be drawn from there was institutional 'advance knowledge of the targeting. However, these questions can only be satisfactorily answered by a Public Inquiry. The documentary evidence certainly suggests that such an inquiry should be held.'[46]

There was no doubt that Nelson was appreciated by his handlers, as witnessed by this extraordinary excerpt from a character statement issued on his behalf by Gordon Kerr:

> I have no doubt in my mind that his motivation was to make up for past misdemeanours, to save life and to bring down, eventually, the terrorist organisations, but I think probably the biggest motivation of all was team spirit and loyalty to the Army…He actually put

country before family, I believe, because of the risks he took and the disruption to his family life. He put country before family and to that extent he was very loyal to the system and it embarrasses me, personally, that the system has been unable to recognise the real difficulties of running agents within a terrorist organisation, has been unable to recognise the dichotomy between terrorist or counter-terrorist situation and a law and order situation, and as a result Brian Nelson is a victim of the system to which he was actually very loyal. I feel a personal moral responsibility to Brian Nelson because whatever he has done or has not done, he wouldn't have done it if I hadn't been responsible for ordering his re-recruitment in January 1987. I believe, however, the real moral responsibility doesn't lie with individuals or any organisations that are involved in this business, but within a system that hasn't been able to come to terms with the peculiarities and the difficulties of the agent work in Northern Ireland.[47]

Revisiting the documentation of the case, and in particular the cross-examination of Colonel Kerr, one is left with a distinct impression that the honourable defence was fundamentally undermined by the dissembling involved. Although by Kerr's own admission the system was incapable of dealing with the complex moral reality of running an effective counter-terrorism operation within the law, Nelson's own actions in not contacting his handlers on any of the cases in which he admitted guilt absolved the system itself of direct responsibility. The army itself viewed Kerr's evidence as opening an important debate. In a letter dated 13 February 1992, the General Officer Commanding wrote to Kerr that he 'had served the army's and, I judge, the national interest extremely well…The official reaction has been to promote a long and overdue focus upon the constraints and contradictions inherent in the agent-running system. Above all, your comments were institutional, rather than individual, thereby leaving the existing critically important personal relationships in Northern Ireland undamaged.'[48]

While the prosecution accepted Nelson's arguments that he had passed on information related to McDaid, it was with regards to Declan McDaid and there could be no suggestion that Nelson had intended to murder Terence. It therefore was decided to accept Nelson's not guilty plea, a decision that the prosecuting counsel, Brian

Kerr, claimed was taken after 'a scrupulous assessment of the possible evidential difficulties and a rigorous examination of the interests of justice', which was an elaborate way of justifying a course of action that served to obviate the need for a more searching inquiry. A review of the grounds given is instructive:

> The amount and nature of the material which the accused passed to those who were responsible for the various incidents;
> The opportunity available to him to communicate with his handler about the information he was passing to other UDA members;
> The degree of involvement, or lack of it, of the plaintiff in the actual attacks as opposed to the supply of information which preceded the plan and its execution;
> The evidence which was available to the Crown, which could have been held to be consistent with purpose or intention on the part of Nelson that McDaid or Slane should not have been murdered.[49]

Despite the glowing testimony at the trial, documentary evidence reveals further interesting examples of conflicting dynamics. First, the testimony at the trial that Nelson had provided information on threats to 217 people, of which only three were killed, suggested that only the provision of credible information from the agent prevented murder. In fact, the soldier involved in collating the information 'said he took every name that was mentioned in MISRs arising out of information provided by Nelson, whether or not a specific threat was mentioned and whether or not that person had been the subject of a planned attack.'[50]

This, however, was more than a question of the unwitting reiteration of facts based on a flawed prospectus. The soldier involved in preparing the document made clear that he was asked specifically by his commanding officer in the FRU to provide numbers, not details. Secondly, Colonel Kerr is alleged to have suggested to Superintendent McFadden, a senior member of the Stevens team, that 'he had made a "script" of his evidence and it was approved by those in authority.'[51] Although Kerr subsequently denied making the comment, he did forward a report to intelligence bosses on 20 May 1992 in which he argued that 'if Nelson had obeyed the advice of his handlers he would never have spoken to the Inquiry Team, would not have divulged his role and would not have been prosecuted.'[52] For Cory, both the evidence at the trial and Kerr's subsequent actions 'raise troubling questions not only as to his conduct but [also] as to the likelihood of collusion by FRU. It reflects a pattern of conduct and an attitude that is consistent with acts of collusion taking place.'[53]

The annual emergency legislation renewal debate process always ensured a succession of platitudes. At the height of the prosecution of the Dirty War, the Secretary of State, Peter Brooke, maintained that 'we shall continue to work unreservedly for the defeat of terrorism with all the means at our disposal that are compatible with the letter and spirit of the rule of law'.[54] Both the spirit and the letter of the law were broken repeatedly by agents of the state between 1988 and the killing of Finucane in 1989. More problematic was the nature of the cover-up. The operation of the Nelson trial and the manner in which the state had prepared the prosecution belied the seriousness with which successive governments worked under that rubric. As Seamus Mallon pointed out:

> It is clear from the transcript taken in a court of law that Colonel J [Gordon Kerr] was, in his own words, in many ways colluding with murder and ignoring it. If that is the case, we had better sit up and end the self-righteousness that is injected into this kind of debate. We should ask ourselves what kind of society is being left for us in the North of Ireland.[55]

The ending of the Nelson trial resulted in the usual demarcation along sectarian lines. The Ulster Unionists saw the problems arising out of a failure to give Special Branch primacy and called for even more restrictive uses of the law. One claimed that the 'best return for that good work is not being achieved in that shortcomings in the law allow the higher echelons of the terrorist organisations — their command and control structures — to remain free to walk the streets with impunity, despite the fact that the RUC has provided high-grade intelligence about those people'. The SDLP's Seamus Mallon saw a different dynamic at work: the injudicious application of the law and its distortion by the activities of the security nexus:

> The public interest requires a system of law enforcement and justice that all can support and in which all can have confidence. Does he [Brian Mawhinney, Minister of State] believe that that is

possible in Northern Ireland, when some sections of the security services are colluding with terrorists, when they are using terrorists as agents while they are involved in terrorist activity, and when some members of the security services are handing out confidential security documents as though they were pen-pal photographs? What changes will he and the Secretary of State demand so that the integrity of the law can be protected from some of those who are charged with enforcing it?[56]

What is striking, however, is that the Nelson trial involved much more detail in terms of other people who were allegedly involved in murder operations. In outlining the prosecution case in the Barrett trial, conspicuous efforts were made not to identify other participants, a state of affairs that cannot be put down simply to improved prosecutorial design or adherence to 'due process'. In 1992 there was no such compunction in naming those who did not face charges, including Jim Spence, the loyalist godfather who controlled the UFF in north Belfast at the time of the Finucane killing. This then begs the question of why so little of the Stevens investigation was entered into the public domain. It leaves unresolved the wider questions of who else was involved in the operation and their connections with the security forces. In this context it is notable that in Justice Cory's report, even the names of those whom Nelson was convicted of conspiring to murder have been redacted.

In order to unravel this mystery it is necessary to revisit contours of the three Stevens investigations and their political import. The first Stevens investigation resulted in ninety-four arrests and the prosecution of forty-seven loyalists. Despite the fact that over 2,000 documents had been leaked from security force installations, mainly from RUC stations and UDR bases, none of the prosecutions involved members of the security forces. Nelson was not charged with complicity in the Finucane murder and the full extent of his involvement only became public as a consequence of a documentary produced by the *Panorama* 'Dirty War' programme and broadcast in June 1992 after Nelson had begun his prison sentence.

As with the Barrett proceedings a decade later, the guilty verdict meant that none of the evidence could be tested, a state of affairs that ensured the code of silence governing the true extent of collusion retained its potency. The stalemate ended with the decision by Johnston Brown, the CID detective who had captured on tape the confession of Ken Barrett as early as 1991, to come forward, first to Stevens and then to the *Insight* programme. Brown, now reaching the end of his police career, broke the code of silence within the RUC by giving a statement detailing his concerns to the Stevens Inquiry about the attempts by Special Branch to stymie his investigation into the Finucane killing following the admission in a car in October 1991.

> I wasn't put under any pressure, I was there voluntarily and I made a statement, a six-page statement outlining as I have with you, my career or involvement in the murder squad in '89 and the running of informants from then until I retired. And setting out exactly what had taken place on the 1st, 3rd and 10th October. And before I would sign it, the Sergeant told me to read the certificate, which took me aback because the certificate sets out quite clearly that if you say anything or do anything, right, and sign anything that you know to be not true or don't believe it to be true or you know it's not true and you sign that, that's perjury. It's as simple as that and I understood that. I wasn't at odds with that, I'd no problem with that. Nonetheless, they were saying to me to be very careful. Was I sure? Could I be wrong? I said no and I signed it. When I signed it the officers just cleared the desk as I had done it thousands of times myself. The atmosphere changed totally. And they were looking at me then like a police suspect and I couldn't understand this and I said what's the problem?

The Stevens' detectives asked Brown whether he would agree that a tape recording of the events would serve as an independent verification of his allegations, a question that immediately put the CID officer on the defensive. They produced a tape dated 3 October, which did not have any mention of Pat Finucane.

> I was aghast, I could see myself facing court for perjury in the full knowledge that I wasn't telling lies. How could this not be changed? How could this be that this tape was in total contradiction to my written records? And then they allowed me to listen to a couple minutes of the tape and said that's all. It was just road noise so I canvassed them and Mr Stevens said allow him to listen to the entire tape, give him paper to write whatever notes he wants, at the end of this note-taking, seize the notes as exhibits.

Within minutes of listening to the tape Brown relaxed. The tape dated itself. As Barrett had got into the car, the conversation began with a discussion of the killing of Henry Fleming Ward, a loyalist killed by a republican splinter group in the Jubilee bar in the Shankill, and a reprisal murder of Hugh Magee, a Catholic taxi driver, as he drove his black hackney through the Oldpark area of north Belfast later that evening, both of which occurred on 10 October 1991, the date of the second interview in which Brown and his colleague had been warned not to mention the Finucane killing.[57] The re-dating of the tape as that of the 3 October meeting, if deliberate, represents a perversion of justice.[58]

> I was incensed. But immediately that I realised that it was the 10th of the 10th '91, Mr Stevens was called down and I told him that this couldn't have been the 3rd of the 10th and he was taken aback. All it had to be was a re-run of the 3rd in line with my notebooks and my journals in the same order as I would have in my notes and that rids Special Branch of the confession. Why this was done and it was done within a week of the confession, it wasn't done in '98, I don't know. You would have to ask Special Branch. Someone in within a week of that confession being in our domain had made the decision not only not to go forward with the investigation but to obstruct and to ensure that anybody like myself or my colleague who took a serious break down coming forward would be ridiculed.

The Stevens team took cognisance of the Brown lead to launch its own operation against Barrett but failed to act immediately on his evidence. The missing tape recording meant that another crucial line of evidence had been destroyed. To this day there has not been an adequate explanation from either the Steven teams or Special Branch as to why this was done. What is clear, however, is that it fitted in to a wider operational reality that governed the prosecution of a Dirty War that remains impenetrable to public accountability.

Chapter 6
Inquiring for Truth

On 23 September 2004 the Secretary of State for Northern Ireland, Paul Murphy, announced that an inquiry would be held into concerns of collusive activities between various sections of the security forces and loyalist paramilitaries in the assassination of Pat Finucane. As London wrestled to find a way through a political impasse occasioned by the continued public failure of the political parties to agree on an overarching settlement, Paul Murphy eventually, and reluctantly, ceded an inquiry. Despite stated concerns that ongoing criminal investigations could be stymied by the staging of an inquiry, London acknowledged that the 'exceptional concerns' arising from the circumstances of the killing and the corrosive effect of its aftermath necessitated action.[1]

The Attorney General, Lord Goldsmith, had provided three rationales for initially advising taking a prosecutorial tack. There were practical, moral and political impediments to the holding of an inquiry. First, 'preparation for cross-examination will deprive the criminal court of a witness's genuine reaction and answer when confronted'. Second, the Stevens investigation was 'too serious to brush aside questions of prosecution'. Third, 'the victims of wrongdoing deserve to see wrongdoers before the courts and, where convicted, punished'. Underpinning this was a stated determination that prosecutions would be 'vigorously pursued, regardless of the position or seniority of the alleged offender'. The ending of the Barrett trial melted away those objections.

What is striking is that those who now face prosecutions are primarily current or past members of the security forces. They would
face jury trials because they were not alleged to be members of
proscribed organisations. This, in turn, raises profound questions of
state legitimacy. If convicted, they could not avail of the early release
terms governing the paramilitaries, an appalling vista indeed, to quote
Lord Denning's memorable phrasing, and one that would be hard to
justify to a British public, particularly while the country is now a
frontline participant in a global war on terror. The decision to hold an
inquiry now jeopardises those prosecutions. Through a spokes-
woman, the Attorney General intimated that those prosecutions were
unlikely. 'In light of the view expressed by the Attorney General that
possibility of further prosecution[s] must be at this stage speculative
as must the potential risk to any prosecution by an inquiry, the
government has determined that the public interest now weighs in
favour of an inquiry.'

By waiving his doubts, the Attorney General is accepting the
conclusion of Justice Cory that the Finucane case 'may be one of the
rare situations where a public inquiry will be of greater benefit to a
community than prosecutions'. However, the Canadian judge maintains that if prosecutions do not proceed, some other way of dealing
with criminal malfeasance must be found. 'If, for example, the person
to be prosecuted is a member of the military, then military discipline
resulting in loss of rank and benefits may be a far greater punishment
and have a far greater deterrent effect than a prosecution.'

Just as the Finucane murder was exceptional, so too was the careful phrasing of the announcement, which allowed the government
considerable room to manoeuvre over the composition, remit and
degree of public oversight involved in the establishment of an inquiry.
'Legislation is needed to provide the tribunal with the powers of the
four other inquiries in Northern Ireland — Bloody Sunday, Rosemary
Nelson, Robert Hamill and Billy Wright. Because this case deals with
issues of national security, much of the proceedings will have to take
place in private', proclaimed the Secretary of State in an interview
carried by the Press Association. 'Details will be made clear when
the legislation emerges but I would suspect much of it will be in
private but some may also be in public, to the extent that it can be
held in public. Obviously that depends on the legislation and on the
tribunal itself.'[2]

In order to protect the government from charges that it had resiled from its commitments at a previous round of talks, held at Weston Park in 2001, Murphy pointed to the findings of the international judge appointed to ascertain the necessity of an inquiry. Peter Cory had recommended an inquiry but conceded that national security issues necessitated caution. He had recommended that 'the hearings, to the extent possible, should be held in public'.[3] For those alleging duplicity, they pointed to the fact that Cory had not intimated that special legislation was a prerequisite.[4] He had also concluded that 'the findings and recommendations of the Commissioners should be in writing and made public', a formulation that could be subverted by the privileging of the competing concept of the public interest, which includes the national security imperative.

As Paul Murphy attempted to clarify the government's position, he served merely to obfuscate. According to the Secretary of State, 'national security' had necessitated the redaction of nine pages from the Cory Report, a subtle shift from the original justification, which posited that the redactions were caused because publication of the offending passages — including, implausibly, section headings — had the potential to prejudice the criminal proceedings against Ken Barrett. Despite the passage of a symbolic life sentence, no attempt had been made to alter the terms or extent of the original redaction. Nor even in announcing the emasculated inquiry, or since, has the Secretary of State prepared to amend the public version of the Cory Report. The failure to put material no longer governed by the already spurious notion that publication could prejudice a non-jury trial into the public domain served merely to raise suspicion about the government's motives.

Given the government's stated determination to get to the truth about the issues arising from the Cory recommendations, the legislative route chosen was also difficult to explain on a rational basis. The stated reason for not introducing an immediate Order in Council was the imperative for parliament — with an inbuilt and unassailable Labour majority — to debate the issues.

The decision was presented as a triumph for democracy because Northern Ireland parliamentary representatives would have the capacity to debate the provisions of the legislation. Left unsaid was the reality that, despite protestations to the contrary, the net effect of the government's approach was to delay the holding of an inquiry

until more favourable terms had been given the legitimacy of a parliamentary patina. The passage of legislation through open sessions of
parliament gives powerful credence to what Leman-Langlois and
Clifford Shearing term 'the process of authorisation'.[5] Even a limited
inquiry has the potential to create versions of the truth, which, while
capable of contestation, set the political agenda.

Reaction to the government's stated objective was swift and
polarised. Speaking for the family, Michael Finucane complained that
what 'we are looking at is an inquiry which is going to be established
by government, probably accountable to government but also controlled and restricted by government'.[6] Later a statement was released
on the Pat Finucane Centre website from the family which expressed
profound suspicion at the decision to await new legislation. 'Special
legislation when it isn't needed can only mean that rather than the
truth emerging what will emerge is cover-up and lies.'[7] In order to
ascertain whether the truth will be served by the terms announced and
later amplified by Paul Murphy, it is necessary to carefully deconstruct
the pivotal last paragraph of the Murphy announcement.

> As in any inquiry, the tribunal will be tasked with uncovering the
> full facts of what happened, and will be given all the powers and
> resources necessary to fulfil that task. In order that the inquiry can
> take place speedily and effectively and in a way that takes into
> account the public interest, including the requirements of national
> security, it will be necessary to hold the inquiry on the basis of new
> legislation, which will be introduced shortly.[8]

Unpacking the paragraph raises a number of profound questions
concerning the extent and remit of the inquiry. What facts are we
talking about? What timescale is the government operating within?
Will the inquiry be limited to tracking direct connections between
handlers and the loyalists involved in the events that led to the shooting and the pulling of the triggers or the wider implications of the
decision not to effectively protect the killers by impeding the criminal
investigation? Will the wider policy dynamics that facilitated the
killing be examined? If so, to what level: unit; military; security nexus,
Whitehall or cabinet? Will the tribunal be given full access to the
information gleaned by the Stevens Inquiry? If not, who will make
that decision? Does speed trump depth and how is effectiveness to be

measured? Should the inquiry be limited to the Finucane murder alone or to other killings in which aspects of the security nexus are implicated? Will the wider institutional framework, including the actions of the Director of Public Prosecutions and the Attorney General in relation to the handling of legal cases involving those alleged to have been implicated in the early 1990s, be explored? Will the briefings that formed the basis of the guilty compromise accepted by the Crown in the prosecution of Brian Nelson in 1992 be privileged or enter into the public domain? Will parties to the tribunal have the right of cross-examination, discovery and disclosure? What precisely is meant by the phrase 'the public interest' and who will decide what it is? Should the public interest be defined in financial, legal, moral or political terms and is there a right of appeal if sessions are conducted in camera? Will the documents on which conclusions are reached be made public? If not will the documents be footnoted to allow future generations of researchers the capacity to reach conclusions once the documents are eventually put in the public domain, or will the publication of an executive summary without annotations suffice and who will make that decision? Finally, what are the grounds for proposing the new legislation and does its pre-ordained passage given Labour's inbuilt parliamentary majority, in turn both legitimise and pre-configure the outcome?[9]

In an interview with the *Guardian*, Geraldine Finucane appeared to compromise on the international dimension of the family's call for an independent public inquiry. However, for her, there could be no compromise on the need for a transparent process in which the wider policy issues could be addressed and those responsible for designing, implementing and monitoring those policies could be held to account. If these concerns were not addressed, what was on offer, she claimed, was merely a 'fiasco and a circus' to which the family would not give legitimacy. 'We will go and see Tony Blair and make it clear that if he presents us with an inquiry that is not public, not judicial and not independent, which is a government investigation, we will not take part.'[10]

Tribunals of Inquiry are political constructs, designed to validate and legitimise certain kinds of 'official truths'.[11] As such they can represent the primacy of the politics of symbolism, creating the illusion of a determination to elicit the causes of failure and ensure that corrective action is taken to remedy past wrongs, when this is not necessarily the reality.[12] It is therefore imperative to ask what is the function of the revealed truth? The decision as to whether or not to establish an inquiry is arbitrary and can result from panic and attempts to shore up legitimacy as well as a genuine attempt to arrive at an adjudication of events for its intrinsic normative value. How and why tribunals are constituted, limited and resourced remains deeply contested and closed to public accountability or transparency. Recent tribunals of inquiry ceded by the British government are instructive in this regard. As Phil Scraton has noted:

> In airing the views of competing interests before impartial arbiters, whose sole objective is to establish publicly the 'facts' through thorough investigation, commissions and inquiries are presented as exemplars of democratic conflict resolution and action...While the potential exists for inquiries to reconcile differences and resolve serious public issues, they are open to management and manipulation. Official inquiries into circumstances that challenge the legitimacy and authority of state institutions are often undermined by partial investigation and restricted disclosure.[13]

In the Saville Inquiry, for example, the terms of reference were deliberately set in such a way as to omit from critical investigation the wider policy implications of the decision to open fire in Derry. The question posed was limited to what factors facilitated the killing. The more politically damaging question of how the now disgraced Widgery judgment was arrived at, a galling 'official truth' that has caused ongoing alienation, is beyond the Saville Inquiry's terms of reference. Even within its limited parameters, the hearings have been shrouded in controversy from the beginning, with legal obstruction a defining characteristic. The resulting wrangling and spiralling costs seriously damaged the credibility of the probe.[14]

When the government established the Saville Commission in January 1998, Tony Blair set out the limitations of the terms of inquiry. According to the Prime Minister, it would inquire into 'a definite matter of urgent public importance, namely the events on Sunday, 30 January 1972, which led to loss of life in connection with the procession in Londonderry on that day, taking account of any new information relevant to events on that day'.[15] He went on to justify the calling of the tribunal on the grounds that 'Bloody Sunday was different because, where the state's own authorities are concerned, we must be as sure as we can of the truth, precisely because we pride ourselves on our democracy and respect for the law, and on the professionalism and dedication of our security forces.'[16] Throughout its public sittings, the Ministry of Defence contested the right of Saville to hear evidence in public, in person, or even in Derry. Crucial evidence was destroyed, including sixteen of the nineteen rifles used and all photographs taken by military photographers.[17] More ominously from the perspective of those interested in the wider dynamic, serving or past agents could refuse or be refused a hearing on the grounds that the substantive issue of the right to life trumps the 'procedural right of ascertaining truth'.[18] The contestation of these competing dynamics resulted in juridical paralysis, which saw proceedings commute between the Guildhall to the High Court.

Even more problematic is the fact that while Bloody Sunday is, in policy terms, a historical footnote, the wider issues surrounding the killing of Pat Finucane remain as salient today as they were in 1989. In fact, given the war on terrorism, they have become even more important. Thus, while undeniably painful for those bereaved by the reckless disregard shown by the paratroopers in 1972, reassessing the verdict of Lord Widgery is relatively painless politically for the government. Opening for inspection the governance and accountability processes, or lack thereof, of the prosecution of counter-terrorism is quite another matter. Crossing the sacrosanct rubicon of due process in a democratic order repeatedly and without effective sanction is a profoundly destabilising and delegitimating process.

Here we face a paradox. In order to ensure that policy recommendations arising from a tribunal of inquiry into these matters are robust, the political and military establishment as well as their agents within the intelligence community, as part of the security forces, must be held accountable for their actions in the design, implementation and prosecution of the Dirty War, a political impossibility in an age of global terror. However, excavating these issues is central to ascertaining the factors that led to the institutionalisation of collusion as a matter of *de facto* if not *de jure* operational policy. In this context, just as the Finucane family remain adamant that they are more interested in ascertaining who pulled the strings rather than the trigger, placing the focus on the individual handlers involved in making the judgement as to whether to intervene to stop murder in order to protect sources represents a stunted view of causation. Such a formulation does little to instil confidence, not least because the Stevens inquiry team has already ascertained who was responsible for agent mishandling. Papers have been lodged with the Director of Public Prosecutions, which has yet to make a judgement on whether to proceed with judicial charges.[19] There is little prospect that an independent tribunal of inquiry could necessarily improve the quality of the paper trail. What is important at this stage is to contextualise that paper trail in order to ascertain why such repeated breaches occurred. To do otherwise ensures the suppression of truth, not its validation.[20]

The handlers operated within a system of control that allowed murder to take place and was not calibrated in the aftermath of demonstrable and repeated failure. As a report issued to the two governments on the tenth anniversary of the killing that prompted the re-entry of John Stevens to the Northern Ireland arena made clear, accountability structures were not publicly validated. According to the report, the Force Research Unit 'broke every rule in the book and committed some of the most serious crimes, including conspiracy to murder, collecting and providing information likely to be of use to terrorists, and directing terrorism.'[21] The report was heavily criticised by Tom King, Secretary of State at the time, who argued on the UTV *Insight* programme that 'there was never any possible suggestion that the authorisation was given to operate outside the law...we had democratic principles to uphold.'[22]

This, however, is precisely the accusation that the public inquiry announced by the government in September 2004 will have to adjudicate if the issue of collusion is to be adequately explained. In his interview with *Insight*, Tom King suggested that the human rights group was scaremongering, masking unsubstantiated allegations without regard for the consequences. These allegations now carry substantial weight because of the investigative power of John Stevens and Justice Cory. Both paint a picture of institutionalised collusion. Stevens suggests that 'the unlawful involvement of agents in murder implies that the security forces sanction killings'. He places responsibility for this state of affairs on a culture in which 'informants and agents were allowed to operate without effective control and to participate in terrorist crime'.[23] Cory goes further, noting that 'army handlers and their superiors turned a blind eye to the criminal acts of

[Brian] Nelson. In doing so they established a pattern of behaviour that could be characterised as collusive.' [24] Cory further notes:

> The records kept in the usual and ordinary sense of the business of FRU leave little doubt that, on occasion, handlers provided information to Nelson that facilitated his targeting activities. While there is no indication that handlers provided information that specifically pertained to Patrick Finucane, this breach of policy is significant, as it demonstrates a general pattern of behaviour on the part of Nelson's handlers that could be considered collusive... [and] had the potential to facilitate the deadly operations planned by the UDA. [25]

This then raises the question of organisational and ultimately political responsibility. The killing of an officer of the court represented a profound assault on each of the key indicators identified by Tony Blair when he convened the Saville Inquiry. If the investigation is to be seen as credible, the wider factors that governed the intelligence community have to be addressed in an open and transparent manner. The grounds that were identified as a necessity for closed sessions during the planned Finucane inquiry raise profound concerns about how 'national security' will be identified and measured and who will be able to avail of, or be smothered by its protective cloak. [26] Instructive here is the application from the Ministry of Defence to the Saville Inquiry to limit questioning of Martin Ingram, a pseudonym used by a former member of the Force Research Unit. The application requested that the following information would not be disclosed by the Inquiry:

(1) the organisation, chain of command, methods of operation, capabilities, training, equipment and techniques of the special units of the armed forces;
(2) the identity and location of the premises of special units of the armed forces; the identities and physical appearance of members and former members of the special units of the armed forces;
(3) any counter-terrorist activities in which Martin Ingram, or any units with which he served, may have been involved, in particular those summarised in the confidential annex to this certificate;
(4) the nature and sources of intelligence information;

(5) any other information which might be useful to terrorist organisations or detrimental to national security.[27]

Given the number of former members of the FRU and indeed loyalist paramilitaries now talking in the media, the question arises as to whether they will be allowed to give evidence in public and whether the government believes that their substantive right to life or that of those whom they implicate trumps public hearing.[28] This was a constant dynamic facing investigative journalists in Northern Ireland throughout the late 1990s and early part of this century. Each television or newspaper editor faced 'gagging orders' from the Ministry of Defence, which were routinely upheld by the courts. In order to demonstrate the sophistry involved, it was only through a gagging order placed on UTV that the army even conceded that the FRU existed.

The justification used was the necessity not to imperil either the sources of intelligence or the means by which it was collected. In affidavits provided to the courts, the Ministry of Defence repeatedly cited the danger that the compromising of agents or their handlers could lead to torture, and ultimately murder. When these matters related to the Force Research Unit, we were told that it had made a contribution to the campaign against terrorism that was disproportionate to its size. The agents were lionised as people who at great personal risk were willing to give detailed information to the army that prevented attacks. The documents make clear that all information provided to the army was passed on to the RUC Special Branch, a formulation that is bitterly contested by senior police officers. More problematically, the Ministry of Defence made clear in its submissions to the court that the release of information about operations could never be released.

As Editor of Current Affairs, I was informed that not only were the tradecraft methods to be kept secret, so too were the terms of the injunction. This dual strategy was ostensibly designed to protect both the personnel who served in the unit, who expected, if captured, to be tortured and killed and to protect the agents who were under constant threat from terrorists. For the Ministry of Defence there was a constant risk that former members of the Force Research Unit could, by virtue of an unauthorised disclosure, inadvertently and unwittingly or maliciously, reveal the identity of other soldiers and agents. That risk was unacceptable to the Crown's legal team. What was particularly striking was the impenetrable nature of the Ministry of Defence's circular logic. According to the affidavits, national security interests could be compromised by the revelation of what precisely the national security concerns were.[29]

In this context, it is worth pointing out the contrast between the unwillingness to compromise 'national security' in the Northern Ireland arena with the transparent manner in which a potentially even more politically destabilising tribunal of inquiry was handled in the summer of 2003. Some of the most powerful figures in the political and media establishment were summoned to the Royal Courts of Justice in London to appear before Lord Justice Hutton as he investigated the death of the weapons inspector David Kelly. Despite the fact that Lord Hutton, in his final report, chose to interpret his remit in exceptionally narrow terms, giving rise to an immediate concern about whom the government chooses to appoint in the Finucane case, the inquiry was distinctive because of the amount of material disclosed on the inquiry website. Notwithstanding Justice Hutton's personal integrity, he appeared to be favourably disposed towards the arguments put forward by the intelligence community. This consideration, no doubt, influenced the government's thinking in seeking his appointment in the first instance. However, the remarkable web resource site does allow for a very different interpretation of the 'facts' adjudicated on by the inquiry chairman. Given the fact that the government has yet to rescind its redactions relating to Ken Barrett, it is highly unlikely that the government will want to repeat the experiment. As David McKittrick, one of the shrewdest observers of Northern Ireland conflict, has observed, 'in a Belfast context, the citing of national security has in the past signalled the non-disclosure of sensitive information'.[30] The question is why?

While much recent media attention, particularly in the United Kingdom, has focused on the specific circumstances surrounding the murder of Pat Finucane, the moral hazard is at once more complex and more profound. And it is in this context that the disclosures on the Hutton website assume critical importance. Given the divided nature of Northern Irish identity, providing full disclosure enables the construction of an alternative to the 'official truth', providing critical insights into the mechanisms that allow for the reflexive erosion of integrity of the British state's capacity to kill in the execution of public policy. Corruption thrives in situations where discretion occurs in the absence of transparency, accountability and impartial enforcement. Precisely because the British government sought to use moral suasion to underwrite its security policy in Northern Ireland, the perception of moral and political corruption has been rendered much more acute.[31]

Problematic at the best of times, the concept of corruption is much more difficult to assess when the gain is to either the state or party political rather than venal, with the potential benefits shrouded in longer-term paybacks. The most widely used definition of corruption dates from a 1967 formulation prepared by the American political scientist Joseph Nye. He argues that 'corruption is behaviour that deviates from the formal duties of a public role because of private-regarding (close family, private clique) pecuniary or status gains.'[32]

Nye's paradigm rests on the assumption that officials — elected and bureaucratic — who subvert the public good for private gain destroy public confidence in the efficacy of the state's ability to be an independent arbiter of competing claims. This formulation has the advantage of precision, but its salience is diluted when applied to the formulation or execution of wider policy issues. It diverts attention away from systemic defects and minimises the responsibility of the component parts of the formal state structure — political parties, institutions, governments — for contributing to, or exacerbating, the extent of the malaise. It is precisely this arena which is the most controversial and difficult to legislate against and which is crucial to understanding the dilemmas that underpinned the Hutton Inquiry and which will also be central to adjudicating the issues in the planned investigation into the killing of Pat Finucane.

The widely used economic concept of principal–agent analysis has been offered as a way forward. Aligning the public interest with the 'principal' and assigning any corrupt activity by either politician or bureaucrat to the role of the 'agent' violating 'principal' trust, it seeks to demonstrate how corruption occurs, while remaining agnostic on the moral aspect. While this is exceptionally useful when examining problems within allegedly rogue units, it is less so when assessing the political reality of principal corruption itself. Extending the analysis of the impact of ethical corruption to the political realm is therefore highly problematic. At what stage does an action become corrupt and how do you stop the entire fabric of politics from itself being labelled as corrupt as opposed to being susceptible to corruption? A third paradigm, which rests on the definition of corruption as being any activity that is contrary to the 'public interest', a formulation closely akin to 'national interest', is too elastic and prone to manipulation to act as a secure anchor for policy choices.

The judicial inquiry led by Lord Hutton has been instrumental in providing compelling insights into the complexity of modern governance. The tragedy surrounding Dr Kelly's death raised issues of profound public importance about choices faced by individuals, institutions and governments in the face of an acute moral dilemma. For both institutions at the heart of the dispute — the government and the BBC — the stakes could not be higher. As the philosopher Onoroa O'Neill has commented, 'in a world in which information and misinformation are generated, in which good drafting is a vanishing art, in which so-called informational products can be transmitted, reformatted and adjusted, embroidered and elaborated, shaped and spun, repeated and respun, it can be quite hard to assess truth and falsehood.'[33]

The evidence uploaded onto the official website offers an unparalleled view of how decisions are made and justified. History must not necessarily wait the customary thirty years: the documents offer the political scientist a unique opportunity to critique in real time the entire process. The paper trail has implicated the most senior officials in both organisations in questionable activities that reveal a deficit of integrity in ethical standards. While the Hutton Inquiry focused on the circumstances surrounding Dr Kelly's death, the wider policy issues raised were unavoidable. The same imperative faces the government as it prepares to design the framework for the examination of the Finucane case. In order to understand why, it is necessary to outline briefly the facts of the Kelly case.

The scientist held a meeting with Andrew Gilligan, Defence Correspondent for the *Today* programme at the Charing Cross Hotel in Central London. In the course of a subsequent broadcast interview on *Today*, Gilligan alleged that the contents of a dossier on Iraq's weapons programme, prepared by the intelligence services for public dissemination, had been 'sexed up'. He further alleged that there were particular misgivings about the insertion of a single-sourced assertion that nuclear weapons could be used within forty-five minutes, a claim Gilligan asserted was untrue and that the government knew to be untrue. The crux of the item was that in order to further the presentational needs of the government, intelligence was processed into propaganda at the behest of Downing Street. In a subsequent article for the *Mail on Sunday,* Gilligan went further. He suggested that his source had claimed that the Director of Communications at Downing Street, Alistair Campbell, had been instrumental in orchestrating the insertion of the forty-five minute claim.

The government demanded an immediate retraction, which the BBC refused to comply with. As the dispute escalated, the Leader of the House, Dr John Reid, spoke darkly of attempts to destabilise the government. 'There have been uncorroborated briefings by a potentially rogue element, or indeed rogue elements, in the intelligence services', he told *The Times.*[34] In a bad-tempered exchange on *Today,* Dr Reid oscillated between speculating that the BBC's source could have been a man in the pub or a printer involved in the production of the dossier, to condemning the lack of loyalty and professionalism of the person involved in the leak.[35]

As the row escalated, Dr Kelly contacted the Ministry of Defence and admitted he could be the source of the contentious report. Despite being assured confidentiality, the Ministry of Defence, with the knowledge — and connivance — of the Downing Street communications directorate, allowed Dr Kelly's name to become public. Forced to appear before the Foreign Affairs Select Committee (while the Director of the Joint Intelligence Committee, Sir John Scarlett, the person most centrally involved in the dossier's presentation, was shielded), Dr Kelly faced withering criticism. Two days after a second appearance, Dr Kelly walked into the woods near his home and committed suicide, thereby setting in motion the Hutton Inquiry itself.

The central issue to be resolved was whether the intelligence picture was wilfully distorted for propaganda purposes. And central to the adjudication of this — beyond the terms of reference of the Hutton Inquiry itself — was a critical assessment of the purpose for putting intelligence into the public domain in the first place in the form of a dossier published on 24 September 2002. This view of unwarranted politicisation of sensitive material certainly held some currency within the intelligence community, according to evidence of a senior chemical weapons inspector who spoke of 'the spin merchants of this administration' in an email to Dr Kelly. In oral evidence, the expert told the Inquiry there was a 'perception that the dossier had been round the houses several times in order to try to find a form of words which would strengthen certain political objectives. The Head of the Joint Intelligence Committee, Sir John Scarlett, had earlier asserted that he retained control of the document at every stage, rejecting suggestions that it had been 'beefed up' by Downing Street.

What has become clear is that each draft went through a cost-benefit analysis by Downing Street, the key variable of which was narrow political gain. The first draft of the dossier was presented to Downing Street on 5 September. It did not include the controversial claim that weapons could be deployed within forty-five minutes, a claim the BBC stated was included at the behest of Downing Street. It has now been established that the government was adamant that the dossier needed 'to be as strong as possible, within the bounds of available intelligence'.[36] The political imperative was enunciated by the Prime Minister's Chief of Staff, Jonathan Powell, in a key email to Scarlett on 17 September: 'The document does nothing to demonstrate any threat, let alone an imminent threat from Saddam.'[37] By the time the dossier was published, the forty-five minute claim, based on 'credible information' from a single source, had been inserted. This definite conclusion was at stark variance with evidence from the Defence Intelligence Service Chief, Brian Jones, who thought the information needed to be heavily discounted. Sir John maintained that the insertion could be justified and remained steadfast in his conviction that there had been no political interference. Interestingly, Sir John also confirmed in evidence that the request for the document in the first place had come from Alistair Campbell, who said he had been authorised by the Foreign Secretary. Sir John was not drawn on his assertion that he had asked for the request to be put in writing or his insistence that his control of the document was also committed to paper.

The question to be resolved is whether the manipulation of language degenerated into wilful distortion for partisan ends? This has implications at three interlinked but subtly different levels: the presentation of the intelligence itself; the proportionality of the government's response to the BBC for broadcasting the allegation that there was unease about the initial exercise; and whether moral certainty occluded rational discourse both in terms of the initial hunt for the person responsible for the leak and the process whereby the weapons scientist was named. It is this allegation of 'deindividuation' in pursuit of presentational superiority (or more banally, vanity and pride) that presented the biggest threat to the government and was potentially most damaging to the credibility of the Prime Minister himself.

To a certain extent, Lord Hutton's findings provided little comfort to either the government or the BBC; the damage caused to both institutions had already occurred. At issue was not so much the veracity of the initial story that sparked the furore, but rather the manner in which both institutions handled the entire Iraq crisis, matters that went beyond the limited terms of reference set by the judge. The BBC's robust public defence of the journalist involved, Andrew Gilligan, has been revealed to be in stark contrast to internal correspondence. Kevin Marsh, the programme's editor, complained of 'flawed reporting', while Richard Sambrook, the corporation's Director of News, had suggested to Geoff Hoon, the Defence Secretary, in the hours before the publication of Dr Kelly's name, that the BBC was considering 'an appropriate use' for the controversial correspondent. Suggestions of managerial bullying of another reporter in what she termed a misguided and wrong strategy to corroborate Gilligan's evidence, denied by senior executives, have tarnished the self-image of the corporation as a defender of truth itself threatened by a paranoid administration incapable of accepting harsh reality. At a strategic level, the BBC's Board of Governor's unquestioning public upholding of its managerial team's response raised profound questions about the corporate governance structures of the BBC. At the very least the public stance is at variance with internal minutes of a key governors' meeting, which paint a very different picture. *Today* was accused of being 'naïve' and its editorial culture was deemed to display 'tabloid or Sunday paper journalism. This should be examined.'[38]

The central problem was that an escalation imperative had already taken hold on both the BBC and the government. As a consequence of its actions, the self-policing paradigm, so jealously guarded by the BBC, was undermined, perhaps fatally. The government's once famed presentation skills have once again come back to haunt the administration. It is precisely because the government has placed morality at the centre of the dispute with Iraq that the allegations that it was derelict in its duty of care to a civil servant for presentational purposes have had such potentially destabilising and explosive consequences. Tom Kelly, one of the Prime Minister's official spokesmen, stated in an email to the Chief of Staff, Jonathan Powell, prior to Dr Kelly's appearance at the Foreign Affairs Select committee: 'This is now a game of chicken with the Beeb — the only way they will shift is if they see the screw tightening.' Tom Kelly gave evidence that the language was unfortunate. The efficacy of this defence may be devalued by repetitious use. He was forced to retract a comparison of Dr Kelly to the fictional fantasist Walter Mitty prior to the inquiry starting.

There was no evidence of a smoking gun, comprehensively falsifying either argument at the centre of this dispute. It came down to a question of interpretation. As noted above, Sir John Scarlett, the chairman of the Joint Intelligence Committee, stated in evidence that there was no suggestion that he ever felt under pressure to change the document for political purposes. This defence was far from conclusive. What was clear was that Downing Street itself played a pivotal role in assessing the raw intelligence, a truth that resulted in the removal of ambiguities. The result was that the realms of politics, impure and unsimple, collided with professional judgements, however obliquely, and politics won.

The Hutton Inquiry revealed the way in which adherence to the internal logic of an ideological project had the potential to corrupt entire organisations by eroding public confidence in the veracity of speech. Deceit is a common currency in politics but reserves can be seriously depleted, a fact explicitly acknowledged with the departure of Alistair Campbell and the overhaul of the entire communications machine in Whitehall. Preaching morality but governing through Machiavellian constructs is a difficult balancing act. The exposure of the true rules of the game has already forced a realignment that usurps the government's advantage in the informational conflict. If power is not knowledge but the ability to disseminate it, then the damage to the credibility of the government is as profound as the tragedy surrounding the unnecessary death of a public servant.

The moral implications of successive governments' decisions in the battle against terrorism have critical implications for public confidence in the legitimacy of the public structures currently being negotiated within Northern Ireland. The reality of counter-terrorism served an important justificatory, if not substantiated, rationale for republican violence. The institutionalisation of emergency measures set a context in which the resultant slip by agents of the state into the widespread acceptance of effective extra-judicial methods and its justification by government and judiciary alike happened by stealth rather than design.[39] Once it occurred, no serious attempt was made to rein it in and when solicitors attempted to use the courts to question the consequences, they were harassed, intimidated and, in the cases of Rosemary Nelson and Pat Finucane, murdered. Smear campaigns were orchestrated in which senior figures in the intelligence community suggested sotto voce that the victims were IRA sympathisers, code for legitimate targets. When this rationale governs policing priorities, particularly in a context in which the security nexus itself occupies an unassailable position, the danger of abuse is enormous.

In order to inform the analysis it is useful to place the policy under a comparative microscope. Providing the military with an overt role in security policy is one that carried grave risks. The military mindset, by definition, operates under looser constraints than that expected of civil societies. One of the first British army commanders in Northern Ireland, Frank Kitson, suggested in an influential book, published in 1971, that the successful prosecution of a counter-insurgency war necessitated the moulding of the criminal justice system as an instrument of state policy. According to Kitson, 'the law should be used as just another weapon in the government's arsenal, and in this case it becomes little more than a propaganda cover for the disposal of unwanted members of the public. For this to happen efficiently, the activities of the legal service have to be tied into the war effort in as discreet a way as possible.'[40] Kitson's critique was not particularly unique; rather it mirrored a practised global phenomenon.

Take this example from Argentina, where the military authorities recruited French theorists of counter-revolutionary warfare to provide a grand strategy for defeating terrorists. These theorists, including Colonel Patrice de Naurois, suggested that guerrillas were successful primarily because they adopted a dual strategy to subvert the state: propaganda to undermine loyalty, and terrorism to undermine the state's morale. To combat this, 'the state needs information as to who the subversives are, where their bases and hideouts are located, and who is helping them. Then the army must centralise and collate its information.'[41]

Underpinning this was a recognition that the army would have to play by different rules. In Argentina, Colonel Roger Trinquier, a veteran of Vietnam and Algeria, was to become a pivotal influence. Trinquier advocated a duel in which 'the terrorist should be treated as an enemy soldier whose army has to be destroyed so that it will be unable to continue fighting'.[42] Not only was there a need to create elaborate counter-revolutionary organisations and intense surveillance, but also the creation of a collaborator network was deemed essential. 'Once a victim confesses, giving names and places, he has no recourse but to continue collaborating. Therefore a practised interrogator will treat his victims with flexibility.'[43] Trinquier was particularly insightful in his view that 'the state must expect that the terrorists will use all the opportunities offered by the criminal laws of procedure to slow down or thwart counter-revolutionary strategy. What they fear most is the suspension of legal guarantees…The state and the army must be prepared, therefore, for a propaganda duel in which they constantly remind the people that their measures have only one purpose: to pursue and wipe out the band of terrorists that are flagellating it.'[44]

Deconstructing this reality is of profound normative value to Northern Ireland. Since the initial publication of the Cory Report, speculation has mounted that the British government is finally prepared to cede some form of Truth and Reconciliation Commission. It is a high-risk strategy and one that has found little mainstream political support. One is reminded of the classic line uttered by the film actor Jack Nicholson in *A Few Good Men*. Charged with bringing the US army into disrepute, Nicholson's character, in an emotionally charged response to prosecutors, retorts: 'You want the truth, you can't handle the truth.'

In the Finucane case, fact is indeed stranger, and more disturbing, than fiction. Evaluating responsibility for his execution requires reassessing old certainties about the role of the state in the management of conflict and its aftermath. Such a process has the potential to be exceptionally destabilising. The incisive deconstruction of the security nexus in South Africa was designed to symbolically strip away the legitimacy of the old regime and, through a process of atonement and forgiveness, generate reconciliation and loyalty to a single new South Africa. In Northern Ireland, where the very existence of the state is still contested, such a process is exceptionally problematic, as a cursory examination of the South African Truth and Reconciliation Commission findings in relation to political and military responsibility for fomenting and targeting communal violence attests.

The TRC concluded that 'clandestine and covert forms of control included…extra-judicial killings and support for surrogate forces'.[45] In an amnesty application to the TRC, one of its key architects, Major General Sakkie Crafford, maintained 'in some cases it was necessary to eliminate activists by killing them. This was the only way in which effective action could be taken against activists in a war situation...to charge someone in the normal court structure and go through the whole process was cumbersome and occasionally totally inadequate and impossible.'[46] Major General Crawford argued that detention could provoke 'added momentum to the liberation struggle. The security police and the country could not afford a Nelson Mandela again.' He outlined three distinct advantages for the state of execution rather than incarceration. Firstly, it acted as a deterrent for activism, creating distrust and demoralisation amongst cadres. Secondly, it reassured white voters that the terrorists were not in control, and, thirdly, that the information gathered by informants was protected. As the state became more practised, the emphasis moved from direct action to fomenting divisions. Intelligence became centralised through the establishment of the Counter Revolutionary Information Target Centre, known by the Afrikaner acronym TREWITS, which drew together the National Intelligence Service, Special Branch and the South African Defence Forces.

According to documents published by the Truth and Reconciliation Commission, the TREWITS was 'a new joint effort by the relevant members of the IG to bring about a solid information base for meaningful counter-revolutionary operational action'.[47] The aim was to 'consolidate, evaluate, interpret and distribute all relevant information with a view to operational actions to realise the Republic of South Africa's counter-revolutionary strategic aim.' As one participant in TREWITS remarked sardonically, 'What did they think we were collecting all this information about addresses, cars, movements for? To send them Christmas cards?'[48]

The TRC rejected any suggestion that extra-judicial killing was the result of rogue agents or units operating outside a framework of security and political control. On the contrary, it argued that while all members of the cabinet were indirectly responsible through omission, all those responsible for the direction of security policy — including the state president and ministers of law and order, defence and foreign affairs — had to take responsibility for 'a process of operationally directed intelligence collection of targeted individuals'.[49]

It is clear that the South African security forces played a major role in the development of 'counter-mobilisation' in order to stymie the political actions of the ANC. As early as 1982, the South African Defence forces argued there was a need to 'exploit and encourage the division between the ANC, Inkatha and the Black Consciousness Movement organisations'. The TRC found that while the origins of conflict, in the Western Cape in particular, lay in historical rivalries, 'these conflicts would not have resulted in the scale of violence and destruction without the permission, facilitation and endorsement of the Security Forces'.[50] It concluded that the subsequent 'failure to prosecute individuals, organisations or groups who attacked supporters of the liberation movements and their property amounted to an endorsement of such actions and, in some instances, a subversion of justice.'[51]

Within Britain, the Northern Ireland conflict was always presented as one in which, because of a residual loyalty to unionism, London was forced to intervene against its wishes. It is an important legitimating strategy, which posits Westminster as a neutral figure attempting to separate feuding and potentially warring communities. This formulation, however, is an intellectual deceit not supported by the facts. The actions of the security forces within Northern Ireland effectively criminalised the state itself. This is not to suggest that the actions of the state justified republican or indeed loyalist violence.

As Michael Walzer has noted, 'we live today in a political culture of excuses'.[52] Walzer offers a useful taxonomy of these excuses, ranging from the weapon of last resort to the easily falsifiable claim that terrorism works, to the claim that 'all politics is (really) terrorism. The appearance of innocence and decency is always a piece of deception, more or less convincing in accordance with the relative power of the deceivers. The terrorist who does not bother with appearance is only doing openly what everyone else does secretly…Terrorism is the politics of state officials and movement militants alike. This argument does not justify either the officials or the militants, but it does excuse them all.'[53]

Sinn Féin's clumsy and ill-advised reaction to the barbaric murder of Robert McCartney caused even more damage to the credibility of the republican movement. Known members of the IRA cut McCartney's throat because of an alleged slight in a Belfast hostelry on 30 January 2005. The bravery of his sisters in confronting the contradictions of a party proclaiming its democratic mandate while effectively shielding the killers from justice has undermined the very basis for the Provisional IRA's existence. Unlike the killing of JoJo O'Connor in Ballymurphy in October 2000, which could also be traced back to the Provisional IRA and which barely registered on the political agenda, the McCartney murder caused a storm of protest. The traction occurred precisely because the 2005 variant of IRA machismo so revolted the republican movement's core constituency. A self-styled 'investigation' by the IRA resulted in the expulsion of three members for conduct unbecoming. Whether the results of that 'investigation' will be passed over to the police or to 'people in authority' to use Sinn Féin's recondite formulation, in order to provide the McCartney family with justice its leadership says is an imperative, is another matter entirely.

The point here is that pleading justification for abuse blurs the lines of responsibility for the decision taken to embark on a course of action that cannot be justified. It is this wider truth that makes an inquiry into state actions in the 1980s and their subsequent cover-up exceptionally problematic and subversive of state legitimacy. Unless there is a parallel truth commission process running alongside formal state judicial investigation, in which loyalist and republican political and military leaders are held to account, the result is that the state itself risks facilitating both a distortion of history and a travesty of justice at precisely the same moment as it ratchets up its own contribution to a wider global, self-proclaimed war on terror.

Here we face an intractable paradox. Precisely because in a global war on terror, actions taken by state actors (or those franchised to act on their behalf, such as the independent contractors employed by the US military to run Iraqi prisons) have consequences far beyond the confines of a small arena, the potential for regional destabilisation if democratic norms are departed from is exceptionally high. Yet, any independent inquiry into past abuses that transfers, or has the potential to transfer, responsibility into the wider political and military chain of command serves only to provide the factual basis for a litany of excuses for the contemporary enemies of the state.

As Michael Ignatieff has observed, the 'rule of law is not compromised by emergencies per se, but by the politicised construal of risk to justify measures that are not actually necessary to meet the threat at hand. It is crucial to distinguish threat assessment from moral repulsion, to separate ethical judgement from actuarial estimation of judgement. The fact that terrorism is an attack on the political character of society does not mean that the society's identity or future is in question.'[54] For both Walzer and Ignatieff, the danger to society is based primarily on the fact that political and military establishments depart too easily and too readily from liberal democratic norms on the basis of unsubstantiated risk assessments. The checks on this process are not necessarily rights but transparency and accountability structures. What is required is access to credible information about how and why decisions are taken, an exceptionally difficult process when consent is manufactured through the prism of a politicised corporate media that is largely accepting of official discourse. Political legitimacy requires that values be taken seriously and law critiqued on the basis of whether it is just as well as justified.[55] The derogation of fundamental rights on the grounds of emergency legislation too easily enacted and rarely seriously challenged has profound moral consequences, as the Northern Ireland experience has demonstrated.

As the government moves towards the establishment of an inquiry into the killing of Pat Finucane, it is imperative that the wider issues are adequately debated in order to ensure that the circumstances that led to documented abuse cannot return. The governance of a war on terror is too important an issue to be left to populism. Unless adequate checks and balances are put in place, the danger of a wider erosion of legitimacy and consequential fracturing of society are acute. Northern Ireland did not feature on the political radar in the rest of the United Kingdom, a reality that effectively allowed the corrosive effect of the security policies adopted to weaken the underlying structure. Given the global implications of the current manifestation of a war on terror, such myopia is unsustainable.

Appendix 1

The Walker Report

Headquarters
The Royal Ulster Constabulary
Brooklyn
Knock Road
Belfast BT5 6LE

23 February 1981
To 'C' Department
Chief Superintendents
Superintendents
Chief Inspectors
Inspectors

1. In January 1980 the Chief Constable commissioned a report on the interchange of intelligence between Special Branch and CID and on the staffing and organisation of units in C1(1) in Crime Branch.

2. The following recommendations, which were made in the report, have been approved by the Chief Constable and will be implemented with effect from 1.3.81.

(1) All CID Agents, Sources or Informants who in the past have or are currently in a position to report on:

(a) Subversive Crime
(b) Non-Subversive Crime
should be declared to D/Chief Superintendent C1 and the Regional D/Superintendent on the attached Pro-forma as at Appendix 'B'.

(2) Detailed instructions regarding the handling of these Agents, Sources or Informants, the preparation of the reports and their dissemination are contained in the attached Appendix 'C'.

3. Arrests
All proposals to effect planned arrests must be cleared with Regional Special Branch to ensure that no agents of either RUC or Army are involved. A decision to arrest an agent must only be taken after discussion between Special Branch and CID. If agreement is not possible the matter will be referred to Assistant Chief Constable level. The charging of an agent must be the result of a conscious decision by both Special Branch and CID in which the balance of advantage has been carefully weighed. (Recommendation 5 — para 11).

4. Recruiting of Agents/Sources
CID Officers must be alert to the possibility of recruiting as agents the individuals whom they are interviewing. When the opportunity to recruit such a person arises, Special Branch must be involved at an early stage both in de-briefing and handling the agent. It is also important to ensure that information provided by the person so recruited is handled in such a way that his value as an agent is not put at risk at an early stage. (Recommendation 6 — para 12).

4. Interviews
(1) Interviews are an important source of intelligence. Even if the individual is not prepared to talk about his own activities for fear of incriminating himself, he may well be prepared to give valuable intelligence about the activities of others.

The process of persuading an individual to talk often requires patience and there may be a temptation for a busy CID Officer to end an interview with someone who is clearly not going to incriminate himself. Even when an admission has been obtained, an individual may be able to give other valuable intelligence. It is imperative that CID Officers seize every opportunity to acquire intelligence on subversive organisations. To this end interviews will be conducted by Officers who are well informed about the individual in custody and supported by those best able to direct the questioning and follow up the intelligence obtained. It is vitally essential that in this area the closest co-operation exist between Special Branch and CID. (Recommendation 7 — para 13).

(2) The following rules will be adopted for interviews:
(a) CID Officers must always be aware of the possibility of obtaining intelligence in addition to admissions. The exploitation of these opportunities requires Special Branch Officers as well as CIU and Collators to support interviews at Regional and Divisional level.
(b) If a CID Officer concludes that a person being interviewed is not going to make an admission but may have intelligence of value, he will arrange for the interview to be taken over by Special Branch.
(c) When a person in custody has made an admission or admissions to CID and the CID Officer feels that that person may have intelligence of value it is desirable that Special Branch be given an opportunity to question such person. In those circumstances CID, on completion of questioning, should prefer charges and, where possible, arrange the Court in such a way that a reasonable period will elapse between charging and appearance in Court to enable Special Branch to question the person concerned for intelligence purposes.

5. Intelligence Briefs
Records should show when intelligence from interviews is handed over by CID. The originator of an intelligence folder will show in his records when intelligence from an interview is received (including nil returns when the interviewee refused to talk) in order that delays in producing reports can be taken up with the CID Officers concerned. (Recommendation 9 — para 18).

6. SB Intelligence — Forms 5/56
Special Branch Officers have been instructed to record as much intelligence as possible on Forms 5/56 passed to CIS.

7. D/Chief Superintendent C1 — Maintenance of index
D/Chief superintendent C1 will maintain an index of the main informants. He will seek from CID Officers a declaration of areas of criminal activity covered by their informants. This survey should be

concluded as quickly as possible. To enable him to exercise better control of this area he needs to know the name of every casual contact or informant of CID Officers. He should establish a procedure for securing these declarations and maintain a secure index in his office for holding the identity of informants. To this end each CID Officer is now required to indicate the contacts he has with the criminal fraternity and the nature of the criminal activity whether 'ordinary' crime or subversive crime upon which his source can supply information. The survey will be carried out immediately by Regional CID Superintendents and a consolidated return forwarded, by hand, to D/Chief Superintendent C1. These returns will be made by each CID Officer completing the pro-forma attached — Appendix 'B'. (Recommendations 13 & 14 — paras 23 & 25).

8. Causal contacts — Collators records

Many Police Officers have in the course of their duties established a wide range of trusted contacts throughout the community whom they may use during enquires of a confidential nature including investigations into crime. Other Police Officers are unlikely to be aware of these contacts and potentially valuable assistance may be lost. Collators will indicate on street and premises location cards the names of the Police Officer(s) having such contacts. Such location cards will show only the name of the street or area and the name of the Police Officer having the contact. Other Police Officers seeking assistance should be referred to the Police Office concerned. No reference as to the identity of the contact will be made on these records. (Recommendation 15 — para 26).

9. Regional Criminal Intelligence Units

All reports by CID of interviews with a subversive connection will be passed direct to CIUs. It is no longer necessary for CIU to maintain the vehicle indices nor should they carry out the basic research into weapons and explosives but rely on DRC and WEIU. DRC or WEIU, as appropriate, will issue to CIUs, on a regular basis, copies of their charts on weapon use. CIUs will receive ICS charts of subversive groups. The Enquiry Bureau in Belfast will be amalgamated with the CIU, Belfast Region. (Recommendation 19–23 inclusive — paras 36–40 respectively).

10. SB Intelligence Briefs for HQ Crime Squad

Special Branch intelligence briefs for Headquarters Crime Squad will now be prepared by ICS. This must be done in a way that provides CID with the information in such detail as is possible, bearing in mind the need to protect sources. When intelligence briefs have been produced it is clearly important that Special Branch Officers involved should, whenever possible, discuss them with the CID Officers who will be conducting the interviews. (Recommendation 25 — para 46).

11. Transfer of WEIU to Special Branch

WEIU with effect from 1 September 1980 was transferred to Special Branch. Any CID requirement on WEIU should be put to Superintendent E3. (Recommendation 28 — para 54).

12. Transfer of DRC to Special Branch

DRC with effect from 1 September 1980 was transferred to Special Branch
(E3). (Recommendation 34 — para 64).

13. Responsibilities D/Superintendent C1(1)

Consequent on the transfer of ICS, WEIU and DRC, the following units — CIS, CIU, Collator and MO — will form a single coherent grouping solely concerned with criminal intelligence. The responsibility of the Superintendent C1 (1) will be:

(a) To ensure that there is an effective interchange of intelligence between Special Branch and CID.
In this he will work very closely with Superintendent E3 Special Branch to see that CID requirements are met by Special Branch.

(1) To develop the criminal intelligence system. This will involve him in regular visits to CIUs and Collators offices; discussions with Divisional and Sub-Divisional Commanders to secure their full support of the system and their co-operation in replacing unsuitable collators.

(2) To ensure that the Criminal Intelligence System is meeting the requirements of CID. (Recommendation 36 — para 66).

14. Special Branch & CID Co-operation

Co-operation between Special Branch and CID should be a matter of conscious policy at all levels. Efforts must be made to develop trusted relationships and maximum liaison. Senior Officers must be prepared to take a firm line where poor relationships are interfering with the efficient conduct of business, even if this entails the transfer of staff who insist on conducting business their own way to the detriment of the overall objectives of the Force.

15. Force Order Ref C352/70 under the same heading dated 8.9.80 is cancelled and should be destroyed

16. All officers under your command should be fully acquainted with these instructions.

J A Whiteside

Assistant Chief Constable 'C'

Copies to:
Chief Constable
Deputy Chief Constable
All Assistant Chief Constables
All Divisional Commanders
All Collators and Field Liaison Officers

SUBJECT: INTERCHANGE OF INTELLIGENCE BETWEEN SPECIAL BRANCH AND CID

1. It was necessary to review the instructions contained in Paragraph 2 of this office's C352/70 dated 8.9.80 and in particular Paragraph 2(ii)C so that the recommendations contained in the above report and approved by the Chief Constable may be fully implemented.

2. Apart from the establishment of a system of reporting information regarding non-subversive crime, the other main purpose of the Report was to ensure that the fullest possible consultation and co-operation exists between SB and CID with regard to subversive crime.

3. These instructions are designed to set out the procedures for reporting on each type of crime, i.e. Subversive and Non-Subversive.

SUBVERSIVE CRIME:

4. The following directions have been approved and will be implemented forthwith except where otherwise stated:

5. All past and current CID agents and sources which have or are supplying intelligence of a subversive nature should be declared on the appropriate pro-forma to The D/Chief Superintendent, C1 and to The Regional CID Superintendent (copies to each by Hand under TOP SECRET cover).

6. The following ground rules will be adopted for agent handling:
(a) An agent or source reporting on subversive organisations should be handled by Special Branch.
(b) If (a) is not possible the agent should be handled and reported on jointly by CID and SB, even though the latter's role be purely advisory.
(c) All intelligence obtained relating to subversives or subversive crime will be reported on Form SB 50 — in the case of joint handling as outlined at (b) above with co-located SB.

7. Were 6(b) is applicable extra copies will be forwarded to:
(1) D/Chief Superintendent, C1
(2) D/Superintendent, C1(1)
(3) The Regional CID D/Superintendent I/c of Officer of origin and
(4) The person i/c of the office of the CID Officer of origin.

8. When Form SB 50 is used for reporting on subversives as in the case of 6(a), (b) above the preparation, handling and passage of these documents will be the responsibility of Special Branch including that of copies to CID as listed above.

9. There are two points to be stressed in relation to the reporting of subversive intelligence:

(1) When Form SB 50 is used rather than a CID 50 and the preparation, handling and passage of these documents is vested in Special Branch these factors alone should assist both Departments in ensuring full co-operation and consultation at the various levels.

(2) It will be unnecessary for CID to undertake the very involved work

in the preparation, handling and passage of these classified documents and avoid the setting up of another channel (apart from SB) of reporting on subversives which would have had the reverse effect to that intended.

10. Supervisory ranks will be responsible for the full implementation of these directions. Any difficulties which may arise should immediately be brought to the attention of Chief Superintendent C1 through the normal chain of Command.

NON-SUBVERSIVE CRIME:

11. Form CID 50 will be used by CID personnel for reporting on clearly non-subversive crime. Dissemination as listed on the form or at the discretion of the CID Officer in charge.

12. Where a report contains both elements, i.e. subversive and non-subversive or where the persons involved are suspected or known to have a previous subversive trace, form SB 50 should be used and disseminated accordingly by agreement with co-located SB.

13. Ultra Sensitive Intelligence touching on Internal Security Intelligence in this category which is clearly of a highly sensitive nature will be handled and disseminated with discretion by the Officer of Origin.

14. It will be the responsibility of all personnel who are furnished with copies of Form SB 50 and/or CID 50s, to make provisions for their proper security. Such documents should not be left lying around when not in use and should not be photocopied in whole or in part without the authority of the officer in charge.

15. The attention of all personnel is drawn to the instructions contained in the Restricted Memo 13/75 dated 25.9.1975 and headed 'Security of Documents' issued to all Chief Officers, Chief Superintendents, Chief Inspector, Inspectors and persons I/c of Stations and also this office directions dated 29.10.80 issued to C1 personnel.

These should be attached to this directive and used extensively for instructional purposes within this Department.

Informant Reference No — Certain regular informants will be allocated a reference number at Headquarters. This number will be used by Officer of Origin on all CID 50 reports emanating from that particular informant.

Casual Contact Identification — A casual contact should be identified by the Officer of Origin by means of an alias or nickname and this should be used in all subsequent reports emanating from that particular informant. Should a casual contact become a 'regular' contact they should be considered for 'registration' at Headquarters.

PART 1
Assessment Codes

A–F relates to the informant only
A — Completely reliable.
B — Usually reliable.
C — Fairly reliable.
D — Not usually reliable.
E — Unreliable.
F — Reliability unknown.

1–6 relates to the information supplied only
1. Absolutely accurate — confirmed by an independent source.
2. Probably true.
3. Possibly true
4. Doubtful.
5. Improbable.
6. Impossible to assess accuracy.

Circumstances in which informant obtained information

Indicates whether he gained it personally or by hearsay or other method.

Degree of Consciousness of informant

Indicates his placing within a group — e.g. Part of a criminal group engaged in Robberies, Burglary, Theft, Handling etc.

High Medium Low

Indicates Handlers overall assessment of informants and information.

Comment by Originator

The originator can recommend the level of dissemination or make any other comments.

Comment of Submitting Officer

Where appropriate the officer in charge Sub-Division/Division/ Region indicate the action taken or directed.

The Cory Report Conclusions

The basic requirements for a public inquiry
1.294 When I speak of a public inquiry, I take that term to encompass certain essential characteristics. They would include the following:-

An independent commissioner or panel of commissioners.

The tribunal should have full power to subpoena witnesses and documents together with all the powers usually exercised by a commissioner in a public inquiry.

The tribunal should select its own counsel who should have all the powers usually associated with counsel appointed to act for a commission or tribunal of public inquiry.

The tribunal should also be empowered to engage investigators who might be police officers or retired police officers to carry out such investigative or other tasks as may be deemed essential to the work of the tribunal.

The hearings, to the extent possible, should be held in public.

The findings and recommendations of the Commissioners should be in writing and made public.

The importance and necessity of holding a public inquiry in this case

1.295 During the Weston Park negotiations, which were an integral part of the implementation of the Good Friday Accord, six cases were selected to be reviewed to determine whether a public inquiry should be held with regard to any of them.

1.296 The Finucane case was specifically chosen as one of the six cases to be reviewed to determine if there was sufficient evidence of collusion to warrant the directing of a public inquiry. In light of this provision in the original agreement, the failure to hold a public inquiry as quickly as it is reasonably possible to do so could be seen as a denial of that agreement, which appears to have been an important and integral part of the peace process. The failure to do so could be seen as a cynical breach of faith which could have unfortunate consequences for the peace accord.

1.297 Further, if as I have found, there is evidence which could be found to constitute collusion then the community at large would, undoubtedly, like to see the issue resolved quickly. This is essential if the public confidence in the police, the army and the administration of justice is to be restored. In this case only a public inquiry will suffice. Without public scrutiny doubts based solely on myth and suspicion will linger long, fester and spread their malignant infection throughout the Northern Ireland community.

1.298 The Attorney General has the difficult and onerous official duty to consider and decide whether prosecutions will have to be brought in light of the further evidence which has been brought to light. If it is determined that prosecutions are to proceed then the public inquiry would in all probability have to be postponed, since it is extremely difficult to hold a public inquiry at the same time as a prosecution. This would be a bitter disappointment to the Finucane family and a large segment of the community. It is a difficult decision that only the Attorney General can make. If the evidence makes it apparent that an individual has committed an offence then as a rule there should be a prosecution. Society must be assured that those who commit a crime will be prosecuted and if found guilty punished.

1.299 If criminal prosecutions are to proceed the practical effect might be to delay the public inquiry for at least two years. The Finucane family will be devastated. A large part of the Northern Ireland community will be frustrated. Myths and misconceptions will proliferate and hopes of peace and understanding will be eroded. This may be one of the rare situations where a public inquiry will be of greater benefit to a community than prosecutions. If, for example, the person to be prosecuted is a member of the military then military discipline resulting in loss of rank and benefits may be a far greater punishment and have a far greater deterrent effect than a prosecution.

1.300 If this public inquiry is to proceed and if it is to achieve the benefits of determining the flaws in the system and suggesting the required remedy, and if it is to restore public confidence in the army, the police and the judicial system, it should be held as quickly as possible.

1.301 There are other factors that will have to be considered. For example it cannot be forgotten that Patrick Finucane was murdered over 14 years ago. Important potential witnesses such as Brian Nelson and William Stobie have died or been murdered. Memories are fading fast. In light of my finding that there is sufficient evidence of collusion to warrant a public inquiry the community might prefer a public inquiry over a prosecution even if it means that some witnesses must receive exemption from prosecution. The difficult decision to be made by the Attorney General will require a careful and sensitive balancing of all the relevant factors.

1.302 Concerns may be raised regarding the costs and time involved in holding public inquiries. My response to that is threefold:

1. If public confidence is to be restored in public institutions then in some circumstances such as those presented in this case a public inquiry is the only means of achieving that goal.

2. The original agreement contemplated that a public inquiry would be held if the requisite conditions had been met. That there is evidence which could constitute collusion has been established in this inquiry. Thus, in this case, the requisite condition has been met.

3. Time and costs can be reasonably controlled. For example, a maximum allowance could be set for counsel appearing for every party granted standing. That maximum amount should only be varied in extraordinary circumstances duly approved by a court on special application.

Counsel and the Commissioner or Commissioners could undertake to devote their full time to the inquiry until it is completed.

If the Commissioner found that the actions of a counsel were unnecessarily and improperly delaying the proceedings the costs of that delay could be assessed against that counsel or his or her client.

1.303 These are simply suggestions for controlling the unnecessary expenditure of public funds. Obviously there are many variations that could be played upon the important theme of cost reduction of public inquiries. If implemented, they could reduce the burden on the public purse and lead to greater harmony and fewer discordant notes in the inquiry process.

1.304 The Good Friday Accord and the Weston Park Agreement, which set out the selected cases as an integral part of the Accord, must have been taken by both Governments to be a significant step in the peace process. Six cases were chosen and the Agreement was negotiated and entered into on the basis that, if evidence which could constitute collusion was found, a public inquiry would be held. In those cases where such evidence has been found, the holding of a public inquiry as quickly as is reasonably possible is a small price to pay for a lasting peace.

1.305 At the time of the Agreement, the parties would have had in mind a public inquiry as that term was known in 2001. Yet all reasonable people would agree that an inquiry should proceed as expeditiously and economically as possible. They are not designed, and should not be considered, as a means of enriching the legal profession. No reasonable person could object to strictures being placed on the inquiry to ensure these goals. These strictures would benefit all.

Appendix 3
Stevens 3 Conclusions

4.1 My third Enquiry began on 19th April 1999. It has, in conjunction with my two previous Enquiries, been the largest investigation undertaken in the United Kingdom. During the course of these three Enquiries 9,256 statements have been taken, 10,391 documents recorded (totalling over 1 million pages) and 16,194 exhibits seized.

4.2 This has led to 144 arrests. So far 94 persons have been convicted. To date 57 separate reports have been submitted to the Director of Public Prosecutions (NI) for his direction. These reports contain the detail of my three Enquiries.

4.3 My recommendations cover the operation of all the security forces in Northern Ireland. They should not be seen in isolation. There have been a number of other reports published in the intervening years since my first Enquiry. The Army undertook a review of their agent handling operations after my first Enquiry had uncovered the criminality of the Army's agent, Brian Nelson. This resulted in the Blelloch report, which established specific guidelines for such operations. More recent reports include the Patten report (1999) on the future of policing in Northern Ireland, the Police Ombudsman for Northern Ireland report on the Omagh bombing (2001) and the report by Her Majesty's Inspectorate of Constabulary into the Police Service of Northern Ireland Special Branch (2002). My recommendations complement and support those contained in them.

4.4 The recommendations arising from my first report and the Blelloch report, together with the recommendations of this report, should be independently reviewed and audited within an agreed time frame.

4.5 My recommendations draw on the information uncovered by my three Enquiries, carried out over the past fourteen years. In most cases the facts have been clearly established; in others the evidence is contradictory and therefore incapable of resolution.

4.6 I have uncovered enough evidence to lead me to believe that the murders of Patrick Finucane and Brian Adam Lambert could have been prevented. I also believe that the RUC investigation of Patrick Finucane's murder should have resulted in the early arrest and detection of his killers.

4.7 I conclude there was collusion in both murders and the circumstances surrounding them. Collusion is evidenced in many ways. This ranges from the wilful failure to keep records, the absence of accountability, the withholding of intelligence and evidence, through to the extreme of agents being involved in murder.

4.8 The failure to keep records or the existence of contradictory accounts can often be perceived as evidence of concealment or malpractice. It limits the opportunity to rebut serious allegations. The absence of accountability allows the acts or omissions of individuals to go undetected. The withholding of information impedes the prevention of crime and the arrest of suspects. The unlawful involvement of agents in murder implies that the security forces sanction killings.

4.9 My three Enquiries have found all these elements of collusion to be present. The co-ordination, dissemination and sharing of intelligence were poor. Informants and agents were allowed to operate without effective control and to participate in terrorist crimes. Nationalists were known to be targeted but were not properly warned or protected. Crucial information was withheld from Senior Investigating Officers. Important evidence was neither exploited nor preserved.

4.10 My enquiries with regard to satisfying the test for prosecution in relation to possible offences arising out of these matters are continuing.

Appendix 4

Statement from the Secretary of State on Finucane Inquiry

23 SEPTEMBER 2004

As I said when publishing Justice Cory's reports, the Government is determined that where there are allegations of collusion the truth should emerge. The Government has consistently made clear that in the case of the murder of Patrick Finucane, as well as in the other cases investigated by Justice Cory, it stands by the commitment made at Weston Park.

However, in the Finucane case, an individual was being prosecuted for the murder. The police investigation by Sir John Stevens and his team continued; and it was not possible to say whether further prosecutions might follow. For that reason, the Government committed to set out the way ahead at the conclusion of prosecutions.

The prosecution of Ken Barrett has now been completed, with Barrett sentenced to life imprisonment for the murder of Patrick Finucane. It is still possible that further prosecutions might result from the Stevens investigation into the murder of Patrick Finucane. Nevertheless, with the Barrett trial now concluded, and following consultation with the Attorney General, who is responsible for the prosecutorial process, the Government has considered carefully the case for proceeding to an inquiry. In doing so, the Government has taken into account the exceptional concern about this case. Against that background, the Government has concluded that steps should now be taken to enable the establishment of an inquiry into the death of Patrick Finucane.

As in any inquiry, the tribunal will be tasked with uncovering the full facts of what happened, and will be given all of the powers and resources necessary to fulfil that task. In order that the inquiry can take place speedily and effectively and in a way that takes into account the public interest, including the requirements of national security, it will be necessary to hold the inquiry on the basis of new legislation which will be introduced shortly.

Appendix 5

The Inquiries Bill
Proposed Provisions

House of Lords, HL Bill 7, 25 November 2004

1 Power to establish inquiry

(1) A Minister may cause an inquiry to be held under this Act in relation to a case where it appears to him that—

(a) particular events have caused, or are capable of causing, public concern, or

(b) there is public concern that particular events may have occurred.

(2) In this Act "Minister" means—

(a) a United Kingdom Minister;

(b) the Scottish Ministers;

(c) a Northern Ireland Minister;

and references to a Minister also include references to the National Assembly for Wales.

(3) References in this Act to an inquiry, except where the context requires otherwise, are to an inquiry under this Act.

2 No determination of liability

(1) An inquiry panel is not to rule on, and has no power to determine, any person's civil or criminal liability.

(2) But an inquiry panel is not to be inhibited in the discharge of its functions by any likelihood of liability being inferred from facts that it determines or recommendations that it makes.

4 Appointment of inquiry panel

(1) Each member of an inquiry panel is to be appointed by the Minister by an instrument in writing.

(2) The instrument appointing the chairman must state that the inquiry is to be held under this Act.

5 Setting-up date and terms of reference

(1) In the instrument under section 4 appointing the chairman, or by a notice given to him within a reasonable time afterwards, the Minister must—

(a) specify the date that is to be the setting-up date for the purposes of this Act; and

(b) before that date—

(i) set out the terms of reference of the inquiry;

(ii) state whether or not the Minister proposes to appoint other members to the inquiry panel, and if so how many.

(2) An inquiry must not begin considering evidence before the setting-up date.

(3) Functions conferred by this Act on an inquiry panel, or a member of an inquiry panel, are exercisable only within the inquiry's terms of reference.

(4) In this Act "terms of reference", in relation to an inquiry under this Act, means—

(a) the matters to which the inquiry relates;

(b) any particular matters as to which the inquiry panel is to determine the facts;

(c) whether the inquiry panel is to make recommendations;

(d) any other matters relating to the scope of the inquiry that the Minister may specify.

12 Power to suspend inquiry

(1) The Minister may at any time, by notice to the chairman, suspend an inquiry for such period as appears to him to be necessary to allow for—

(a) the completion of any other investigation relating to any of the matters to which the inquiry relates, or

(b) the determination of any civil or criminal proceedings (including proceedings before a disciplinary tribunal) arising out of any of those matters.

(2) The power conferred by subsection (1) may be exercised whether or not the investigation or proceedings have begun.

(3) A notice under subsection (1) may suspend the inquiry until a specified day, until the happening of a specified event or until the giving by the Minister of a further notice to the chairman.

(4) A member of an inquiry panel may not exercise the powers conferred by this Act during any period of suspension; but the duties imposed on a member of an inquiry panel by section 8(3) and (4) continue during any such period.

(5) In this section "period of suspension" means the period beginning with the receipt by the chairman of the notice under subsection (1) and ending with whichever of the following is applicable—

(a) the day referred to in subsection (3);

(b) the happening of the event referred to in that subsection;

(c) the receipt by the chairman of the further notice under that subsection.

17 Restrictions on public access etc.

(1) Restrictions may, in accordance with this section, be imposed on—

(a) attendance at an inquiry, or at any particular part of an inquiry;

(b) disclosure or publication of any evidence or documents given, produced or provided to an inquiry.

(2) Restrictions may be imposed in either or both of the following ways—

(a) by being specified in a notice (a "restriction notice") given by the Minister to the chairman at any time before the end of the inquiry;

(b) by being specified in an order (a "restriction order") made by the chairman during the course of the inquiry.

(3) A restriction notice or restriction order must specify only such restrictions—
(a) as are required by any statutory provision, enforceable Community obligation or rule of law, or
(b) as the Minister or chairman considers to be conducive to the inquiry fulfilling its terms of reference or to be necessary in the public interest, having regard in particular to the matters mentioned in subsection (4).

(4) Those matters are—
(a) the extent to which any restriction on attendance, disclosure or publication might inhibit the allaying of public concern;
(b) any risk of harm or damage that could be avoided or reduced by any such restriction;
(c) any conditions as to confidentiality subject to which a person acquired information that he is to give, or has given, to the inquiry;
(d) the extent to which not imposing any particular restriction would be likely—
(i) to cause delay or to impair the efficiency or effectiveness of the inquiry, or
(ii) otherwise to result in additional cost (whether to public funds or to witnesses or others).

(5) In subsection (4)(b) "harm or damage" includes in particular—
(a) death or injury;
(b) damage to national security or international relations;
(c) damage to the economic interests of the United Kingdom or of any part of the United Kingdom;
(d) damage caused by disclosure of commercially sensitive information.

(6) Subject to any restrictions imposed by a restriction notice or restriction order, the chairman must take such steps as he considers reasonable to secure that members of the public (including reporters) are able—
(a) to attend the inquiry or to see and hear a simultaneous transmission of proceedings at the inquiry;
(b) to obtain or to view a record of evidence and documents given, produced or provided to the inquiry.

(7) No recording or broadcast of proceedings at an inquiry may be made except—
(a) at the request of the chairman, or
(b) with the permission of the chairman and in accordance with any terms on which permission is given. Any such request or permission must be framed so as not to enable a person to see or hear by means of a recording or broadcast anything that he is prohibited by a restriction notice from seeing or hearing.

18 Further provisions about restriction notices and orders

(1) Restrictions specified in a restriction notice have effect in addition to any already specified, whether in an earlier restriction notice or in a restriction order.

(2) Restrictions specified in a restriction order have effect in addition to any already specified, whether in an earlier restriction order or in a restriction notice.

(3) The Minister may vary or revoke a restriction notice by giving a further notice to the chairman at any time before the end of the inquiry.

(4) The chairman may vary or revoke a restriction order by making a further order during the course of the inquiry.

(5) Restrictions imposed under section 17 on disclosure or publication of evidence or documents continue in force indefinitely, unless—
(a) under the terms of the relevant notice or order the restrictions expire at the end of the inquiry, or at some other time, or
(b) the relevant notice or order is varied or revoked under subsection (3), (4) or (7).
This is subject to subsection (6).

(6) In so far as the restrictions apply in relation to information—
(a) given to or created by an inquiry, and
(b) kept (in any form) after the end of the inquiry by or on behalf of a Minister, they cease to have effect at the end of the period of thirty years following the date on which the inquiry came to an end.

(7) After the end of an inquiry the Minister may, by a notice published in a way that he considers suitable, vary or revoke a restriction notice or restriction order containing restrictions on disclosure or publication that are still in force.

(8) In this section "restriction notice" and "restriction order" have the meaning given by section 17(2).

23 Publication of reports

(1) It is the duty of the Minister, or the chairman if subsection (2) applies, to arrange for reports of an inquiry to be published.

(2) This subsection applies if—
(a) the Minister notifies the chairman before the setting-up date that the chairman is to have responsibility for arranging publication, or
(b) at any time after that date the chairman, on being invited to do so by the Minister, accepts responsibility for arranging publication.

(3) Subject to subsection (4), a report of an inquiry must be published in full.

(4) The person whose duty it is to arrange for a report to be published may withhold material in the report from publication to such extent—
(a) as is required by any statutory provision, enforceable Community obligation or rule of law, or
(b) as the person considers to be necessary in the public interest, having regard in particular to the matters mentioned in subsection (5).

(5) Those matters are—
(a) the extent to which withholding material might inhibit the allaying of public concern;
(b) any risk of harm or damage that could be avoided or reduced by withholding any material;
(c) any conditions as to confidentiality subject to which a person acquired information that he has given to the inquiry.

(6) In subsection (5)(b) "harm or damage" includes in particular—
(a) death or injury;
(b) damage to national security or international relations;
(c) damage to the economic interests of the United Kingdom or of any part of the United Kingdom;
(d) damage caused by disclosure of commercially sensitive information.

(7) In this section "report" includes an interim report.

Notes

Chapter 1 (pp. 1–19)

1. 'Policing the Police', *Insight*, 17 April 2001.
2. The Sentence Review Board has maintained that Barrett is not eligible for release on the grounds that he is serving his sentence in an English jail. Given that Barrett was transferred to England in order to ensure his safety, the rationale seems tendentious. Barrett's lawyers are appealing the decision.
3. The legislation was published on 25 November 2004 as the Inquiries Bill. Under Section 17 restrictions can be placed on either 'attendance' or 'disclosure or publication of any evidence or documents given, produced, or provided to an inquiry'. These restrictions can be either mandated by the chair of the inquiry or by a relevant minister 'at any time before the end of the inquiry'. Specifically the Bill allows for restrictions on grounds of 'damage to national security'. See Inquiries Bill, 25 November 2004, HMSO.
4. *Cory Collusion Inquiry Report*, HC470, 1 April 2004, London: HMSO. Alongside the Finucane case, Cory investigated three other contentious murders in Northern Ireland: Robert Hamill, who was set upon by a loyalist mob in a late-night fracas in Portadown on 27 April 1997; Billy Wright, the incarcerated leader of the Loyalist Volunteer Force, in the high-security Maze Prison on 27 December 1997; and Rosemary Nelson, a prominent solicitor, in Lurgan on 15 March 1999. In all four cases, Justice Cory adjudicated that there was compelling evidence to merit holding public inquiries. The British government ceded inquiries into the Wright and Hamill cases immediately on publication of the reports on 1 April 2004. Plans to hold the inquiry into Rosemary Nelson's killing began after the formal end to an external investigation into the murder in 2004.
5. Liam Clarke, 'Cory will offer little comfort to families seeking the truth', *Sunday Times*, 4 April 2004.
6. *Stevens Inquiry 3*, p. 15.
7. Ibid., p. 16.
8. Ibid., p. 16.
9. *Cory Report*, p. 18.
10. *Cory Report*, pp. 21–2.
11. For an indication of how the intelligence community operated, see *Report of the Inquiry into the Circumstances Surrounding the Death of Dr David Kelly C.M.G. (The Hutton Report)*, HC247, 28 January 2004. Full text available online at *http://the-hutton-inquiry.org.uk/content/rulings.htm*. See also *Review of Intelligence on Weapons of Mass Destruction (The Butler Report)*, HC898, 27 October 2004. Full text available online at *http://www.butlerreview.org.uk/report*.
12. See Anthony McIntyre, 'Modern Irish Republicanism and the Belfast Agreement: Chickens Coming Home to Roost or Turkeys Voting for Christmas', in Rick

Wilford (ed.), *Aspects of the Belfast Agreement* (Oxford 2001). See also Anthony McIntyre, 'Modern Irish Republicanism: The Product of British State Strategies', *Irish Political Studies*, 10 (1995), 97–122.

13. 'Policing the Police', *Insight*, 17 April 2001.

14. Quoted in Jack Holland, *Phoenix, Policing the Shadows* (London 1996), p. 76. Phoenix was one of the senior intelligence officials aboard a helicopter that crashed on the Mull of Kintyre in June 1994 killing all crew and passengers.

15. Evidence in the trial of Brian Nelson, January 1992, cited in Nicholas Davies, *Dead Men Talking* (Edinburgh 2004), p. 144.

16. This blurring was apparent from the very beginning of the Troubles. See Colm Campbell and Ita Connolly, 'A Model for the "War Against Terrorism"? Military Intervention in Northern Ireland and the 1970 Falls Curfew', *Journal of Law and Society*, vol. 30, no. 3, September 2003. In their excavation of the Falls Curfew, which they conclude was 'probably unlawful', Campbell and Connolly note 'a fracturing of administrative, legal and political authority'. The authors explicitly suggest that 'as recent controversy over agent-handling indicates, this problem of divided and dysfunctional Northern Ireland control mechanisms may not have been solved'.

17. Two of Pat Finucane's brothers were members of the IRA. For a portrait, which is based on interviews with the family, see the useful, but flawed, Kevin Toolis, *Rebel Hearts, Journeys Within the IRA's Soul* (London 1995), pp. 84–191.

18. The process was so ingrained that it prompted an exceptionally hostile report from the UN Special Rapporteur on the Protection of Judges and Lawyers in 2002. The author of that report, Param Cumaraswamy, re-entered the Northern Ireland maelstrom in the aftermath of the 2004 Cory Report with his observation that 'justice delayed is justice denied'. See Rachel Andrews, 'Former top UN official slams Finucane inquiry delay', *Sunday Tribune*, 4 April 2004.

19. *Hansard*, 17 January 1989, col. 508.

20. *Cory Report*, citing SB 20836, p. 92.

21. *Cory Report*, p. 92.

22. *Hansard*, 17 January 1989, col. 511.

23. Only Barrett and Stobie (on conspiracy) were charged with involvement in the Finucane murder. Although evidence existed from Stobie (then a Special Branch informer) as early as 1990 that Nelson was implicated, he did not face charges before his death in 2003. Stobie was gunned down by associates soon after his trial collapsed in December 2001. Jim Spence, although named in documentation, not least by Barrett, is not the subject of police investigation by Stevens or the Police Service of Northern Ireland.

24. 'A Licence to Murder', *Panorama*, 19 June 2002. See also the pivotal documentary 'The Dirty War', also broadcast by the *Panorama* series on 8 June 1992, three months after Brian Nelson, the army's primary source of information on loyalist targeting, was convicted of ten counts of conspiracy to murder. As noted, despite the evidence linking him to the Finucane killing, he was not charged with this offence.

25. British Irish Rights Watch, *Deadly Intelligence: State Involvement in Loyalist Murder in Northern Ireland* (London 1999).

26. 'A Licence to Murder', *Panorama*, 19 June 2002.

27. *Cory Report*, pp. 51–3.

28. *Cory Report*, pp. 46–7

29. *Cory Report*, p. 93.

30. 'A Licence to Murder', *Panorama*, 19 June 2002.

31. 'Justice on Trial', *Insight*, 7 December 2001.

32. *Cory Report*, pp. 98–9.

33. All quotations from Dan Keenan, 'SF, SDLP criticise Finucane inquiry delay', *Irish Times*, 2 April 2004.

34. Frank Millar, 'Government in London distances itself from Cory Report', *Irish Times*, 2 April 2004.

35. It is a deeply dispiriting reality that the question of who constitutes a victim and therefore merits sympathy is a deeply contested one in Northern Ireland. For a typology see Bill Rolston, *Unfinished Business: State Killings and the Quest for Truth* (Belfast 2000), p. xi. See also Kieran McEvoy and Ruth Jamieson, 'State Crime by Proxy and Juridical Othering', *British Journal of Criminology* (2005 forthcoming). This dynamic still afflicts Northern Irish society, see Colin Knox, 'See No Evil, Hear No Evil', *British Journal of Criminology* 42 (2002), pp. 164–85 and Paul Dixon, 'Political Skills or Lying and Manipulation? The Choreography of the Northern Ireland Peace Process', *Political Studies*, 50 (2002), pp. 725–41.

36. Confidential source. It is not this book's design to populate its content with unsourced quotations. This, however, is an important admission from a serving intelligence officer that should be brought to the public domain.

37. Murray Edelman, *The Politics of Symbolism* (Chicago 1964).

38. For a full discussion of the implications of this extraordinary state of affairs, see Chapter 6 below.

39. A similar imperative governed previous investigations, including those conducted by John Stalker into allegations of shoot to kill in the 1980s. Within the RUC/PSNI that process continued through into the late 1990s, even after the establishment of the office of the Police Ombudsman.

40. *Cory Report*, p. 96, citing Document no. E2/8621-G2(CI), dated September 1990.

41. 'The Dirty War', *Panorama*, 8 June 1992.

42. Ibid.

43. *Cory Report*, p. 96.

44. The alleged activities of 'Stakeknife', the British government's most highly placed agent within the IRA, are discussed in Davies, *Dead Men Talking*, and Greg Harkin and Martin Ingram, *Stakeknife* (Dublin 2004). For a scathing analysis of the Stakeknife controversy, which sees its publication as an attempt to divert attention from the issues raised in the Finucane case, see Martin Dillon, *The Trigger Men* (Edinburgh 2004), pp. 268–76.

45. Jimmy Burns, 'Peace hope hit as police blame IRA for bank robbery', *Financial Times*, 8 January 2005.

46. See Colm Campbell, Fionnuala Ní Aoláin and Colin Harvey, 'The Frontiers of Legal Analysis: Reframing the Transition in Northern Ireland', *Modern Law Review* 66:3 (2003), pp. 317–45.

47. For general discussion see Graham Ellison and A. Mulcahy (eds), 'Policing in Northern Ireland', *Policing and Society* 11 (2001), pp. 3–4.

Chapter 2 (pp. 20–53)

1. In 2000 the government published the *Review of the Criminal Justice System in Northern Ireland*. Full text is available online at *www.nio.gov.uk/mainreport.pdf*. The authors recognised that 'we report at one point of time and as part of a wider political process which continues to develop and will develop further as this report is debated and implemented. The extent to which our proposals should be taken forward in any given scenario is a matter for political judgement, and we express no views on transitional or interim arrangements which may prove necessary as a result' (par. 1.12, p. 4). The terms of reference provided to the Review committee meant that it was designed to offer potential solutions rather than investigate past failings and the report was published with a major caveat: 'We do not express any opinion about the validity of views about past events and wish to stress that where we suggest change, this should not in itself be taken as implying criticism of what has gone before' (par. 1.20, p. 7). For an overview of the political considerations of managing the peace process see Paul Dixon, 'Political Skills or Lying and Manipulation? The Choreography of the Northern Ireland Peace Process', *Political Studies*, 50 (2002), pp. 725–41. For an overview of the moral considerations inherent in the political compromise see Colin Knox, 'See No Evil, Hear No Evil', *British Journal of Criminology* 42 (2002), pp. 164–85.

2. See Kieran McEvoy and Ruth Jamieson, 'State Crime by Proxy and Juridical Othering', *British Journal of Criminology* (2005 forthcoming).

3. See for example Fionnuala Ní Aolain, *The Politics of Force: Conflict Management and State Violence in Northern Ireland* (Belfast 2000); Bill Rolston, *Unfinished Business: State Killings and the Quest for Truth* (Belfast 2000).

4. For a discussion on the perceived necessity among nationalists to change the culture of policing as a consequence of the distortions caused by operating within a 'war' framework, see Robin Wilson, *Order On Policing: Resolving the Impasse Over the Patten Report* (Belfast 2000), p. 4. For a wider appreciation of the issues involved in changing an underlying police culture, see Peter Waddington, 'Police (Canteen) Sub-Culture, An Appreciation', *British Journal of Criminology* 1999, vol. 39, no. 2, pp. 287–309, and Janet Chan, 'Changing Police Culture', *British Journal of Criminology* 1996, vol. 36, no. 1, pp. 109–34.

5. *Disturbances in Northern Ireland: Report of the Committee Appointed by the Governor of Northern Ireland*, Cmnd 532 (Belfast 1969), p. 91.

6. Justin O'Brien, *The Arms Trial* (Dublin 2000), pp. 1–32.

7. Eamon McCann, *War and an Irish Town* (London 1989), p. 99.

8. *Violence and Civil Disturbances in Northern Ireland in 1969: Report of Tribunal of Inquiry (Scarman Report)*, p. 74.

9. Ibid, p. 80.

10. In this regard, it is interesting to note the conclusions of an earlier tribunal under Lord Cameron, who noted that while IRA personnel were active in NICRA, they were not in a dominant enough position to direct its policy. See *Cameron Report*, pp. 53–6.

11. See Justin O'Brien, 'The Arms Trial Revisited', in *The Modern Prince, Charles J. Haughey and the Quest for Power* (Dublin 2002), pp. 25–55, and Justin O'Brien, *The Arms Trial* (Dublin 2000), pp. 214–24.

12. Cabinet Minutes, 16 August 1969, cited in *Committee of Public Accounts, 1968–69/70*, p. 29.

13. For a scathing assessment written from a position sympathetic to the position taken by the Official IRA in the split, see Anonymous, *Fianna Fáil and the IRA* (Dublin undated). See also the work of Henry Patterson, *The Politics of Illusion: A Political History of the IRA* (London 1997), pp. 121–35, and *Ireland Since 1939* (Oxford 2002), pp. 173–80.

14. *Irish Times*, 24 October 1970.

15. See 'Northern Ireland, Text of a Communique and Declaration issued after a meeting held at 10 Downing Street on 19 August 1969', cited in Colm Campbell and Ita Connolly, 'A Model for the "War Against Terrorism"? Military Intervention in Northern Ireland and the 1970 Falls Curfew', *Journal of Law and Society*, vol. 30, no. 3, September 2003, pp. 341–75.

16. Ibid, pp. 350–52.

17. Ibid.

18. BBC, *Panorama*, 6 July 1970, cited in O'Brien, *The Arms Trial*, p. 161. For a discussion of the critical importance of the Falls Road curfew within Northern nationalism, see Paddy Devlin, *Straight Left: An Autobiography* (Belfast 1983), p. 134.

19. *Irish Times*, 13 July 1970.

20. *Irish Times*, 14 July 1970.

21. For a discussion of the legal implications see Ní Aolain, *The Politics of Force*, pp. 38–41.

22. Thomas Hennessey, *A History of Northern Ireland 1920–1996* (Dublin 1997), p. 190.

23. Ministry of Defence Statement, 11 February 1971, cited in J. Bowyer Bell, *The Irish Troubles* (Dublin 1993), p. 197.

24. *Irish Times*, 10 August 1996, cited in David McKittrick, Brian Fenny, Chris Thorton and Seamus Kelters, *Lost Lives* (Edinburgh 2000), p. 80.

25. By the time internment was eventually phased out in 1975, no less than 1,800 were killed.

26. Cited in Hennessey, *A History of Northern Ireland*, p. 195.

27. Ní Aolain, *The Politics of Force*, p. 21.

28. See *Compton Report into Security Force Behaviour in August 1971*, Cmnd 4823, HMSO 1971; *Parker Report into Interrogation Procedures of Suspected Terrorists*, Cmnd 4901, HMSO 1972; *Diplock Report of Commission on New Legal Procedures to Deal with Suspected Terrorists*, Cmnd 5185, HMSO 1972.

29. For a discussion on the moral hazard involved in privileging this form of governance, see Michael Ignatieff, *The Lesser Evil: Political Ethics in an Age of Terror* (Edinburgh 2004).

30. Just as the British government adjusted its position, so too did the IRA, meting out street justice to those who dared to provide information to the security forces. The range of gruesome humiliation ranged from tarring and feathering girls seen with British soldiers to abduction and murder. Summary justice in the form of a bullet in the back of the head was the standard punishment meted out to informers, whose bodies were left on country lanes. For a number of families, the grief was compounded by the fact that the bodies were never found. In one

of the most notorious cases, involving Jean McConville, a mother of ten from west Belfast, more than thirty years elapsed before her body was found on a beach in County Louth. She was eventually buried in October 2003, providing a limited form of closure. The IRA apologised for her killing but its level of genuine remorse has to be discounted given the organisation's suspected role in the abduction of a dissident republican and Special Branch informer in South Armagh in April 2003, six months earlier.

31. Confidential Downing Street Minutes, 1 February 1972, reproduced as Appendix 1 in Don Mullan, *Eyewitness Bloody Sunday* (Dublin 1997).

32. Paul Bew and Gordon Gillespie, *Northern Ireland: A Chronology of the Troubles* (Dublin 1993), p. 44.

33. *Widgery Report*, Conclusion 10, cited in Mullan, *Eyewitness Bloody Sunday*, p. 25. Dublin critically dissected the findings of the initial inquiry in a public document published by the Government Publications Office in 1998. See *Bloody Sunday and the Report of the Widgery Tribunal* (Dublin 1998). The report amplified much of the evidence produced by Mullan. The British government announced a second tribunal of inquiry in 1998, chaired by Lord Saville. It has yet to pronounce its findings but its terms of reference set a cut-off point of the day of the killing, leaving the political implications of Widgery unexamined. In closing submission, Christopher Clarke, counsel for the inquiry, noted that it was impossible to ascertain which soldiers fired the shots and whether there was evidence of pre-planned strategy. He noted that the soldiers' evidence was at times contradictory and that the tribunal would have to assess whether 'various members of the platoon refashioned their evidence to provide retrospective justification for their movements' (p. 2). The advocate notes that the soldiers believed that they were under threat but Clarke notes that the discrepancies in the soldiers' evidence could 'indicate confusion or collusion on his part or the imperfections of the statement-taking process' (pp. 9–10). When discussing claims by the soldiers that they only fired at known targets, Clarke concludes: 'It will be for the Tribunal to determine, as far as it can, how many of these reported sightings are reliable and to form a view of the number, if any, of unidentified gunmen and bombers who were present on the day and of the number of dead or wounded individuals whose names are not known. Soldiers have given evidence of firing at gunmen, nail-bombers and in many cases of their belief that they had hit their targets, none of these civilian gunmen or bombers has ever been identified' (p. 121). See Christopher Clarke, 'Closing Submission', Bloody Sunday Inquiry, 23 November 2004. Full text available online at: *http://www.bloody-sunday-inquiry.org/index2.asp?p=3*. Soldiers interviewed after the counsel to the inquiry gave his closing submission complained bitterly about the way in which they had been treated, see Joshua Rosenburg, 'Bloody Sunday Inquiry Treated IRA Suspects Better Than Us, Say Soliders', *Daily Telegraph*, 24 November 2004. See also Angelique Chrisafis, 'Gaps, Contradictions and the Pain of Truth', *The Guardian*, 24 November 2004.

34. An influential report by a New York-based legal human rights group noted sardonically that 'although paramilitaries were to be presented as "ordinary criminals" they were not to be tried under ordinary criminal law'. See Lawyers'

Committee for Human Rights, *Beyond Collusion: The UK Security Forces and the Murder of Pat Finucane* (New York 2002), p. 2.

35. Following pressure from the European Court of Human Rights, the government ceded the Bennett Commission in 1979, which recommended that detainees should gain access to their solicitors after forty-eight hours and that CCTV cameras should be placed in interrogation suites in order to minimise allegations of abuse. See *Report of the Committee of Inquiry into Police Interrogation Procedures in Northern Ireland*, Cmnd 7497, HMSO 1979 (The Bennett Report).

36. See *Donnelly v. United Kingdom (No. 1)* Applications Nos. 5577/22, 5533/72 43; *Collected Decisions* (1973), 122; *Ireland v. United Kingdom*, 1976 Y.B. ECHR 512. See also Amnesty International, *Report of an Amnesty International Mission to Northern Ireland* (London 1978). Attempts by the British government to counter the negative international publicity backfired when the influential Bennett Report found that in certain cases injuries had been inflicted by the jailers. See *Report of the Committee of Inquiry into Police Interrogation Procedures in Northern Ireland*, Cmnd 7497, HMSO 1979 (The Bennett Report).

37. *An Phoblacht/Republican News*, 1 September 1979.

38. For a discussion of the ideological imperatives governing the first Thatcher administration, see Stuart Hall, 'The Great Moving Right Show', *Marxism Today* (January 1979), pp. 14–20. For Hall, 'the language of law and order is sustained by moralisms ... where the great syntax of "good" versus "evil", of civilised and uncivilised standards, of the choice between anarchy and order constantly divides the world up and classifies it into its appointed stations.' Hall points out that at the heart of the Thatcher experiment was a belief that society was ungovernable without the firm application of the law to instil order. Crucially this was 'harnessed to and, to some extent, legitimated by a popular groundswell below'. If the state was threatened, then only definitive action could save it from itself. This domestic policy imperative set a political context for the justification of extraordinary measures in the battle against the IRA that intensified rather than weakened as the conflict mutated. See Stuart Hall, 'Authoritarian Populism', *New Left Review* 151 (1985), pp. 115–24. I am grateful to Phil Scraton at the School of Law, Queen's University, Belfast, for bringing these references to my attention.

39. 'Dying for Ireland', *Insight*, UTV, 27 February 2001.

40. O'Brien, *The Modern Prince, Charles J. Haughey and the Quest for Power*, p. 79. The prison dispute has spawned a number of excellent works. See David Beresford, *Ten Men Dead* (London 1994); Liam Clarke, *Broadening the Battlefield: The H Blocks and the Rise of Sinn Féin* (Dublin 1987); Richard English, *Armed Struggle* (London 2003), in particular, pp. 187–226; and Ed Maloney, *A Secret History of the IRA* (London 2002), pp. 205–16. There have also been a number of documentaries. The author was the producer of a major film for the *Insight* series for UTV, 'Dying for Ireland', broadcast on the twentieth anniversary of the start of the second hunger strike, on which the account that follows is largely based.

41. 'Dying for Ireland', *Insight*, UTV, 27 February 2001.

42. Ibid.

43. Interview with author, February 2001.

44. The question of responsibility for the ending of the hunger strike still provokes considerable controversy among analysts and within the Republican movement itself. Ed Maloney writes that the secret nature of the discussions between MI6 and the Belfast leadership 'raised dark questions elsewhere in the Provisionals, suggesting that the Belfast leaders would go to any length to end the protest'. See Maloney, *A Secret History*, p. 207. By contrast, Richard English sees strategic guile on behalf of the British government in isolating the hunger strikers as the key determinant. See English, *Armed Struggle*, p. 195.

45. Brendan McFarlane, interview with author, February 2001.

46. Anglo-Irish Summit Communique, 8 December 1980, reprinted in Martin Mansergh (ed.), *The Spirit of the Nation: The Collected Speeches and Statements of Charles J. Haughey 1957–1986* (Cork 1986), p. 406.

47. 'Dying for Ireland', *Insight*, 27 February 2001. In her memoirs, Mrs Thatcher agreed with the Republican movement on the terms of the conflict. 'The IRA and the prisoners were determined to gain control of the prison and had a well-thought-out strategy of doing this by whittling away at the prison regime...[by ensuring through obstruction] that their crimes were political, thus giving the perpetrators a kind of respectability, even nobility. This we could not allow.' See Margaret Thatcher, *The Downing Street Years* (London 1997), p. 390.

48. Interview with author, February 2001.

49. Cited in English, *Armed Struggle*, p. 206.

50. English, *Armed Struggle*, p. 206, emphasis in original.

51. Paul Bew and Gordon Gillespie, *Northern Ireland, A Chronology* (Dublin 1992), p. 135.

52. Ní Aolain, *The Politics of Force*, p. 76.

53. Ibid.

54. McCauley was later to be arrested in Colombia, tried and acquitted of training leftist guerrillas in exchange for weapons.

55. John Stalker, *Stalker* (London 1988), p. 253.

56. Brendan O'Brien, *The Long War* (Dublin 1995), pp. 60–61.

57. Stalker, *Stalker*, p. 55.

58. See Ní Aolain, *The Politics of Force*, pp. 59–64. Ní Aolain remarks that while she 'does not suggest that there is a political text which explicitly gives a green light to active counter-insurgency under new rules of engagement...there was a discernible shift in the empirical patterns of state confrontation with paramilitary actors in the 1980s in Northern Ireland...In legal terms, they illustrate a shifting approach to a permanent emergency situation, which displays unacknowledged low-intensity armed conflict characteristics...In particular, it seems that suspicion or actual membership of a proscribed organisation in Northern Ireland substantially weakens the right to life of those suspected' (pp. 63–4).

59. See Tom McGurk, 'Licenced to Kill', *Sunday Business Post*, 23 June 2002. Citing a security source as evidence, McGurk argues that a revenge motivation for IRA killings was never credible. 'It always smacked of careful organisation and planning...The rationale [for the British security services] was that since they could only fight one side in the war and sooner or later the IRA campaign would provoke a similar loyalist reaction — from the outset they had to become involved

in that loyalist reaction. Since it was all inevitable anyway, the security services should control it and where possible use it for their own purposes in the war against the IRA.'

60. For a scathing assessment of the supergrass system see Amnesty International, *Northern Ireland Killings by the Security Forces and the 'Supergrass' Trials* (London 1988).

61. Following defenestration in the European Court of Human Rights (ECHR) in Strasburg, Britain formally derogated from the International Covenant Civil and Political Rights and the European Convention on Human Rights, citing the pressures placed on the state by an organised terrorist campaign. In a ruling on 29 November 1988 the ECHR found that Britain had violated the rights of an IRA suspect by detaining him without charge. See *Brogan and Others v. the United Kingdom*, Eur. Ct. H.R., Series A, no. 145-B (29 November 1988). Pat Finucane was the solicitor handling the case.

62. Denzil McDaniel, *Enniskillen: The Remembrance Sunday Bombing* (Dublin 1997).

63. This change in policy has provoked bitter debate both within republicanism and among analysts. For competing academic perspectives see English, *Armed Struggle*, pp. 244–60, and Maloney, *A Secret History of the IRA*, pp. 318–25.

64. Address to SDLP annual conference, *Irish News*, 28 November 1988, quoted in English, *Armed Struggle*, p. 240.

65. *Republican News*, 28 June 1984.

66. *Republican News*, 22 November 1984.

67. Maloney, *A Secret History of the IRA*, p. 304. For Maloney, the suspicion within the IRA that the unit was compromised from within was even more destabilising than the loss of experienced operatives (p. 305). Maloney argues that the leader of the unit, Jim Lynagh, represented a visceral form of republicanism, hostile to any attempts to dilute the republican message, and speculates on his likely opposition to the current peace process (p. 311). While the evidence of a leak from the headquarters staff is inconclusive, Maloney argues that putative plans for a split in 1987 left the unit exposed within the organisation and that 'the vertical IRA structures introduced by [Gerry] Adams…combined with the greater political control exercised over operational matters made it easier, not harder, for British intelligence to penetrate the IRA's nerve centres' (p. 317). Indicative of the schism within the republican movement was the fact that the family of Padraig McKearney refused to allow Martin McGuinness to address the oration marking the first anniversary of the killing. See O'Brien, *The Long War*, p. 152.

68. Maloney, *A Secret History*, p. 319.

Chapter 3 (pp. 54–77)

1. See Maloney, *A Secret History*, pp. 329–32; Dillon, *The Dirty War*, and Davies, *Dead Men Talking*, pp. 187–201. Maloney suggests there may have been a leak in west Belfast and across the border in Louth. Dillon argues that the disappearance of McCann and Farrell from Belfast automatically triggered an alert. Davies places, without providing documentary evidence, the blame directly on Stakeknife, the army's most notorious agent within the ranks of the IRA.

2. English, *Armed Struggle: A History of the IRA*, p. 257.

3. See Murray Edelman, *The Politics of Misinformation* (New York 2001).

4. In making this decision, the British government was following a precedent set by the Irish government, which had banned Sinn Féin from the airwaves in 1973. In the immediate aftermath of the IRA ceasefire the British government was the first to lift its prohibition. Ireland did not formally follow suit until 1997.

5. Kevin Toolis, *Rebel Hearts* (London 1995), p. 179.

6. Ian Jack, *Gibraltar* (London 1988), p. 34. See also Toolis, *Rebel Hearts*, pp. 176–80.

7. See *McCann vs. United Kingdom* (1995), para. 128. This evidence refers to a sourced interview conducted by Julian Manyon and Harry Debelius of Thames television with Augustin Valladolid from the security services in Madrid. According to Debelius, an extensive operation was mounted involving cars, helicopters and officers stationed at fixed observation points.

8. *McCann vs. United Kingdom*, para. 2.

9. Ibid., para. 201.

10. Ibid.

11. See Peter Taylor, *Provos: The IRA and Sinn Féin* (London 1998), p. 268.

12. Cited in David McKittrick et al., *Lost Lives* (1999), p. 1113.

13. Cited in Bew and Gillespie, *Northern Ireland: A Chronology of the Troubles*, p. 212.

14. Tim Pat Coogan, *The Troubles* (London 1994), p. 313.

15. *McCann vs. United Kingdom*, para. 205. As Ní Aolain has pointed out, 'it is this postulation, this framing of the right to life, as a right which belongs to those transgressing the law as much as those who observe it, which is at the heart of the court's judgement.' See Fionnuala Ní Aolain, *The Politics of Force* (Belfast 2000), p. 201.

16. Michael Stone, 'Portrait of a Killer', *Insight*, 19 October 2000.

17. Writing in the *Irish Times* days after the attack, Kevin Myers, an ardent critic of republicanism, noted: 'This was not simply bravery; this was heroism, which in other circumstances, I have no doubt, would have won the highest military decoration. Victoria Crosses have been won for less.' Cited in McKittrick et al., *Lost Lives*, p. 1117.

18. Quoted in Dillon, *The Trigger Men*, p. 205. Dillon points out that Stone demanded respect as an operator, leaving cartridges at the scene of his killings as a calling card. The tactic was replicated in further shootings. Dillon continues that Stone was, in all likelihood, run as an agent of British intelligence, without his knowledge (p. 207).

19. Davies, *Dead Men Talking*, p. 127. Davies argues that the South Africa connection solidified Nelson's reputation with both MI5 and the FRU, with both sides attempting to lure him back to Northern Ireland. Although MI5 offered a more lucrative package, Nelson had 'more faith that Military Intelligence [FRU] would fulfil their side of the bargain' (p. 129). 'Military Intelligence offered Nelson a deal: £300 a week in cash, a reasonable but not a flash saloon car, a house in Belfast and a cover — a job as a taxi driver' (p. 128). Davies further reports that the FRU connived with MI5 and MI6 and German intelligence to have it reported that Nelson had won £30,000 in a lottery, giving a convenient cover story for Nelson's ability to resettle in Belfast. While the FRU succeeded in gaining operational control over Nelson, other intelligence agencies viewed his re-insertion into the

paramilitary fulcrum as something to be exploited. According to one recent account, MI5 and the FRU arranged for Nelson to be given specialist training 'in computer techniques — the compiling, storing and sharing of data'. See Dillon, *The Trigger Men*, p. 253. Justice Cory is silent on many of these controversies. On the South African weapons shipments he contends that the evidence is 'frail and contradictory', although he notes that the fact that the FRU paid for Nelson's expenses indicates a high level of trust between Military Intelligence and their agent. See *Cory Report*, paras. 1.53–1.54, p. 26

20. Michael Stone, *None Shall Divide Us* (Belfast 2003).

21. Mark Devenport, *Flash Frames* (Belfast 2000), p. 42.

22. Ibid., p. 43.

23. *Irish Times*, 18 November 1988.

24. Lawyers' Committee for Human Rights, '*Beyond Collusion: The UK Security Forces and the Murder of Patrick Finucane*' (New York 2002), p. 6. Brian Gillen, on whose behalf the *habeas corpus* petition was lodged, told the New York lawyers that during an interrogation police officers remarked, 'It would be better if he were dead than defending the likes of him. We can give them [detained loyalist paramilitaries] his details along with yours' (p. 4).

25. *Cory Report*, p. 92.

26. *Cory Report*, p. 91.

27. *Cory Report*, p. 60.

28. *Cory Report*, pp. 60–61.

29. *Cory Report*, p. 62.

30. For full details of the Brian Nelson involvement, see Chapter 5 below.

31. Lawyers' Committee for Human Rights, *Beyond Collusion*, p. 4. The report also highlights other innovative applications of the law, including a successful challenge in January 1989 to the systemic use of solitary confinement as an instrument of policy. The report notes portentously that 'less than two weeks before he was murdered, Finucane filed two applications with the European Commission on Human Rights challenging the legality of the UK's derogation from the European Convention on Human Rights' (p. 5). Just as important as the high-profile work was Finucane's capacity to use inquest procedure and the Diplock courts to demand disclosure and then cross-examine Special Branch or other intelligence agency officers, who risked perjury every time they entered the witness box. The result was that cases were dropped rather than risk the publicity that Finucane could generate. With success came an exponential increase in personal risk to the lawyer. The risk was magnified precisely because if the Crown dropped a prosecution, Finucane was able to launch civil proceedings for malicious prosecution. Again the only way to stop disclosure was to settle.

32. See *Finucane vs. United Kingdom* (Application No. 29178/95), p. 2. In an interview transmitted by *Panorama*, Gillen alleged: 'They [RUC detectives] told me that my solicitor was a Provo, he's just the same as you. We'll have him taken out.' See 'A Licence to Murder', *Panorama*, 19 June 2002.

33. John Ware, 'Time to Come Clean Over the Army's Role in the "Dirty War"', *New Statesman*, 24 April 1998.

34. 'A Licence to Murder', *Panorama*, 19 June 2002.

35. 'A Licence to Murder', *Panorama*, 19 June 2002.
36. *Stevens 3*, p. 11.
37. *Cory Report*, p. 61.
38. Justice Cory reports that as early as July 1988, three prominent solicitors (Finucane, P.J. McGrory and Oliver Kelly) were being targeted by loyalist paramilitaries. He cites a report from another source (CF 10 July 1988) that 'Target O (Sos [Solicitor]) spends a lot of time in [Bar name redacted] Antrim Road in the company of [name redacted] Solicitor (Sos). NB every Sunday Target O visits the [Bar name redacted] always some music. Parks the car (Merc) out on the road i.e. unprotected, he is always with his son (also Sos).' Cory is scathing that neither this information nor a further source report (CF 17 February 1989) obtained just days after the Finucane killing, suggesting that the same solicitor was at risk, were passed on. Cory concludes 'thus within days of Patrick Finucane's murder there was evidence to suggest that other solicitors were also targets yet nothing was apparently done to prevent further loss of life. Target O was never warned by FRU or RUC SB, although an officer involved in the Stevens 1 Inquiry did warn him after the team obtained the information.' See *Cory Report*, para. 1.105, p. 39.
39. In a scathing indictment, Cory concludes in relation to Special Branch that contrary to its self-promotion as an agency that protected life irrespective of background, 'generally UDA threats appear to have been ignored. This discrepancy in the treatment of PIRA and UDA targets may be indicative of a selective, perhaps subconscious bias on the part of Special Branch. It may well be that only a portion of the population was receiving effective protection against the threat of loyalist violence.' See *Cory Report*, p. 90.
40. See *Stevens 3*, p. 11.
41. *Cory Report*, p. 92.
42. UN Basic Principles on the Role of Lawyers, Principle 18, cited in Lawyers' Committee for Human Rights, *Beyond Collusion*, p. 9.
43. *Hansard*, 17 January 1989, col. 509–11. When Finucane was murdered six weeks later Mallon contended that Hogg's statement had created the 'climate and the context within which this kind of murder has taken place'. See *Irish Times*, 14 February 1989. Mallon also claimed in an interview with the paper that 'I got the distinct impression he [Hogg] had been asked to put these matters on the record and the more I read of the *Hansard*, the more I believe this to be the case. I thought he was a Patsy at the time and I still believe that to be the case.' See Ella Shanahan, 'The tag end of a long line of Hoggs', *Irish Times*, 15 February 1989. In his third report into collusion, John Stevens concluded, 'to the extent that they [Hogg's comments] were based on information passed by the RUC, they were not justifiable and the Enquiry concludes that the minister was compromised.' See *Stevens 3*, p. 11.
44. Letter from Michael Davey to Douglas Hogg excerpted in 'Solicitors' fury over Hogg claims', *Irish News*, 19 January 1989.
45. P.J. McGrory Statement excerpted in 'Solicitors' fury over Hogg claims', *Irish News*, 19 January 1989.
46. 'Time for full human rights', *Irish News*, 19 January 1989.
47. 'King storms back at human rights critics', *Irish News*, 20 January 1989.

48. *Irish News*, 24 January 1989.
49. Ibid.
50. 'SDLP, Labour anger at guillotine vote', *Irish News*, 24 January 1989.

Chapter 4 (pp. 78–105)

1. Cited in evidence, Dan Keenan, 'Family see prosecution as distraction from wider issue of RUC and British collusion', *Irish Times*, 14 September 2004.
2. *Cory Report*, para. 1.15, p. 12.
3. Lawyers' Committee for Human Rights, *Beyond Collusion*, p. 12.
4. *Beyond Collusion*, p. 11; see also *Finucane vs. United Kingdom*, 1 July 2003, para. 10.
5. Michael Finucane, 'They killed my father', *Guardian*, 13 February 2001.
6. 'UFF claim that Finucane was an IRA officer denied', *Irish Times*, 14 February 2004.
7. As noted in Chapter 1 above, a prosecution is a symbolic formality. Those who carried out the killing were members, at the time, of paramilitary groups, who benefit from the early release scheme that has seen all of those convicted of terrorist crime prior to the signing of the Agreement released back into society.
8. Michael Finucane, cited in 'Murder in Mind', *Insight*, 20 June 2004.
9. Statement of Geraldine Finucane to Commission on Security and Cooperation in Europe, United States Helsinki Committee, Washington DC, 5 May 2004.
10. See Angelique Chrisafis, 'New inquiry calls after Finucane guilty plea', *Guardian*, 14 September 2004.
11. Because Barrett pleaded guilty, the full details of the operation were not disclosed in court. Useful summaries are to be found in David Leppard, 'Met Chief accused of flawed sting to trap hitman', *Sunday Times*, 29 August 2004; Rosie Cowan, 'A tale of cover-up and conspiracy', *Guardian*, 14 September 2004; and Dan Keenan, 'Stevens Inquiry set up elaborate sting to trap Barrett', *Irish Times*, 14 September 2004.
12. Statement carried in Sharon O'Neill, 'Confession must now lead to a public inquiry', *Irish News*, 14 September 2004.
13. See, for example, interview with Dave Cox conducted by Seamus McKee on *Good Morning Ulster*, BBC Radio Ulster, 14 September 2004.
14. Judgement granting leave to appeal, 11 June 2004. Judgement available online at *http://www.madden-finucane.com/douments/pat_finucane/11jun04.htm*. Full details of the note were lodged in an affidavit provided by Peter Madden on 26 May 2004 to the Northern Ireland High Court and quoted extensively in the 11 June judgement.
15. See judgement allowing Geraldine Finucane disclosure of all documentation sent to the government by the Stevens team, 11 June 2004. Justice Gillen's conclusions merit airing: 'The applicant's case, *inter alia*, is that the government is deliberately attempting to frustrate the holding of a public inquiry into the death of Patrick Finucane. One issue relevant to this is clearly whether or not there is evidence, as suggested in the Winter note, that members of the Stevens Inquiry were being encouraged to say that there was a whole string of prosecutions in the pipeline and that they were being used to try to block a public inquiry in the face of opposition from the members of that inquiry. Thus there are grounds for

argument that the approach adopted by the respondent and the evidence relied upon by the deciding authority not to hold a public inquiry is in some respects incorrect or inadequate. The respondent seeks to challenge the weight of the assertions in the Winter note. I consider that there is a clear risk of injustice, not to say denial, of the requirements of logic and fairness if these communications were not produced in the hope of establishing the true facts one way or another. I make this order not simply because the applicant would justifiably otherwise entertain a smouldering sense of injustice, but because in my view it is necessary for the fair disposal of this case and justice requires it be done. This order is of course without prejudice to the right of the respondent to raise any issue of public interest immunity arising out of my order or to apply to delete irrelevant parts of the communications.' Justice Gillen refused disclosure requests for the information provided to the government by either the Attorney General or the Director of Public Prosecutions. Judgement available online at *http://www.madden-finucane.com/douments/pat_finucane/11jun04.htm.*

16. 'Pressure mounts for Finucane inquiry', UTV, *http://u.tv/newsroom/indepth.asp?pt=n&id=50282.* See also Gerry Adams, 'Don't dodge the issue of collusion', *Guardian*, 14 September 2004.'There is a remarkable reluctance for the British government to get at the truth of these matters. Why is this? Having spoken to Tony Blair and his colleagues on this issue many times I know they are very conscious of the fact that Pat Finucane's killing is only the tip of the iceberg… Collusion and, specifically, the killing of Pat Finucane are serious matters which the British government cannot continue dodging, especially in the context of acts of completion as defined by Mr Blair for these negotiations.'

17. Pressure mounts for Finucane inquiry', UTV, *http://u.tv/newsroom/indepth.asp?id=50282&pt=n.*

18. 'Government urged to set Finucane inquiry date', UTV, *http://u.tv/newsroom/indepth.asp?id=50294&pt=n*; see also Michael Finucane's interview with Rosie Cowan of the *Guardian*. Michael Finucane argues: 'We are as much in the dark after this prosecution regarding the exact involvement of the security forces as we were beforehand….The answers lie in Britain, in Downing Street, Whitehall and with the Ministry of Defence.' See Rosie Cowan, 'Guilty plea does not lift the lid', *Guardian*, 14 September 2004.

19. 'Solicitor shot dead', *Irish News*, 13 February 1989.

20. 'Justice in the firing line', *Irish News*, 13 February 1989.

21. 'Bullets and words', *Irish Times*, 16 February 1989.

22. 'Protest sent to British cabinet at Hogg remark', *Irish Times*, 14 February 1989.

23. Ibid. An indication of just how devalued decency had become as a consequence of a generation of violence was evidenced by the polarised political reaction. The Democratic Unionist Party for example, through its avuncular press officer, Sammy Wilson, criticised what he termed the 'hysterical reaction of the SDLP' to the Finucane murder while 'remaining silent while Protestants were being butchered by the IRA'.

24. This also formed the backdrop of the *Panorama* investigation, see 'A Licence to Murder', *Panorama*, 23 June 2002. Following Barrett's guilty plea, security sources also briefed the Press Association that the second killer, believed to be Spence

himself, was still a serving Special Branch agent.

25. 'Justice on Trial', *Insight,* 4 December 2001.

26. Ed Maloney, 'The Informer', *Sunday Tribune,* 6 June 1999, cited in *Beyond Collusion,* p. 31. In a more detailed account given to Neil Mulholland and cited in the *Cory Report,* Stobie went further, saying that 'he had supplied the guns for the attack and had driven one of the cars to the site but not the lead car. He also admitted that he had driven the getaway car.' See *Cory Report,* para. 1.193, p. 70.

27. McKittrick et al, *Lost Lives,* p. 1098.

28. It was the Stevens Inquiry decision to break this compact that was to lead directly to the charging of Stobie and his subsequent murder in 2001. His defence was premised on the grounds that he was an agent of Special Branch at the time and had alerted his handlers of the impending hit on 'a top Provie' but they failed to act on the intelligence. The officer in charge of the Stevens Inquiry at that time, Hugh Orde, made clear that there was no alternative but to charge Stobie. 'Our decision was to follow the evidence; the evidence took us to Stobie. We presented the case in the form of an additional witness statement, which was assigned to a Director who reviewed the case and made a decision to charge Stobie with the murder of Patrick Finucane and Adam Lambert.' This raises the uncomfortable question as to why Stobie was not charged along with the other members of the gang in 1991 and why, even after his involvement in the Finucane murder, the RUC did not revisit the ambivalent consequences of operationalising the Walker guidelines.

29. *Beyond Collusion,* p. 31.

30. *Cory Report,* pp. 65–9.

31. This information relates to a feud which began with the killing of Billy Quee, a close associate of a loyalist godfather, Jim Craig, on 9 September. On 23 September, ten days after Stobie warned his handlers that the UDA unit were about to strike, Gerard Slane was killed. Brian Nelson was to play a central role in the targeting of Slane, as evidenced from the military contact sheets provided to the Stevens Inquiry and published by Cory. See Chapter 5 below.

32. *Cory Report,* p. 71. For a full examination of the issues involved in the trial see *Beyond Collusion,* and 'Justice on Trial', *Insight,* 4 December 2001.

33. *Stevens 3,* p. 16.

34. See *Patten Report on the Future of Policing* (1999).

35. *Irish News,* 27 November 2001.

36. See the commentary released by the Pat Finucane Centre, available online at: *http://www.serve.com/pfc/pf/pf12122001a.html.* This rationale for the killing of Stobie forms an important backdrop to the *Panorama* investigations into collusion, which suggested that not only did the UDA commander, Jim Spence, set up the Finucane killing with the connivance of a rogue RUC Special Branch officer, but he was also instrumental in the killing of Stobie and the subsequent targeting of Ken Barrett, the last surviving direct source linking back to the murder team. *Panorama* reports that when Spence learnt that Stobie was talking to journalists in July 2001, he said to Barrett, 'Fuck this. Something will have to do done. Stobie will be lucky if he sees his fucking trial.' See 'A Licence to Murder', *Panorama,* 23 June 2002.

37. Justice Peter Cory interview, 'Murder in Mind', *Insight*, June 2004.
38. Maloney's account was published subsequent to Stobie's arrest and questioning by the Stevens team. In an attempt to ward off prosecution, Stobie authorised Maloney to publish his 1990 interview. It appeared as 'The Informer', *Sunday Tribune*, 6 June 1999. Perhaps significantly, Stobie never disputed the Maloney interpretation of his story. Maloney refused to divulge his notes of the interview but this did not prevent Stevens from pressing ahead with charges against Stobie on 23 June. The evidential basis was the alternative interview provided by Stobie to Neil Mulholland of the *Sunday Life*, which had been in police possession since the early 1990s. (It was Mulholland's refusal to give evidence on medical grounds that was to lead to the collapse of the Stobie trial.)
39. *Cory Report*, paras. 1.214–234, pp. 75–81.
40. *Stevens 3*, p. 8. The Cory Report tracks the history of a Browning pistol (not the one linked to the Finucane shooting) recovered by Special Branch in 1989 from Stobie and subsequently returned. Stobie claimed that the firing mechanism had been 'filed down', rendering the gun inoperable, a fact that he claimed had compromised his cover. In fact, the gun was used in several more shootings, leading to the killing of six people. In December 1991, the Browning was used to kill Aidan Wallace as he played snooker in a Belfast bar. It was also used in the killing of five people on an attack on Sean Graham's bookmakers on the Ormeau Road. See *Cory Report*, para. 1.244, p. 86. Ken Barrett pleaded guilty to stealing the weapon from a UDR barracks on the Malone Road in Belfast. Dressed in a UDR uniform, Barrett had entered the complex with a colleague and had simply requested two SA-80 rifles, four magazines and two Browning pistols for target practice. In evidence read into the court, Barrett intimated to undercover police officers that some high-level collusion had taken place because the cameras had been deliberately turned off. He was recorded as saying, 'Do you think that just happens?' It took the army four days to even notice that the guns were missing. See Chris Thornton, 'Government set to gag Finucane report', *Belfast Telegraph*, 14 September 2004, and Chris Thornton, 'Mystery of the army's stolen guns', *Belfast Telegraph*, 14 September 2004. See also 'Gun returned to UFF killed six', *Irish News*, 2 December 2003; 'Smoking gun in the report', *Irish News*, 3 December 2003.
41. *Cory Report*, para. 1.199, p. 71.
42. Ed Maloney, 'The Informer', *Sunday Tribune*, 6 June 1999.
43. *Beyond Collusion*, p. 32.
44. *Cory Report*, para. 1.187, p. 68.
45. Ken Barrett claimed in an interview with *Panorama* that he had received a telephone call from a police officer who told him that vehicle checkpoints in the vicinity had been cleared. 'The decision was taken and that was it. There was none of this fucking about, driving here and driving round there. The decision was taken. Bang. Let's go. That's how quickly it happens.' See 'A Licence to Murder', *Panorama*, 19 June 2002. Cory notes this in his report but finds no evidence to suggest that the checkpoints were deliberately removed to facilitate the murder.
46. *Cory Report*, para. 1.213, pp. 74–5. Whether Cory goes further into the detail of these issues is difficult to ascertain because the next section of the report is

dedacted. In his conclusion, however, Cory decries the Special Branch failure to act on information that 'a top UDA official had asked Stobie to provide a 9 mm Browning pistol for a "hit on a top PIRA man". This information was not apparently pursued.' Similarly, 'just three days after the murder, Stobie reported that he had been asked by the same UDA official to pick up and hide a 9 mm Browning. No steps were taken to recover or trace this weapon, although there was every reason to believe that it was the firearm used to kill Finucane. The failure to act on information received in 1989, both before and after the Finucane murder, is indicative of collusion.' See *Cory Report*, para. 1.292, p. 104.

47. Interview notes, cited in *Beyond Collusion*, p. 34.

48. Cited in *Finucane vs. United Kingdom*, para 34. This refusal to acknowledge his knowledge that Finucane was a target was designed, in large measure, to minimise his exposure to a conspiracy charge based on direct knowledge of an identifiable target. There were sound legal reasons for believing that this defence could work. It was used successfully in the Brian Nelson trial in 1992.

49. 'Root and Branch', *Spotlight*, 21 May 2002; 'A Licence to Murder', *Panorama*, 19 and 23 June 2002.

50. *Cory Report*, , para. 1.292, pp. 105–6.

51. The Browning pistol was subsequently recovered in a separate operation in July 1989 although no tests were carried out. Despite the failure to close the case, the gun was transferred back to the army in 1995, where for as yet undetermined reasons the decision was taken to replace 'the barrel and slide of the pistol, the two parts of the gun that leave evidentiary marks on the slug and shell of bullets'. The New York Lawyers investigating the case were perplexed at this 'deeply troubling' course of events. 'The army had therefore removed (and presumably destroyed) crucial evidence in one of the most controversial murders in Northern Ireland's history, a controversy with the Army firmly at its center.' See *Beyond Collusion*, p. 32.

52. See *Cory Report*, para. 1.200, p. 72. How the CID reacted to this information is unclear, as vital paragraphs that follow have been redacted on grounds of national security.

53. *Beyond Collusion*. p. 36.

54. *Finucane vs. UK*, para. 19.

55. 'Policing the Police', *Insight*, 17 April 2001. Brown's partner, Trevor McIllwrath, verified the Brown account in an interview in December 2001. See David Gordon, 'Stobie saved my life — Ex-RUC Man', *Belfast Telegraph*, 13 December 2001. In a sinister development, an anonymous letter was sent to the UDA in 1994 claiming that Brown was passing information to republicans about named loyalists. Stobie had intercepted the letter and passed it to an RUC detective who passed it directly to Brown. Brown does not know where the authorship originated but suspects that it came from within the security services. Brown, who is very careful with language, postulated to New York Lawyers that there is speculation that it emanated from Special Branch. See *Beyond Collusion*. p. 60.

56. Jason Benetto, 'He had the eyes of a cold-blooded serial killer', *The Independent*, 14 September 2004.

57. Cited in Alan Erwin and Deric Henderson, 'Undercover police reveal callousness of killer Barrett', *Irish News*, 14 September 2004.

58. 'Policing the Police', *Insight*, 17 April 2001.
59. See Johnston Brown interview with New York Lawyers, cited in *Beyond Collusion*, p. 62.
60. *Beyond Collusion*, p. 59. Brown also claimed that Barrett had been told by Special Branch of his [Brown's] intention to use the confession as a means to bring him to court, a scenario, which, if proven, represents a damning indictment of Branch methods. Not only was an active line of inquiry closed off, but, more seriously, a colleague's life was put at unacceptable risk. See *Beyond Collusion*, pp. 59–60.
61. 'Justice on Trial', *Insight*, 7 December 2001.
62. 'Justice on Trial', *Insight*, 7 December 2001. Rice was also the solicitor representing Ken Barrett.
63. 'A Licence to Murder', *Panorama*, 19 June 2002.
64. 'A Licence to Murder', *Panorama*, 23 June 2002. An important allegation that has not received much coverage is the suggestion by Ware, which is not directly sourced, that details provided by Barrett to a handler within Special Branch were passed on to loyalist paramilitaries in early 2001. If true, this suggests that police complicity in the directing of terrorism, even by a rogue officer, is a continuing reality and that the reforms introduced in intelligence policing have had limited effect.
65. See Chris Thornton, 'Coldblooded killer', *Belfast Telegraph*, 14 September 2004.
66. David Leppard, 'Met chief accused of flawed sting to trap hitman', *Sunday Times* 29 August 2004. Barrett is engaging in hyperbole here. Finucane was shot fourteen times.
67. David Leppard, 'Met chief accused of flawed sting to trap hitman', *Sunday Times*, 29 August 2004.
68. Anthony Harvey QC, cited in 'Finucane killer could be free in 8 months', UTV, *http://u.tv/newsroom/indepth.asp?pt=n&id=50438*.
69. Anthony Harvey QC, cited in Deric Henderson and Gary Kelly, '22 years for Finucane's killer', *Independent*, 17 September 2004.
70. 'Finucane killer gets 22 years', BBC News Online, *www.bbc.co.uk*; 'Finucane killer jailed for 22 years', *www.guardian.co.uk*.
71. See 'UK: Public Inquiry must be held into Finucane killing'. The press release then sets out the terms of such an inquiry in striking language: 'The inquiry should focus on collusion by state agents with loyalist paramilitaries in Patrick Finucane's killing, on reports that his death was the result of state policy, and on allegations that different government authorities played a part in the subsequent cover-up of collusion in his killing.' Available online at *http://web.amnesty.org/library/Index/ENGEUR450222004*.

Chapter 5 (pp. 106–26)

1. John Stalker, *Stalker* (London 1988), p. 262.
2. Ibid., p. 263.
3. Ibid., p. 67. Stalker also complained of how those involved in undercover operations were debriefed in what he termed a 'Chinese parliament' in which a collective version of the 'truth' was arrived at, which was justified on the basis of protecting innocent lives and protecting informants, without whom the battle

against terrorism would be compromised. In what was later to become exposed as systematic policy through the Cory Report, the intelligence reports on Michael Tighe posthumously linked him to the IRA simply because he was shot by an anti-terrorist unit.

4. Stalker, *Stalker*, p. 73.
5. Ibid., p. 76.
6. John Stevens, *Summary Report*, 17 May 1990, para. 41.
7. *Beyond Collusion*, p. 17. The lawyers make the point, however, that Stevens had also stated that 'at no time was I [Stevens] given the authority by either the Chief Constable of the RUC or the Director of Public Prosecutions to investigate the murder of Pat Finucane' (p. 18).
8. In an ironic twist, the decision on publication now rests with the former chief officer on that inquiry, Hugh Orde, who was appointed to lead the Police Service of Northern Ireland in 2002. Despite the fact that the Finucane component of the investigation is now complete, Orde has made no movement towards publication.
9. *Stevens 3*, p. 13.
10. *Stevens 3*, pp. 13–14.
11. See *Cory Report*, para. 1.306–1.311, pp. 113–15. The Canadian judge had already completed his report calling for an independent inquiry into the circumstances surrounding Pat Finucane's killing and filed it with the Canadian High Commission in London when important contextual evidence relating to the trial of Brian Nelson was provided to the judge. The evidence, relating to attempts to protect Nelson from prosecution on grounds of protecting national security, were deemed by the judge to be of vital importance for those charged with holding an inquiry. Cory responded by releasing an addendum to his final report. The communication validated claims made in 1992 in John Ware's investigation for *Panorama*, which suggested that the Director of Public Prosecutions had been sent a letter from the Northern Ireland Office commending Nelson and advocating the non-pursual of charges against him. See 'The Dirty War', *Panorama*, 8 June 1992.
12. *Hansard*, 28 April 1998, col. 75.
13. See 'A Licence to Murder', *Panorama*, 19 June 2002.
14. *Stevens 3*, p. 13.
15. *Hansard*, 14 May 2003, cols. 70–72.
16. Ibid., col. 87.
17. Ibid., col. 81.
18. Ibid., col. 82.
19. Ibid., col. 88.
20. Ibid., col. 89. In an interview for the *Panorama* programme, however, broadcast prior to the release of the Stevens Report, a senior member of the investigation team suggested that collusion was in fact built into the policy dynamic. Commenting on Brian Nelson's role in the killing of Terence McDaid, Detective Nicholas Benwell stated: 'I think it's a dreadful situation. He's passing it [information] to other groups of killers who are completely outside even his control and his handlers are just following on and letting him do it. It's a recipe for

absolute disaster.' Benwell went on to say that he did not find it believable that either Nelson or the FRU were unaware that Finucane was being targeted. See 'A Licence to Murder', *Panorama*, 19 June 2002.

21. Dillon, *The Trigger Men*, p. 257.

22. See *Cory Report*, paras. 1.55–1.60, pp. 26–8.

23. *Cory Report*, p. 27, citing CF 7 September 1987, item 6.

24. *Cory Report*, para 1.57, p. 27.

25. In an interview for the television series *Loyalists*, broadcast in 1999, another senior paramilitary, Bobby Philpott, claimed that he was receiving information from 'all branches: RUC, army, UDR. I was getting documents daily. I was getting so many documents I didn't know where to put them.' When asked what sort of documents, Philpott replied, 'Intelligence reports, photos, what colour socks republicans was wearing, what sort of cars they drive, where they lived, their safe houses.' Philpott conceded that without that degree of help, the UFF could not have achieved their target rate. Material cited in British Irish Rights Watch, *Justice Delayed: Alleged State Collusion in the Murder of Patrick Finucane and Others* (February 2000), para. 2.1. Again, this issue can only be satisfactorily addressed when all documents are released.

26. See *Cory Report*, p. 35.

27. Ibid.

28. Ibid.

29. A similar dynamic governed the handling of the INLA feud in 1996, in which ten people were killed as the organisation imploded. Interestingly, it was Nelson who facilitated the murder of James Craig by the UDA for consorting with the IPLO over ways in which to carve up the extortion rackets in the city less than a month after the Slane killing. Nelson provided a videotape recorded by undercover operatives of Craig meeting republicans in city hostelries just after the republicans had murdered John McMichael, the loyalist leader who began the investigation into Craig's activities. See Martin Dillon, *The Dirty War* (London 1988), pp. 443–58.

30. McKittrick et al, *Lost Lives*, p. 1988.

31. *Irish News*, 12 August 2000.

32. *Cory Report*, para 1.63, p. 28. See also Nicholas Davies, *Ten Thirty Three* (Edinburgh 1999), pp. 130–34. Davies claims that the initial suggestion that Declan McDaid be targeted came from the FRU.

33. 'Fifteen charges against Nelson dropped and guilty pleas accepted', *Irish Times*, 22 January 1992. For full details see Chapter 6 below.

34. *Cory Report*, paras. 1.65–1.66, p. 29.

35. Evidence of Colonel Gordon Kerr in *Regina vs. Nelson*, 29 January 1992.

36. 'A Licence to Murder', *Panorama*, 19 June 2002.

37. *Stevens 3*, p. 16.

38. Note here the remarkable similarities to the posthumous references to Michael Tighe's republican background in the shoot to kill investigation.

39. Ibid. This allegation was denied by Colonel Gordon Kerr, the officer commanding of the FRU. In evidence to Nelson's trial, Kerr claimed, 'There is a further suggestion that Nelson proliferated intelligence documents and as a result put lives at risk on a long-term basis. This rather political allegation seems to me

more designed to justify the actions of the Stevens Inquiry.'

40. See *Cory Report*, p. 55. This also involved giving Nelson latitude to take part in criminal activity. In his report, Justice Cory reports that 'the documents reveal that very often, the concern was not with the illegality of Nelson's actions, but rather the fear that he might get caught and thereby compromise his security.' See *Cory Report*, p. 52, citing CF 24 November, CF 6 December 1989, CF 3 May 1988, CF 10 January 1989.

41. See, for example, an exchange quoted by Nicholas Davies between Nelson and his handlers after the killing of Terence McDaid. 'We fucked up, got the wrong man, that's all. It was his brother we were after. Anyway it is one less Mick to worry about; that's the way we look at it.' One of the senior FRU handlers, fed up with Nelson's cavalier attitude challenged him: 'You told us that the UDA were a professional outfit and then you go and fuck up something like this. What the hell do you think you are playing at?'

'Don't have a go at me,' Nelson pleaded in a pathetic way. 'That side of it is nothing to do with me. That's operational. I just supply the intelligence, the facts, and they do the rest.'

'But that is precisely the point,' the FRU handler retorted. 'You are the intelligence officer and the information you gave your men was obviously inaccurate. As a result some poor innocent bastard died and you sit there and tell us that it doesn't matter. Well, it does matter and the sooner you learn that fact, the better for you and for us.' See Nicholas Davies, *Ten Thirty Three*, pp. 133–4. Davies based his book on a number of interviews with FRU personnel. It was the subject of a court injunction served on the nebulous grounds of the need to protect national security. This does not necessarily mean that the allegations contained in the book are true, and Davies' failure to source the interviews makes it hard to accurately gauge his interpretation. In a subsequent account, Davies changes tack and suggests that the FRU wanted to know what was going on within the UDA and that the aggressive targeting was not part of the original arrangement. See Nicholas Davies, *Dead Men Talking* (Edinburgh 2004), pp. 132–3. However, given the paucity of the written paper trail in relation to a number of controversial killings, including that of McDaid, the issues raised by the former handlers form a very useful line of inquiry to pursue.

42. *Cory Report*, p. 42.

43. Ibid., p. 43.

44. Ibid., p. 43.

45. *Cory Report*, p. 47. The UDA paramilitary Ken Barrett claims that Nelson was more centrally involved. In his secretly recorded interview with *Panorama*, Barrett alleges: 'Brian knew what we were fucking doing. Brian took me up to the fucking place. Do you know what I mean? Brian showed me the [photograph] once and that was all I needed to know.' See *Panorama*, 'A Licence to Murder', 19 June 2002. Another BBC documentary series, *Spotlight*, travelled to Canada in 2002 to interview Finucane's neighbours at the time of the killing. Shown a picture of Nelson, they confirmed that they had witnessed Nelson cleaning windows in the street in the lead-up to the killing. See also Dillon, *The Trigger Men*, p. 262.

46. *Cory Report*, p. 51. Stevens draws a narrower conclusion about Nelson's personal involvement: 'Nelson was aware and contributed materially to the intended attack on Finucane. It is not clear whether his role in the murder extended beyond passing a photograph which showed Finucane with another person [McGeown], to one of the other suspects [Jim Spence]. Nelson was re-arrested and interviewed. There was no new evidence and he was not charged with any further offences.' See *Stevens 3*, p. 10.

47. Evidence of Colonel Gordon Kerr in *Regina vs. Nelson*, 29 January 1992. Nicholas Davies claims in *Dead Men Talking* that Nelson was in effect a double agent, who had told the UDA as early as 1987 that British Intelligence had recruited him. Davies claims that while the FRU wanted to gain information about loyalists, Nelson in contrast was much more interested in gaining information from military intelligence in order to more accurately target republicans. See Davies, *Dead Men Talking*.

48. See *Cory Report*, p. 58. Cory expresses incredulity at this formulation.

49. 'Murder charges dropped "in interests of justice"', *Irish News*, 23 January 1992.

50. *Cory Report*, p. 57.

51. Ibid., p. 57.

52. Ibid., p. 58.

53. *Cory Report*, p. 59.

54. *Hansard*, 12 March 1990, col. 32.

55. *Hansard*, 10 June 1992, col. 399.

56. *Hansard*, 30 Janaury 1992, col. 1058.

57. For details of the Harry Ward and Hugh Magee killings see McKittrick et al., *Lost Lives*, pp. 1251–2.

58. Rearranging police records to fit later agendas is not unusual within the Northern Ireland context, or indeed to matters pertaining to the Irish question in Britain. A similar dynamic governed the deliberate 'process of review and alteration' of police statements prior to the Taylor Inquiry into the Hillsborough tragedy, in which 96 football supporters were crushed to death at the main football stadium in Sheffield on 15 April 1989. For full details see Phil Scraton, *Hillsborough: The Truth* (Edinburgh 2000).

Chapter 6 (pp. 127–49)

1. See David McKittrick, 'Ministers announce inquiry into Finucane murder but fail to ease fears of cover-up', *Independent*, 24 September 2004. See also Chris Thornton, 'U-turn on Finucane case', *Belfast Telegraph*, 24 September 2004.

2. Paul Murphy cited in Press Association, 'Go-ahead for Finucane Inquiry', UTV Online. Available at *http://u.tv/newsroom/indepth.asp?pt=n&id=50667*.

3. *Cory Report*, para. 1.294, p. 108. For a full list of Cory's requirements, see Appendix 2.

4. Cory did highlight the need to control costs and to ensure that the inquiry was expedited, but his remarks were framed as 'simply suggestions for controlling the unnecessary expenditure of public funds' to ensure that the inquiry was not 'a means of enriching the legal profession'. See *Cory Report*, para. 1.303–1.305, p. 111.

5. Stéphane Leman-Langlois and Clifford Shearing, 'Repairing the Future: The South African Truth and Reconciliation Commission at Work', in George Gilligan and John Pratt, *Crime, Truth and Justice* (Cullompton 2004), p. 223.

6. Michael Finucane Interview, *Evening Extra*, BBC Radio Ulster, 23 September 2004, cited in 'Go-ahead for Finucane Inquiry', BBC Online, available at *http:// news.bbc.co.uk/1/hi/northern_ireland/3679358.stm*.

7. Finucane Family Statement, 23 September 2003. Text at *http://www.serve.com/ pfc/pf/040923pf.html*.

8. Statement by Secretary of State, Paul Murphy, 23 September 2004. Full text available at *http://www.nio.gov.uk/media-detail.htm?newsID=10299*.

9. For a comprehensive overview of the issues involved in establishing inquiries, and their strengths and weaknesses, see Gilligan and Pratt, *Crime, Truth and Justice*.

10. Rosie Cowan, 'Finucane family attack secretive murder inquiry as fiasco and circus', *Guardian*, 24 September 2004. For the wider demands of the family see statement released by Peter Madden, 'Truth or Continuing Cover-Up: A Full Public Judicial Inquiry Now', 12 February 2002. Full text available online at *http://www.serve.com/pfc/pf/pf12022002b.html*.

11. See George Gilligan, 'Official Inquiry, Truth and Criminal Justice', in Gilligan and Pratt, *Crime, Truth and Justice*. Gilligan contends that the Stevens Inquiry 'seems to defy specific classification as a tool of vested interests of the state' (p. 17). While at surface level this is true, the difficulty is that beyond two short summaries, the content of the Stevens investigation has not been public, thereby ensuring that the inquiry fits into Gilligan's wider argument that inquiries serve to 'act as a convenient mechanism of legitimation for the state' (p. 18). For a critical assessment of the role of inquiries within the Northern Irish context, see Bill Rolston and Phil Scraton, 'In the Full Glare of English Politics: Ireland, Inquiries and the British State', *British Journal of Criminology* (2005 forthcoming). The authors conclude: 'There is clear evidence that many inquiries were established and designed specifically as weapons of the state in an ongoing political war…. Internment, interrogation, rules of evidence, proscription of named organisations, abolition of jury trials, political status and its replacement by criminalisation, underpinned nine inquiries: Compton, Parker, Diplock, Gardiner, Shackleton, Bennett, Jellicoe, Baker and Colville. These inquiries were established to justify derogation from the "normal" rule of law.' As the authors point out, the choice of language deployed in the terms of reference is indicative. The Baker Inquiry is prefaced by the legend 'Accepting that temporary emergency powers are necessary to combat sustained terrorist violence…' (Cmnd 9222:1). Likewise, Jellicoe's report begins, 'Accepting the continuing need for legislating against terrorism…' (Cmnd 8808:iv). From their exhaustive analysis of previous tribunals of inquiry, the authors come to a dispiriting if justifiably cynical conclusion: 'These inquiries were not established to restore public confidence in the impartiality of the rule of law *within* the North of Ireland, but rather to give that appearance to a British and international audience. The law was used for political ends. They narrowed the field of inquiry, avoided obvious and objective conclusions that might show state forces in a bad

light, delayed reporting to mute the impact of negative criticism of the report and ensured that security force personnel would not be prosecuted or reprimanded for their actions.'

12. Murray Edelman, *The Symbolic Uses of Politics* (Urbana 1985).

13. Phil Scraton, 'From Deceit to Disclosure: The Politics of Official Inquiries in the United Kingdom', in Gilligan and Pratt, *Crime, Truth and Justice*, p. 49. See in particular his criticism of the successful attempts by police officers to carefully filter evidence to the Hillsborough Inquiry, a process that had the implicit support of the inquiry chairman (pp. 53–8). Critiquing inquiries within Northern Ireland, Scraton concludes that 'official inquiries have been staged, managed and manipulated to obstruct disclosure and promote accounts in keeping with a broader political agenda' (p. 63). See also Phil Scraton, *Hillsborough: The Truth* (Edinburgh 2000).

14. A similar dynamic has eroded confidence in the various tribunals of inquiry in the Republic of Ireland. See Justin O'Brien, 'Unravelling the Project: The Impact of the Tribunals', in *The Modern Prince, Charles J. Haughey and the Quest for Power* (Dublin 2002), pp. 147–70. See also Paul Cullen, *With a Little Help From My Friends: Planning Corruption in Ireland* (Dublin 2002).

15. For detailed information on the inquiry see its website *www.bloody-sunday-inquiry.org.*

16. Full text of the statement is available at *www.bloody-sunday-inquiry.org/index2.asp? p=1.*

17. See Bill Rolston, *Unfinished Business: State Killings and the Quest for Justice* (Belfast 2000), p. 9.

18. See Eamon McCann, 'Finucane inquiry probably doomed by earlier judicial hearings', *Sunday Tribune*, 19 September 2004. McCann makes the further point that there cannot be an appeal to the Human Rights Act to guarantee an effective and independent investigation. The European Court ruled in October 2002 that Britain had violated Article 2 of the European Convention on Human Rights by not providing effective investigations into controversial murders. The enactment of the Human Rights Act in 2000 ended the derogation from European Convention, thus paving the way for fresh investigations. The House of Lords ruled in March 2004 that the legislation does not apply to those killed prior to the introduction of the statute in October 2000. Ironically, the test case involved the 'shoot to kill' incidents of 1982, a case that Finucane himself had been heavily involved in while it progressed through the Northern Ireland courts.

19. Although as noted above the change in the advice given by the Attorney General to the government that it was 'speculative' that a prosecution would take place makes it a reasonable assumption to conclude that it is unlikely that the DPP will, in fact, proceed.

20. See Amnesty International Statement, EUR 45/023/2004, 23 September 2004. In a strongly worded statement, the human rights group stated that it 'strongly suspects that the UK authorities are using "national security" to curtail the ability of the inquiry to shed light on state collusion in the killing of Patrick Finucane; on allegations that his killing was the result of an official policy and that different

government authorities played a part in the subsequent cover-up of collusion in his killing. With this announcement, the UK authorities are making the "public interest" subservient to "national security". Conversely, Amnesty International believes that the public interest can only be served by ensuring public scrutiny of the full circumstances of Patrick Finucane's killing and its aftermath.'

21. 'Licenced to Kill', *Insight*, 30 January 2001.

22. Cited in 'Licenced to Kill', *Insight*, 30 January 2001.

23. *Stevens 3*, para. 4.8–4.9.

24. *Cory Report*, para. 1.287, pp. 102–3. Cory goes on to state that 'the documents in themselves or taken cumulatively can be taken to indicate that FRU committed acts of collusion. Further, there is strong, if in some instances, conflicting documentary evidence that FRU committed collusive acts. Only a public inquiry can resolve the conflict' (para 1.289).

25. *Cory Report*, para, 1.286, p. 102.

26. For a list of the key provisions in the Inquiries Bill, see Appendix 5. In this context it is worth considering one of the main conclusions of the British Irish Rights Watch report forwarded to the government in 1999. It states: 'We believe that far from having as its aim the saving of life, the aim was to direct loyalist violence against republican targets — it was in effect a policy of shoot to kill by proxy.' See 'Licenced to Kill', *Insight*, 30 January 2001. This wider context involves allegations of complicity in a range of other killings. The pressure group Relatives for Justice campaigns on the basis that it wants to know 'the chain of command that devised and executed collusion'. See press release 'Relatives of victims point finger at chain of command', 24 June 2001. Full text available at *www.relativesforjustice.com*. An inquiry limited to the Finucane murder without reference to other murders in which the FRU is allegedly implicated will do little to assuage concerns of a cover-up.

27. See Ruling on Admissibility of Evidence by Martin Ingram, 15 April 2003. Full text available online under Tribunal Rulings at *www.bloody-sunday-inquiry.org*. Justice Saville concluded that 'with information bearing on the special units of the armed forces, intelligence details and counter-terrorist activities, [t]he Tribunal has accepted that course where members of the Security Service are involved. We have followed our usual practice of reading that material for ourselves but not disclosing it to the interested parties. Article 2 of the European Convention on Human Rights dictates such a course notwithstanding the Tribunal's desire that the Inquiry should be public.' For Justice Saville, 'clearly, the unrestricted dissemination of such matters could be damaging to national security and, to the extent that the material may lead to the disclosure of Martin Ingram's identity, could constitute a threat to his safety.' Justice Saville concluded that the fairest way of adjudicating on the Ministry of Defence's argument was for interested parties to provide a synopsis of questions. 'The Tribunal will consider each synopsis. If persuaded that it raises matters of relevance, it will give Martin Ingram and those represented by the Defence Secretary an opportunity to object on human rights or public interest immunity grounds.' The net effect of this strategy was to give the Ministry of Defence an effective veto.

28. See Maurice Fitzmaurice, 'Finucane Inquiry', *Daily Mirror*, 24 September 2004. The former member of the FRU, who uses the pseudonym Martin Ingram, told the *Mirror* that he 'fear[ed] this whole thing is going to be a sham', precisely because of the difficulty in calling agents and handlers to testify.

29. As Editor of Current Affairs for UTV, the author was subject to two applications to the court by the Ministry of Defence for programmes to be injuncted. The first programme, 'Licenced to Kill', was transmitted on 30 January 2001 following an independent adjudication by the court. The second programme was never broadcast. The station fought the action on the grounds of its freedom to broadcast. The Ministry of Defence dropped its injunction unexpectedly in April 2001, by which stage the programme had been overtaken by events.

30. David McKittrick, 'Ministers announce inquiry into Finucane murder but fail to ease fears of cover-up', *Independent*, 24 September 2004.

31. When the South African government established a Truth and Reconciliation Commission (TRC), Pik Botha, the former Minister of Foreign Affairs, suggested in a fax to party leader F.W. de Klerk on 5 May 1997 that the entire cabinet of the National Party should apply for amnesty. De Klerk rejected this as it effectively recognised that the state itself was a terrorist actor, a formulation that had enormous implications for conceptions of history and legitimacy. See Alex Boraine, *A Country Unmasked* (Oxford 2000), p. 162. Boraine, a deputy chairman of the TRC, was later described in de Klerk's biography as complicit in the creation of an artificial truth. 'Beneath an urbane and deceptively affable exterior beat the heart of a zealot and an inquisitor.' Quoted in Boraine, *A Country Unmasked*, p. 169. While not suggesting that the degree of complicity in the UK is in any way comparable to that in South Africa, the exchange between Botha, Boraine and de Klerk is instructive. Even if for self-serving reasons, the former minister was accepting a degree of collective responsibility to a body that was established to provide closure to the past. In the United Kingdom context, the difficulty centres on the interconnected reasons that both Labour and Conservatives presided over the concealment of material facts for political reasons, a decision that had occasioned profound moral hazard.

32. Joseph Nye, 'Political Corruption: A Cost-benefit Analysis', *American Political Science Review* (1967), p. 417.

33. Onoroa O'Neill, 'Trust and Transparency', *Reith Lectures 2002* (London 2002), 24 April 2002. Text at *http://www.bbc.co.uk/radio4/reith2002*.

34. *The Times*, 4 June 2003.

35. *Today*, BBC Radio 4, 4 June 2003.

36. *Financial Times*, 27 August 2003.

37. *Sunday Times*, 24 August 2003.

38. *The Guardian*, 25 August 2003.

39. See for example the rationale used by Lord Denning to refuse an appeal from the six Irish people jailed for the Birmingham pub bombings. Lord Denning suggested their release would open an 'appalling vista' in which 'the police were guilty of perjury...of violence and threats that the confessions were involuntary and improperly admitted in evidence and that the convictions were erroneous'. Cited in Phil Scraton, 'From Deceit to Disclosure: The Politics of Official

Inquiries', in Gilligan and Pratt, *Crime, Truth and Justice*, p. 65.

40. Frank Kitson, *Low Intensity Operations* (London 1971), p. 69.

41. Paul Lewis, *Guerrillas and Generals: The Dirty War in Argentina* (London 2002), p. 139.

42. Ibid., p. 140.

43. Ibid., p. 141.

44. Ibid., p. 141.

45. *Truth and Reconciliation Commission of South Africa Report* (Cape Town 1998), vol. 2, p. 165.

46. Ibid., p. 221.

47. Ibid., p. 278.

48. Ibid., p. 287.

49. Ibid., p. 288.

50. Ibid., p. 308.

51. Ibid., p. 312.

52. Michael Walzer, *Arguing About War* (New Haven 2004), p. 52.

53. Ibid., pp. 56–7.

54. Michael Ignatieff, *The Lesser Evil, Political Ethics in an Age of Terror* (Edinburgh 2004), pp. 51–2. While I find myself in agreement with Ignatieff's broad argument, his empirical analysis of the Northern Ireland conflict is weaker. He argues that Britain was successful in preserving 'constitutional normality; without careful control of the military and police power, the British might well have lost the battle for moderate nationalist opinion in Ulster' (p. 72). He cites the RUC as being responsible for collusion but states that the wider security nexus is not, allowing him to claim that the British strategy was a successful template. Given the conclusions reached by Justice Cory about wider collusive activities by the army and MI5, this is a highly questionable assumption.

55. Jean-Marc Coicaud, *Legitimacy and Politics* (Cambridge 2002).

Index

Adair, Johnny, 95
Adams, Gerry, 52, 57, 65, 81, 119
agents. *see* informants and agents
Allister, Jim, 13
Amnesty International, 105
Anglo-Irish Agreement 1985, 51
Anglo-Irish secretariat, 83
Annesley, Hugh, Chief Constable, 16, 107
Argentina, 144–5
Armagh women's prison, 57
arms trial, 26–7
Attorney General. *see* Goldsmith, Lord

B Specials, 21, 30
Ballykelly bomb, 48
Barrett, Ken, 2, 3, 10, 11, 12, 18, 89, 114, 137
   and Brown, 94–9
   confession tape, 96–9, 125–6
   and *Panorama*, 101–3
   on Special Branch, 72
   trial, 80–82, 103–5, 112, 124, 127, 129
BBC, 5, 56, 69, 101–2
   Hutton Inquiry, 138–43
Belfast, 23, 126
   Falls Road curfew, 29, 30
   IRA, 24, 25
Belfast Agreement, 112
Bell, Ivor, 57
Blair, Tony, Prime Minister, 14, 18–19, 131, 132–3, 135, 141
Blaney, Neil, 26–7
Bloody Sunday, Derry, 3, 128
   inquiries, 34–5, 132–3
Bolton, Roger, 64
Brady, Kevin, funeral of, 68–70
Brady, Patrick, 66–7

Brighton bomb, 36
British Army, 8, 28–9, 50, 54. *see also* FRU; SAS
   attacks on, 31, 36, 46, 55, 68–70
   Bloody Sunday, 34–5
   checkpoints, 12
   collusion, 14–17, 106–7
   informants, 113, 115, 121
   internment, 31–3
   primacy over RUC, 22
   Saville Inquiry, 133
British Embassy, Dublin, 34
British government, 31. *see also* national security
   Anglo-Irish Agreement, 51
   and Finucane murder, 83, 129–34
   and hunger strikes, 38, 41–3
   Hutton Inquiry, 138–43
   IRA attacks on, 110
   as neutral, 147
   sends army to NI, 27–8
   state assassination alleged, 79–80
British Irish Rights Watch, 10, 11, 15, 81, 105
   report, 109–10
Brooke, Peter, 123
Brown, Johnston, 80, 95–9, 103, 104, 124–6
Burns, Sean, 47–8

Cameron, Lord, 23
Campbell, Alistair, 140, 141, 143
Canepa, Joseph Luis, 61
Carrickmore, IRA in, 64
Carroll, Rory, 48
Castlereagh station, 35–6, 40, 71, 85
   break-in, 17, 18
Chichester Clark, Sir James, 31

Churchill, Winston, 28
Civil Authorities (Special Powers) Act
  (NI), 33
civil rights movement, 23–5, 28
Coalisland ambush, 53
collusion, 3–7, 9–10, 134–5
  Barrett trial, 81–2, 105
  definition of, 3, 5
  justification for, 15–17
  Nelson, 115–21, 134–5
  RUC, 14–17
  Stobie, 84–9
  UDA publishes material, 106–7
Colombia, 17
Commission of Security and Co-oper-
  ation in Europe (CSCE), 79–80
Committee on the Administration of
  Justice, 105
Conservative Party, 28, 36–7, 110, 114
  security policy, 76–7
Conway Hotel bomb, 57
corruption, 137–8
  principal-agent analysis, 138–40
Cory Report, 3–5, 9, 70–71, 73, 83–4,
  86–8, 107, 128, 145
  Barrett, 104
  collusion, 16–17, 134–5
  Conclusions of, 160–63
  FRU, 11
  Nelson, 114–21, 122–3
  obstruction of, 15, 92, 110
  redactions, 5, 124, 129
  responses to, 12–14
  Stobie, 88–9, 90–91
Cox, Commander David, 80, 81
Crawford, General Sakkie, 145–6
Criminal Evidence Order, 76
Criminal Investigation Department
  (CID), 7, 44, 80, 85, 87, 124–5
  and Barrett, 95–6, 98–100
  Finucane murder, 82
  relations with Special Branch, 94–5
  and Stobie, 88, 93
Criminal Justice Review, 21
Criminal Justice (Temporary
  Provisions) Act 1970, 29

Criminal Law (Northern Ireland) Act
  1967, 49

Davey, Michael, 75
de Naurois, Colonel Patrice, 144
'Death on the Rock', 63–4, 77
decommissioning, 20–21
Defence, Ministry of, 110
  defence of FRU, 135–7
  and Dr Kelly, 140
  and Saville Inquiry, 133
Defence Intelligence Service, 141
Democratic Unionist Party (DUP), 13,
  21, 68
Denning, Lord, 128
Derry, 24–5, 30, 133. see also Bloody
  Sunday
Devenport, Mark, 69
Devlin, Bernadette, 28
Dickson, Brice, 45
Diplock courts, 35, 40
Director of Public Prosecutions (DPP),
  81, 105, 131, 134
  false evidence to, 108
'dirty protest', 37
Dirty War, 16–19, 55, 83–4, 101, 113–14,
  123, 126
  accountability, 18, 133–4
  pressure for investigation, 109
Dobson, Frank, 76
Downing Street attack, 110
Dropping Well bomb, 48
Dublin Castle summit, 1980, 41
Durkan, Mark, 13

E3, 6–7
Easter Rising commemoration, 25
Economist, The, 31
Eksund gun-running, 51
emergency legislation debates, 123–4
Emergency Provisions Act 1973, 35
English, Richard, 42–3, 55
Enniskillen bomb, 1987, 51, 54, 59, 66,
  84
ethnic cleansing, 36, 50
European Commission, 63

European Convention on Human
Rights, 49, 74
European Court of Human Rights, 8,
32, 73, 74, 75
Gibraltar, 59, 62, 63, 64–5

Falklands Crisis, 36
Farrell, Danny, 60–61
Farrell, Mairéad, 54–5, 57–8, 60–61, 62–3
Faul, Monsignor Denis, 42
Faulkner, Brian, 31
Fianna Fáil, 26–7, 83
Fine Gael, 27
Finucane, Geraldine, 2, 78–80, 81, 82, 83
Helsinki testimony, 88
and inquiry, 131
and Stevens team, 112
Finucane, Michael, 79, 82
on inquiry, 130
Finucane, Pat, 57, 70, 144
career of, 8–9
family of, 9
murder of, 78–105, 124
Cory Inquiry, 2–6
description of, 78–9, 96, 97
government statements, 113–14
implications of, 1–2, 13–14
inquest, 93–4
inquiry sought, 13, 127–49, 149
Nelson involvement, 124
obstruction, 94–5, 125
preparations for, 9–12
responsibility for, 19, 45, 118–19, 145
Secretary of State statement, 166–7
source material mishandled, 89–105
targeting, 71–7
weapon, 89–90, 92–3
Finucane, Seamus, 57
Flanagan, Ronnie, 109–10
Force Research Unit (FRU), 7, 18–19, 68,
74, 111. *see also* intelligence services
collusion, 134–5
and Finucane murder, 9–11
information withheld, 15
Ministry's defence of, 135–7
and Nelson, 115, 116, 117–19, 122–3

Foreign Affairs Select Committee, 140
14th Intelligence unit, 43, 47
Free Presbyterian Church, 23

gagging orders, 136
Garda Síochána, 50
gerrymandering, 23
Gibraltar shootings, 54–65, 69
car bomb, 61
'Death on the Rock', 63–4, 77
eyewitnesses, 62, 64
rules of engagement, 60
Gibson, Lord, 49–50
Gillen, Brian, 71
Gilligan, Andrew, 139–40, 142
Glasgow Rangers Supporters Club,
Highfield, 6–7, 47–8, 89–90
Goldsmith, Lord, Attorney General,
105, 127, 128, 131
Good Friday Agreement, 1998, 2, 20–21,
45
releases, 67
Gough Barracks, Armagh, 35–6
Grew, Dessie, 53
Grew, Seamus, 48
Guardian, 131
gun-running, 51

Hackett, Dermot, 67
Hailsham, Lord, 34
Hamill, Robert, 128
Harte, Gerard and Martin, 52–3
Harvey, Andrew, 103–4
Haughey, Charles, 26–7, 38, 41, 42, 83
Heath, Ted, 34
Helsinki Committee, CSCE, 79–80, 88
Hermon, Lady, 112
Hermon, Sir Jack, Chief Constable, 9,
16, 49, 107, 112
Hillery, Patrick, 29
Hogg, Douglas, 9, 70
statement on lawyers, 74–6, 82–3
Home Office, 16
Hoon, Geoff, 142
Howe, Geoffrey, 63
Hughes, Anthony and Oliver, 52

Hughes, Brendan, 38–40
Human Rights First, 105
Hume, John, 51–2
hunger strikes, 22, 27, 51, 65, 70
  criminalisation, 37–43
Hunt Report, 30
Hussein, Saddam, 19, 141
Hutton Inquiry, 5, 137, 138, 139–43

Ignatieff, Michael, 148–9
informants and agents, 99, 145
  British Army, 15–16
  handling of, 6–8
  Nelson, 114–21
  protection of, 108–9
  Special Branch, 11–12
  Stobie, 84–9
Ingram, Adam, 111
'Ingram, Martin', 135–6
Inquiries Bill, 2004, 168–73
Insight, 134
  Brown, 95–8, 125
  Finucane, 83, 84, 88, 90
  Stone, 65
  Walker Report, 44, 99
intelligence services, 23–4. *see also* collusion; informants and agents
  accountability, 99–100, 113, 137–8
  army control of, 28
  changing legal environment, 33–7
  corruption of, 137–8
  extra-judicial methods, 143–4
  Gibraltar shootings, 54–65
  informant protection, 109
  in Northern Ireland
    criminalisation and hunger strikes,
     37–43
    descent into violence, 22–33
  primacy of, 15, 43–7
  prosecution of members, 128
  in Republic, 25–7
  security nexus, 20–53
  shoot-to-kill controversy, 47–53
  and threat to Finucane, 71–7
internment, 31–3, 33
interrogation methods, 32

Iraq War, 19, 148
  Hutton Inquiry, 138, 139–43
Irish government, 51
  arms trial, 26–7
  and Finucane murder, 82–3
  and hunger strikes, 38, 41–2
  response to troubles, 25–7, 29–30
Irish National Liberation Army (INLA),
  36, 48, 86
Irish News, 82
Irish People's Liberation Organisation
  (IPLO), 86, 116
Irish Republican Army (IRA), 6, 8, 19,
  45, 52, 70, 74, 118, 144. *see also* hunger
  strikes
  attacks in Britain, 13, 36, 110
  ceasefire, 1994, 14
  and civil rights movement, 24–5
  counter-terrorism, 16–19
  ethnic cleansing, 36, 50
  Gibraltar shootings, 54–65
  growth of, 25, 28–9, 31
  informants, 7
  and internment, 32–3
  Milltown cemetery killings, 65–8,
    69–70
  and Northern Bank raid, 17, 21
  policing issue, 20
  and RUC tactics, 47–53
  and solicitors, 9, 10, 74
  split, 27
Irish Times, 32, 82–3

Joint Intelligence Committee, 18–19, 58,
  140–41, 143
Joint Security Committee, 31–2
Jones, Brian, 141
jury trials, 35

Kelly, Dr David, 137, 139–40, 142–3
Kelly, Gerry, 13
Kelly, Captain James, 27
Kelly, John, 27
Kelly, Tom, 142–3
Kennedy, Jane, 113–14, 114
Kerr, Brian, 121–2

Kerr, Lt Colonel Gordon, 7, 116, 117, 122, 123
  and Nelson, 119, 120–21
King, Tom, 83, 134
Kinnego Embankment bomb, 47
Kitson, Frank, 144
Kosovo, 5

Labour Party, UK, 76, 111, 114
  Finucane inquiry, 129–34
Lambert, Adam, 11, 84–5
Law Society, 75
Leman-Langlois, S. and Shearing, C., 130
Lenihan, Brian, 41
Libya, 51
Long Kesh, 34, 37
Loughgall ambush, 52, 53, 54, 55
loyalist paramilitarism, 1–2. *see also* collusion
  attitude to Finucane, 70–71
  murder gangs, 50
  security infiltration, 51, 83–9, 106
  Stalker on, 109
  Stone, 65–8
  threat to Finucane, 9–12, 71–7
Loyalist Volunteer Force (LVF), 50
Lynch, Jack, 26, 30
Lyttle, Tommy 'Tucker', 18, 71–2

McCann, Daniel, 54–5, 57–8, 60–61, 62–3
McCann, Eamon, 24
McCartney, Robert, 147–8
McCaughey, Martin, 53
McCauley, Martin, 48, 108
McDaid, Declan, 117, 121
McDaid, Maura, 116–17
McDaid, Terence, 86, 116–18, 121, 122
McFadden, Supt, 122
McFarlane, Brendan 'Bik', 40
McGeown, Pat, 11, 70, 120
McGlinchey, Dominic, 48
McGrory, P.J., 64, 75–6
McGuinness, Martin, 52, 65, 68
McKearney, Tommy, 38
McKenna, Sean, 39–40

McKerr, Gervaise, 47–8, 49, 73, 74
McKittrick, David, 137
McMichael, John, 67–8, 115
McNamara, Kevin, 112, 114
Magee, Hugh, 126
Maginn, Loughlin, 106
Mail on Sunday, 140
Mallon, Seamus, 9, 75, 76–7, 123–4
Maloney, Ed, 88, 90, 91, 92
Marsh, Kevin, 142
Mawhinney, Brian, 123–4
Mayhew, Sir Patrick, 50
Maze prison, 57
  hunger strikes, 37–43
media
  manipulation, 43
  and security policy, 56–7
Mercer, Patrick, 113
Metropolitan Police, 8, 58
MI5, 18–19, 19, 46, 47–53, 87
  report on Finucane, 73–4
  Tighe audiotape, 108
MI6, 18, 39, 46, 58
Milltown cemetery
  British army deaths, 55, 68–70
  Stone shootings, 55, 65–8
Molyneaux, Jim, 14, 64
Morrison, Danny, 37–8
Mountbatten, Lord Louis, 36–7
Mowlam, Mo, 66
Mulholland, Neil, 88, 89, 92, 100
Mullaghmore bomb, 36–7
Mullin, Brian, 52–3
Murphy, Paul, Secretary of State for NI, 2, 3
  Finucane inquiry, 127, 128–9, 130
Myers, Kevin, 32

Napier, Oliver, 76
National Crime Squad, 102
national security, 2–3, 5
  government policy, 55–7, 74–7, 110–14, 123, 143–4
  NIO policy, 14–15
Nationalist Party, 25–6, 33
Neave, Airey, 36

Nelson, Brian, 7, 10–11, 15, 16, 18, 71, 74,
        83
    arrest leak, 111
    in Cory Report, 114–21
    and Finucane murder, 73, 119–20, 124
    handling of, 134–5
    information withheld, 92
    murders by, 116–18
    role in UFF, 68
    Stalker on, 109
    trial, 105, 121–6, 131
Nelson, Rosemary, 9, 13, 128, 144
New York Lawyers' Committee for
    Human Rights, 99, 109
Newman, Kenneth, Chief Constable,
        43
Ní Aolain, Fionnuala, 33, 47
Nicholson, Jack, 145
Northern Bank robbery, 17, 21
Northern Ireland Assembly, 9, 13, 20–21
Northern Ireland Civil Rights
    Association (NICRA), 24, 26
Northern Ireland Human Rights
    Commission, 45
Northern Ireland Office, 46, 76–7, 82,
        100
    security policy, 14–15
Northern Ireland Secretary, post of,
        35
Nugent, Kieran, 37
Nye, Joseph, 138

O'Brien, Brendan, 49
O'Connor, JoJo, 147
Official IRA, 27, 32
O'Hare, Paschal, 82
Oldfield, Maurice, 46
Omagh bomb, 17–18
O'Neill, Onora, 139
O'Neill, Sir Terence, 24, 31
Operation Demetrius, 32–3
Operation Satiety, 102
Orange Order, 30
Orde, Hugh, Chief Constable, 17, 100,
        104

Paisley, Rev Ian Kyle, 23, 41
Palace Army Barracks, Holywood, 78
Panorama, 16, 29, 64, 103, 116
    'A Licence to Murder', 10, 11, 12, 72
    Barrett, 101–3
Pat Finucane Centre, 130
Patten Commission, 17, 21
peace process, 5, 113
People's Democracy, 25
Phoblacht, An, 37
Phoenix, Ian, 7
Police Service of Northern Ireland
    (PSNI), 8, 17, 21–2, 104
policing. see intelligence services
Policing Authority, 7, 45
population movement, 26
Powell, Jonathan, 141, 142
Press Association, 128
Prevention of Terrorism Act, 8, 35, 64,
    74–6, 82–3
principal-agent analysis, 138–40
Prior, James, 48
prisoners
    hunger strikes, 37–43
    mistreatment of, 71
Provisional IRA. see Irish Republican
    Army (IRA)
Public Accounts, Dáil Committee of,
        26

Quee, Billy, 116
Queen's University, 57

Real IRA, 17–18, 45
Red Hand Defenders, 87–8
Reid, Father Alex, 69
Reid, Dr John, 140
Rice, Joe, 100, 103
right to silence, 76–7
Robinson, John, 49
Ross, Dr, 39
Royal Ulster Constabulary (RUC), 58,
    98. see also intelligence services;
    Special Branch
    and BIRW report, 109–10
    changed to PSNI, 21–2

and civil rights movement, 24–5
collusion, 4, 12, 14–17, 72–3, 106–7
and Finucane, 8, 9, 93
informants, 7, 108–9
information withheld, 14, 15
intelligence failures, 23–4
and internment, 32
leaks, 124
and Nelson, 115
shoot-to-kill controversy, 47–53, 74
Special Branch primacy, 6–8, 43–7
St George's Cross, 21–2
and Stalker, 15, 107–8
and Stevens, 15–16
Ryder, Chris, 45

St Mathew's church, defence of, 28–9, 30
Sambrook, Richard, 142
Sampson, Colin, 50
Sandhurst Military Academy, 34
Sands, Bobby, 39, 40, 42, 70
SAS, 18–19, 47, 53
    Gibraltar shootings, 54–65
Savage, Sean, 54–5, 57–8, 60–61, 62–3
Saville Inquiry, 3, 132–3, 135–6
Scarlett, Sir John, 140, 141, 143
Scarman Tribunal, 24–5
Scraton, Phil, 132
Seapark fire, Carrickfergus, 110–11
sectarianism, 22–3, 36
    murders, 50, 84–5, 106, 126
shoot-to-kill controversy, 47–53, 55, 74, 107, 112
Simpson, Det Supt Alan, 78, 92, 93–4
Sinn Féin, 9, 20, 21, 51, 66, 74
    accused of fascism, 52
    and Cory Report, 12–13
    ends abstention, 52
    Finucane murder, 81–2
    and hunger strikes, 38
Slane, Gerald, 116, 120, 122
Social Democratic and Labour Party (SDLP), 13, 21, 27, 33, 51–2, 75
    and Nelson trial, 123–4
South Africa, 68, 145–7

Spain, 54, 58, 64
Special Branch, RUC, 2, 5, 14, 18–19. *see also* collusion; intelligence services
agents, 83, 84–9
attitude to Finucane, 70–71
and Barrett, 80, 89, 96–9, 103, 104
and CID, 94–5
downgraded, 22
and Finucane murder, 9–10, 12, 71–7, 89–91, 92, 125–6
and FRU, 136
informants, 11–12, 112
Omagh bomb, 17–18
primacy of, 6–8, 123
    institutionalised, 43–7
shoot-to-kill controversy, 47–53
and Stalker, 108
and Stobie, 89–91, 92, 93
and Stone, 68
Spence, Jim, 10, 83, 101, 124
Stakeknife, 17
Stalker, John, 48–50, 107–8
    autobiography, 107, 109
Standing Advisory Commission on Human Rights, 76
Stevens, Sir John, 3–4, 6, 48, 72, 107, 116
    and Barrett, 102–3
    and FRU, 120
    investigations of, 80–81, 109, 124–6, 127, 130
    assessment of, 111–15
    collusion, 134
    obstruction, 14–16, 110–11
    public summary, 2003, 110–11
    Reports, 83–4, 86–7
    third investigation, 100, 164–5
    on leadership, 105
    on Nelson, 118
    Omagh reports, 17–18
    on PSNI, 104
    and Stalker report, 107
    statement, 80–81
    and Stobie, 89, 92, 100
Stobie, William, 10, 82, 96, 104, 116
    as agent, 11–12, 84–9
    murder of, 18, 87–8, 100–101

trial, 18, 91, 100, 112, 114
warns of Finucane attack, 73, 89–93
Stone, Michael, 65–8, 96
Stormont parliament, 23, 29, 30–31, 115
prorogued, 1972, 33
spy-ring, 17
Sunday Life, 88
Sunday Times, 103
Sunday Tribune, 88
supergrass trials, 50
Sutcliffe, Peter, 96

Tactical Action Group, 18–19
Tactical and Coordinating Groups, 73
Tasking and Co-ordinating Group,
46–7
Taylor, John, 112–13
terrorism. *see* national security
Thames Television, 56
'Death on the Rock', 63–4, 77
Thatcher, Margaret, 36–7
hunger strikes, 38, 41–2
Tighe, Michael, 48, 108
Times, The, 140
Today, 139–40, 142
Toman, Eugene, 47–8, 49
TREWITS, 146
Tribunals of Inquiry, 2–3, 132–4, 137
Trimble, David, 13
Trinquier, Colonel Roger, 144–5
Truth and Reconciliation Commission,
South Africa, 145–7
Tuzo, General, 31

Ulster Defence Association (UDA), 7, 67,
68, 115, 116
Finucane murder, 71–2, 73–4, 78–105
leaks intelligence material, 106–7
and Nelson, 122
Stobie in, 84, 86, 87–8, 91

and Stone, 66
targets, 120, 135
Ulster Defence Regiment (UDR), 21, 115,
124
Ulster Freedom Fighters (UFF), 10, 11,
18, 67, 84, 96, 124
and Barrett, 101
files, 115
Nelson in, 68, 74
targets, 106, 117
Ulster Resistance, 68
Ulster Television (UTV), 83, 136
Ulster Unionist Party (UUP), 13, 14,
20–21, 30, 64, 123
Ulster Volunteer Force (UVF), 50
United Nations Basic Principles on the
Role of Lawyers, 75
United States of America (USA), 148
University of Ulster (UU), 47

Voice of the North, The, 26, 27

Wakeham, John, 76
Walker Report, 6–7, 43–4, 45, 46
guidelines, 94, 96, 99, 112
shoot-to-kill controversy, 47–53
text of, 150–59
Walzer, Michael, 148–9
Ward, Henry Fleming, 126
Ware, John, 71–2, 101
Warrenpoint bomb, 36, 46
Weir, Justice, 103, 104–5
West, Harry, 30
Weston Park talks, 2001, 129
Whitelaw, William, 28
Widgery Inquiry, 34–5, 132, 133
Windelsham, Lord, 77
Winter, Jane, 81
World War II, 36
Wright, Billy, 128